An American Marriage

HILARY MASTERS

An American Marriage

The Macmillan Company

Collier-Macmillan Ltd., London

. . . ESPECIALLY *Polly*

HISTORIANS *who write in aristocratic ages* are wont to refer all occurrences to the particular will or temper of certain individuals; and they are apt to attribute the most important revolutions to very slight accidents. Historians who live in democratic ages . . . attribute hardly any influence to the individual over the destiny of the race, nor to citizens over the fate of a people; but, on the other hand, they assign great general causes to all petty incidents.

—ALEXIS DE TOCQUEVILLE

An American Marriage

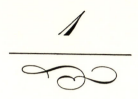

L ET ME TELL YOU ABOUT MY WIFE.
She was sick half the night, gagging and heaving all over the place and finally making the last trip to the commode on her hands and knees, crawling up the narrow steps to the tiny landing where the equipment was installed when modern plumbing came to this forsaken country. Perched is more the word for the installation. There is no other room up there against the roof line, and the commode and its accompanying finger bowl of a sink are enclosed on three sides by sheets of pressed cardboard and reached by a precarious, narrow stairway that hugs the side of the stairwell.

Sometimes, sitting there, it is easy to imagine a gentle swaying motion as if one were sitting in the top of a tall tree. And it is especially spooky at night, the narrow, steep stairs leading up to the door of the small cubicle—all too easy to imagine Charles Laughton, a candle held just below the points of a wing collar, emerging with a satisfied and relieved mien.

My wife is up and down those steps all night. I must have slept through the first time but I catch her coming down after some subsequent upheaval and she gives me a reproachful look. Her darling eyes of black myopia glisten

under an ebony fall of hair and the olive sheen of her
skin is pink with the exertions of vomiting. She is so childlike, so adorably sexy that I would almost take her in my
arms then and there had she not been vomiting. Also, she
probably would have stiff-armed me over the low, shaky
banister and down into the deep stairwell I'd go.

After the last trip, made on her hands and knees as I
say—excellent buttocks thrust above trim, muscular thighs
though the soles of the rather large feet a bit callused and
dirty—after this last trip with my encouragement just a
step behind, she says she is too weak to crawl back down
to our bedroom so I sit her down on the top steps, lean
her against the inside wall and go for supplies. I nearly
break my neck in the bedroom, catching my feet in the
straps of her brassiere thrown on the floor by the armoire.

Now the bedroom nearly takes up the whole second
floor of this house—if the small platform supporting the
toilet and sink can be called a third floor. The bedroom
is thirty-five feet wide, the approximate width of the house
itself, and twenty feet deep, and into it our landlord placed
only the essentials: a bed, a double wardrobe and one
chair. The great emptiness of the place is multiplied by
two large mirrors facing each other from opposite walls
and hung from the fifteen-foot ceilings on cables the size
of those that suspend the George Washington Bridge.

In such a vacuum, one can imagine the importance this
one chair assumes. We use it for a clothes rack, a bookshelf, a bureau and even for certain sexual experiments, the
latter usage curtailed when one of the curved, Queen
Anne arms broke away to leave a nasty exposure of jagged
dowels.

I locate the cigarettes, matches, the bottle of magnesium-
gel beneath the clothes and papers piled on the chair. On

the floor beneath it is the drinking cup and the large scallop shell we had found on the beach in Wellfleet last summer—and doesn't that seem like a long time ago?—and brought with us as a remembrance of the New World here in the old. I hurry back, hoping she has not tumbled down the stairs, but she still leans against the pressed tin wall, a weary demonstrator. I fix her a cup of gel and sit down beside her.

"Ah, Hamlet," she sighs, "what would I do without you?"

Now my name is not Hamlet, I hasten to add, but Hamilton and I'm called Ham by most people, but early in our relationship, my wife—then my student—invented this diminutive form for moments of stress.

"What would I do without you?" she repeats between courageous slurps of the gel.

Our brief marriage has already been complicated by a series of mistakes, commencing with the pregnancy, that brought us to the top tread of an Alpine stairway of a dilapidated town house in a foreign capital. She blamed me for the conception and more particularly for the sickness and the changes in her body, changes which I, at least at this point, find very appealing, just as she blamed me for all the other honest mistakes.

How many are aware that there are two distinctly different universities named for this capital city. Alclair University. The name summons the magic of a royal charter, Tudor dining halls, the world-famous library and especially the department of government—my field. But all of this belongs to the University of Alclair and not to Alclair University. The latter is a state institution founded no more than fifty years ago for the education of the lower class and with a curriculum weighted toward nursing and bookkeeping. It is famed for a collection of stuffed Arctic birds bequeathed by an archbishop whose early missionary work took him among the Laplanders. And even after meeting Professor Crawford and Mrs. Waters, two exchange compatriots who had made the same mistake on their application forms, Patricia still blames me for not knowing the difference between the two schools.

Then there's this cluddy house, to use a local term. American naïveté perhaps allowed me to take the landlord's assurances of furniture at face value. But it was a fault on the side of Good, for I treat all men as honest and when the landlord said the house was to be furnished I assumed it would be furnished.

The bedroom is actually the best of the lot. The living room contains one sofa, one table, a magazine rack and a coal scuttle. There's an enormous Chinese Chippendale table in the dining room with nine matching chairs and a television set upon a tea wagon. Both rooms, like the bedroom upstairs, feature great mirrors hung above high, marble mantels. There's an umbrella stand and a grandfather's clock in the hall. The kitchen, down a half flight of steps in the rear, and apparently converted from a servant's small room, boasts a stove, a refrigerator the size of an orange crate, a sink and a breakfast shelf with two stools. The stools we bought. And beneath is a full-size basement, the rooms locked and nailed shut, apparently containing our landlord's valuables, except for the vast, tiled chamber that had once been the kitchen in this town house's heyday, now crumbling and smelling like the men's room of a derelict vaudeville house.

So this is our condition as the clock at the bottom of the stairwell strikes eleven times which means it's three in the morning. Three in the damp morning in the capital of Alclair as I sit on a stair outside the toilet, sit beside my mistress of three months and my bride of four, a total of seven short months if not including our teacher-student relationship.

The difference between Patricia Gates, daughter of the late Colonel and Mrs. Edmond Gates, and Mrs. Hamilton Phillips, wife of the soon-to-be-recognized authority on medieval guilds, is enough of a one to make her two separate people. She had not been an outstanding student and she had been, at first, only one of the many who sat before me every morning at Scott Junior College, knitting needles clicking off the hour with an occasional pause to note a date relevant to the development of Western democracy. No more need be said of Scott Junior College except that it is the remnant of a female seminarianism that continues to send home bills for pen points and ink. And the bills are paid.

But there was a challenge in this frivolous atmosphere, for when I regarded my class every morning, I reminded myself I held in the palm of my intellectual hand, so to speak, not only the flower of American womanhood but the fruit of American industry and enterprise. The long-legged blonde in front was American T & T, the brunette with the fetching lisp was Peabody Coal, and so forth. It seemed that I, in no small way, could influence and be responsible for the growth of our gross national product.

For actually, the real education never took place in class but in those informal, chatty get-togethers in my office when the girls would drop by to discuss our nation's problems and other developments. And the confidence that developed in this delicate relationship between teacher and pupil carried over to their trusting me with their personal problems. The door of Hamilton Phillips' office was always open and I'm proud to say that they came to me as to an older brother and their confidence was never betrayed.

So Patricia Gates, an average student with healthy thrust of breast beneath a Brooks Brothers shirt, appeared at my door one day. The light from my window opaqued her horn-rimmed glasses or else I would have detected the glint of an extracurricular problem in the dark eyes. She began with a question concerning the reconciliation of the secret treaties with Wilson's Fourteen Points but I could see her interest was feigned. The fine articulation of her knees above knubby high socks came into play as one leg swung up and down. Then after the third cigarette and second cup of coffee, the little hot plate always at the ready, and after we had disposed of Hitler's claims to the Ruhr Valley, the real matter came out.

"I think I'm tagged," she said, cracking her gum. She pushed her glasses up above the hair band.

"Tagged?"

"Tagged. Knocked up. With child." Now this was not the first time my office walls had heard such information, and I was prepared. I set aside *The World Since 1914* and unobtrusively arranged the box of Kleenex and bottle of camphor near at hand. But without her glasses, such secrecy was unnecessary and without her glasses her rather plain face, quickened by the lustrous, dark orbs now exposed, assumed the fascination of those nearsighted madonnas so partial to the Renaissance. The Kleenex and camphor were put away.

"No, I'm not sure," she answered my question, non-chalantly regarding her midriff, "and God knows, I shouldn't be. But I've never been overdue before and Cindy . . ."

"We mention no names, Miss Gates," I told her, wondering how many "befores" there had been.

"Well, one of the girls said you might know of a doctor —just in case."

"You've been misinformed," I told her promptly. Her mouth stiffened and she ground out her cigarette, resigned to her fate. Pity crept into compassion, feelings I had never held out to the others, as beautiful as some of them were. But this plain, barely pretty girl with her problem evoked my interest. "Can you talk it over with your parents?"

"The Colonel is dead," she replied, the glasses now back on her nose. "And it would positively fracture Mother. Actually, she's my foster-mother—I'm adopted—which is all the more reason why I can't tell her. She'd take it as the final fact of her failure of responsibility. You know what I mean? It's one thing to miss with a child of your own, but to go out of your way to get one, to adopt one, and then muck it up—oh, Christ, it's too depressing." She rose as if to leave but stopped at the small bookcase and thumbed through *This Age of Conflict* (Chambers, Harris and Bailey).

"I can imagine how depressed you are."

"Depressed!" She closed the book and slumped, slouched is more the word, back into the chair. "How would you feel if you thought you were carrying a member of the Yale class of '88?"

"The boy in question attends Yale?" I tried to speak as evenly as possible.

"Well, actually, what's worse—it might be UConn."

"UConn?"

"Yes, they're so square at UConn, a real nowhere."

"You mean there's more than . . ."

"Well, it was a big weekend," she replied. "Also, there was this very distinguished professor at UConn I wanted to meet—his name is Armbrewster, do you know him? Anyway, I got someone to take me down there the same weekend of the Yale-Harvard game, he happened to be going there and . . ."

"I'm afraid I don't understand, Miss Gates. What does this professor . . .?"

"No, it's a long story and has nothing to do with tum-tum here." She patted the front of her skirt. "How old are you, Mr. Phillips?"

"I'm thirty-five."

"You look older."

"Older?"

"Well, no, actually, you look younger, but you seem older, act older."

"We're getting away from the subject," I said. She continued to look at me, eyes even more enlarged by the glasses, and, with a pencil, coiled a lock of black hair. Her teeth tested the resiliency of the eraser. Ignoring this disturbing inspection, I advised her as best I could; not to be rash and to prepare to discuss the matter with her foster-mother. There the matter ended. She swung out of my office with a moving bravado.

And a few days later, I remember I was reviewing a lecture on the establishment of the World Court, I heard someone say, "Hey!" I turned around and peering around the doorway was Patricia Gates. There was a broad smile on her face and her glasses glinted merrily. Before I could say anything, she nodded and said, "Quiet flows the Don," and disappeared. But I could never forget that face. She was beautiful.

The same face now leans against the clammy tin sheathing that covers the wall of this Alclair house as I peer through the banister down into the oblivion of the front hallway, sixty feet below.

"We can't sit here all night," I say finally.

"I can try." Her voice is weary.

"Let me help you down. You must get some rest." I put my arms around her, a hand inadvertently brushing one breast.

"Hands off the glands, you bastard," she snaps.

"I'm sorry, it was an accident." She allows me to pull her up and guide her down the narrow stairs.

"You can say that again," she says. "Oh, Jiminy! Are you sure this is the way Mary did it?"

"Mary who?" She pauses at the foot of the stairs to look at me or try to look at me, for her glasses are on the floor by the bed. "Come now, Pat, lie down. Can I fix you some broth?"

"Aggh." I stretch out beside her. "I'm sorry, Hamlet, this can't be much fun for you either. Maybe it'll pass in a few days. But the thought of sex gives me the squeamies."

"That's all right." Her hand seeks mine and squeezes it. "You're a peacharino. Sleepy?"

"No."

"Neither am I, but I'm exhausted." She sighs. "Well, what will we do? I know," after a moment's thought. "Tell me the reasons why the United States never joined the League of Nations."

And I do.

Dawn comes to Alclair not on rosy fingers but on a

damp, gray cloth that is rubbed across the faces of the buildings and wiped into the crevices of the narrow, winding streets. It leaves a dull film, slippery and slightly colored by the particles of soot that charge the morning air from thousands of brick chimneys and the grates of soft-coal fires below. It is remarkable to me that in a country where central heating has yet to find a word in the old vocabulary the fireplaces and the attendant grates are so small. About the size of a letter box, they are, and if one's posterior is larger than average there is a perpetual chill around the flanks.

Such a backside, amplified by the thick tweed of her suit, appears before me this morning as I walk to my first class. Mrs. R. L. (Maxine) Waters would be a substantial figure in any landscape, nor was it only her hulk which claimed her place. Everything about her bespoke a person of some importance. Her gray eyes, sharp and questioning, "stitched" a listener's attention and among a group they stabbed from one to the other, sewing up relationships into a pattern of her own liking. But it was her voice, a commanding, martial organ wherein the original Midwestern accent sometimes marched through and overpowered the cultivated Eastern seaboard, that inevitably cut a place for her in any gathering as surely as steel cuts butter.

"Good morning, Mrs. Waters," I say, rounding her from the left. She is preoccupied, and walks head bent over the briefcase clutched against a great bosom. Her face had probably been called "handsome" in her youth; the features strong, that is to say there was no question that she had a brow, a nose and a pair of lips and all well fashioned but still not particularly feminine, not particularly petite. Now, she turns her face to me and smiles and it is an amazing effect, for I am looking at a girlish grandmother; the gay, unrestored remnant of a flapper.

"Mr. Phillips, good morning."

We continue to walk in silence across Liberty Park, beneath the dripping trees and around the hedges of steaming rhododendrons, for the sun is making its daily attempt to break through. Before us, across the square and behind a tall picket fence of iron, rises the dull red ramparts of Alclair University, looking every brick crenellation the trade school built by the British for colonial minions.

"It's shocking," Mrs. Waters says suddenly. "Shocking."

"Hmmn, shocking?"

"I've just been to the library at the University," and by this she indicates the good place, "and do you know they do not have one volume of Jeffers?"

"Jeffers?"

"Robinson Jeffers." Her lips purse, her eyes grow hard. "Banned. Yes, I inquired and it seems none of his books were ever allowed in this country. How am I supposed to give them any idea of The Movement without Jeffers?" Mrs. Waters' specialty is American Lit. Her shoulders shrug. "Of course, he can be a bit raunchy at times. I recall my husband once told me . . ."

And I am given a lengthy report of Mrs. Waters' husband's feelings on Robinson Jeffers. We all learned quickly that those two words, "my husband," prefaced an opinion or a remark for which an informal group, a roomful of academics, government dignitaries, a hall of students —indeed, the entire world, if possible—was expected to pause, to listen and to profit from. Along with her size, her eyes and the armor-piercing voice, these two words assured her a focal point in any gathering, magically. They were almost always pronounced in a deceptively soft, crooning tone, the large face thrust out, lids half shading the eyes and the wattles of her neck taut and quivering with the anticipation of their effect.

("Who the hell is her husband?" I asked Jack Crawford after the first couple of these performances. We were having an afternoon break in his office. He brushed tobacco crumbs from his gray moustache, smiled and continued pouring the whiskey.

"Robert Lewis Waters," he announced, capping the whiskey, "was a minor Southern poet of some distinction." The description was made with all the cool tolerance of a New Englander (Harvard '22) speaking of an outsider who had made it. "He preceded Ransom and that bunch by about ten years, which indicates that timing is almost as important as craft." He paused to taste both the whiskey and his theory. "Yes, almost as important. Actually, he reintroduced, or is sometimes credited with reintroducing, the bizarre themes of C. Brockten Brown, Poe and all that we now associate with Southern literature. A little too tied up with the nineteenth century in terms of form, Bryant and all, to be read much these days, though."

He had handed me an anthology of poetry, one finger inserted in the back pages where cameo portraits of the authors were located. I saw the picture of a long-faced man in his middle age. He wore a soft-collar shirt, open at the neck. The high brow was surmounted by a heavy pompadour, a lock of hair falling down over the eyes. The look was frank and with some humor. It was not a face easily imagined on the same pillow with Mrs. Maxine Waters.

"You may borrow that, if you like," Crawford told me. "How do you like this local swill?" he asked, gesturing to the whiskey. I returned the book, said I found the whiskey drinkable and noted that his shelf contained an extensive collection of American poetry. Jack Crawford, Professor Emeritus of Egyptology, teaches Ancient History at Alclair.)

" . . . but he was always a gentleman. And he built that stone house he lived in with his own hands. My husband planted a tree there when we visited him, you know." Maxine Waters and I just manage to reach the traffic island set in the middle of Gonorah Street.

The morning torrent of cars, trucks, motor scooters and carts swirls around us. Battalions of cyclists wheel to the right and in through the open gate of Alclair, students pedaling crickety bikes toward the warm hearth of higher education. And above us towers the huge stone figure of the revolution's hero, epitomizing all those who fought for this country's independence. He is a unique figure. He stands, feet apart, cap low over his eyes and trench coat belted and flapping in the winds of change. Negligently he holds a Thompson submachine gun across his middle. Think of Gattamelata poised perfectly in his square in Padua, of Golden Joan in Place Concorde or even of that simple farmer in Concord, hesitantly picking up the slim musket, and compare them all with this nation's version of Machine-gun Kelly, and you have a fair idea of this place.

Maxine Waters stands beneath this boorish though effective figure of social change, indignant and outraged by the morality of a particular if not all revolutions. And finally, the traffic policeman, wearing the identical trench coat as our heroic friend above, though black, holds back the traffic and waves us across.

"Look here," I say as we stand in the foyer of Main Hall, bound together by the fact of being Americans,

"Thanksgiving is coming up. Why don't we get together for Thanksgiving? We can have all the trimmings at our house. Pat would love it," I say, wondering how to break the news to my wife. The great head comes up, the eyes roll and a most marvelous smile approves the idea. "How grand," Maxine Waters says. "And I can bring the cranberry sauce. I have a wonderful recipe for cranberry sauce. It was my husband's mother's."

The study of history has left me unsentimental and why I made that suggestion in the crowded foyer, jostled by the soot-scented scholars of the lower middle class, I do not know. Perhaps it was the irreverent classlessness of that jostling, the lack of distinction among the scarves and caps and lumpy jumpers that pressed upon us or the cold, farcical attempt at neoclassicism of that foyer that provoked the spontaneous suggestion. In any event, as I watch Maxine Waters shouldering her way through this crowd to the morning class in American Lit., sans R. Jeffers, I realize I am committed. One does not make idle invitations to Mrs. Robert Lewis Waters.

I spend too much time, and too early, describing Maxine Waters. I began by talking about my wife, and it is really only her I want to talk about. But in order to do so, I must describe others, invest in scenery and personae in order to present her to best advantage, though at the risk, finally, that she may not be seen on stage at all. Patricia Simpson Gates. She fell like a petal upon the still surface of my being.

After that day in my office, after that moment of gorgeous hilarity when she assured me her menses were once again functioning, I watched her with more than usual interest. In time, I could identify her loose-kneed lope of a walk from across the Scott campus. I looked for her straight spine in the hallways or the rounded, childish hand which signed her papers, setting them aside to be read last. And once in class, halfway through the Triple Entente, I heard my monologue stop—stopped dead by that face framed in black hair and the far look in the eyes behind the harlequin-frame glasses. I was fascinated with her even though I suspected the haunting distance in her eyes probably reflected the tedious decision of which Ivy League champion would enjoy her this weekend rather than the world-shaking suspense of the Bosnian crisis.

But in her defense, her adventures and their number were no more than what I judged, from the informal coffees in my office, her classmates at Scott Junior College experienced. The difference with Patricia Gates is that she discussed them point-blank; no arch allusions, no meaningful silences, no coy glances. And in her forthright, sometimes humorous accounts of the actual event—the shocking immoral behavior on American campuses so denounced and simultaneously promoted by both *The Reader's Digest* and *The Police Gazette*—lay the suggestion that the event itself was unimportant, a mere physical act unrelated to good or bad, corruption or innocence. I have referred to her in a sentimental lapse as a blossom. She was a wild flower in a cultivated and well-manured forest of gardenias.

Though there were girls at Scott more beautiful in the ordinary sense, Patricia Gates outdistanced them all in the number of invitations to ski weekends, hops, homecomings, class musicals, sugaring-offs or whatever. This was not remarkable given her self-advertised availability and the way such information passes through the intracampus underground of the All-Americans in residence. Her popularity set her apart; she was isolated by the hypocritical and probably envious regard of her fellow demivirgins.

But one could see in her walk and in her almost arrogant shift of shoulder that she would have been a loner in any event. What was remarkable is that she never returned to the same campus twice except for a second visit made to Princeton. These single appearances were not due to any personal failing of hers, as the volume of subsequent invitations proved the contrary, but from a carefully plotted plan of her own design. It was as if she was working her way through *Lovejoy's College Guide* (how apt the author would never know his name to be) and methodically checking off the Eastern schools. And, in fact, there was such a book.

I discovered the book, along with the hint that there was more to her adventures than the mere cataloguing of fraternity frictionals.

It was a bright afternoon in March. There was no warning in the sunlight that played upon the daffodils by the tennis courts, none in the warm blustery air that nourished the robins chirping on the green, absolutely nothing in the view from my office window that would indicate this day to be one of the last free days I was to spend on earth.

Yet I should have been warned by the way Patricia Gates swung into my office, disturbing a sheaf of term papers with a swipe of knitting bag. The alarm should have rung when she sat down, negligently swinging one leg over the other and pulling a heavy strand of hair across her face. The warning *should* have rung, triggered by my reaction, by the joyous though silent way I greeted her almost clumsy entrance, the neat pinkness of her knees and the moving, Chaplinesque self-parody of the hair gesture. But who would ring and who would answer?

"You're going to Brown this weekend," she said, coming to the point immediately.

"Well, yes. I'm going up to visit a friend there," I answered. The friend was a twenty-nine-year-old blonde in the philosophy department with whom I had been having one of those healthy, rational affairs common to Academia. Gretchen and I would meet periodically and moreover she had written me there was an opening in the history department which might be of interest.

"I've never been to Brown," Pat Gates said.

"Really?" She had leaned forward to search inside her knitting bag. The bright yellow shift was very becoming and I could only think of the triteness, fresh as a daisy, when I looked at her.

"Well, I was invited to the Senior Chorus last year," she recalled with a grimace, "but he was only a freshman and didn't know anyone, so I didn't go." She held a small brown notebook now, its pages filled with a schoolgirl printing. It was a list of some kind and I could see over the top of the book—"Colgate—Cornell—Dartmouth"—that it was an alphabetical list of schools. Lines had been drawn through them all except—she turned back a page and found the spot—"Brown U."

"Do you know a Professor Owen McEdwards?" she asked, reading the brief paragraph under the institution's name. "English Department, Blake Specialist. AB Chicago. Rhodes. MA, PhD Harvard. Publications: MLA *Harper's*, *Lit Review*, *Western Humanities*, etc. Also *William Blake, A New Study*, Macmillan. Also, *Poems*, Roundtable Press."

She had finished and looked up at me, one finger adjusting the glasses upon her nose, and the cant of her head, as if from the habit to keep them positioned, gave a disquieting hauteur to her heart-shaped face. She had read the facts of the professor's career as if they were ingredients in an omelet and now she silently awaited my answer.

"No, I don't know him. I've never heard of him," I finally said.

"But your friend—would he know him?"

"She probably would know him," I answered, noting the feminine pronoun caused a flicker in the large, dark eyes. Another warning bell ignored; it had amused me to see that blink.

"Well, do you think *she* could arrange a meeting for me? That is, if you would give me a ride up there?" She grinned and I grinned.

More warning bells. My head resounded like Notre Dame as my deaf heart stumped about in my chest. There was balance and order outside my window and I looked at the neat lawns, the manicured hedges around the entrance. I even went to the window, turned my back upon her and for several seconds watched two students lob a tennis ball back and forth, back and forth across a slack net. She had continued to talk.

". . . in the way. I can take care of myself. All you have to do is give me a ride up and back, arrange for the meeting and tell me where to meet you coming back. I can find a place to stay," she said casually. The lawn, the hedges, the players on the court disappeared, replaced by a black nothingness, momentary but frightening enough. I had reached out a hand, like a blind man, to grip the window casement.

"Very well," I turned back to her. "I will give you a ride; however, since I am to be responsible for you, we shall observe all the rules as if we were here on campus. I will want to know where you are at all times. In your room—and I will choose the hotel—but in your room at eleven o'clock. All . . . any other appointments except with this professor must have my permission."

She nodded her head, impatient with the details. "But you will get the appointment for me?"

"Yes. I'll call this evening." She put the notebook back in her knitting bag, smiled and stood up. I no longer could trust my senses, my perceptions, but I could have sworn that she pushed out her breasts needlessly. "Why do you want to meet this professor at Brown?"

"Well," she paused by the doorway, one foot angled to the other, and shrugged, "he might be my father."

"I am glad we could have this little chat," Dean Morraugh is saying in the syrupy clack of an accent the natives have here with English, "because I think it so important that you are comfortable and at ease and we are so grateful to have you with us. How are you getting on? Is your house comfortable? Is there anything you need? You Americans are so self-sufficient, you won't mind, you won't be insulted, if I be the mother hen with you. It's a gesture of our native hospitality, purely."

His office is a high-ceilinged room with tall windows that look out over Liberty Park and the National Gunman below. Glass-fronted bookcases face one wall and a coal fire snaps in a marble fireplace across the room. A great, square mirror hangs above. The furniture is large and of a mahogany as black as ebony and almost as heavy. On top of the bookcases are busts of Swift, Burns and several patriots unknown to me. There is also a stuffed bird, apparently part of the Archbishop's collection.

"There we are," he says, handing me a mug of the hot tea he had been brewing when I entered. "Salnfah," he salutes me in the Old Tongue and we drink. His eyes peer over the mug, and with the genial roundness of his face obscured by the mug, these "globs of cooling pig iron," as Crawford describes them, are startling in their fierce expression. They are anomalous to the soft roundness of the rest of him, the pudgy hands—two fingers missing on the left one—the melon-shaped head, the short legs and the tiny, delicate feet. It is only when the rest of the face is masked, as it is now by the steaming mug, and one sees the eyes by themselves, that it is possible to believe the stories about the Dean as a young revolutionary, in the old times when he was known as Gil Morraugh, the Bloody Whip of the West.

"And your wife?" he is asking. "How is she getting on? Have you secured a proper doctor for her? We have, you know, a first-class lying-in here. I shall make a note for the missus to call upon Mrs. Phillips as soon as you're settled and fine. Now then, Mr. Phillips." The amiable chatter disappears. We are serious. "Isn't that peculiar," he interrupts himself. "I knew a chap named Phillips once. English, of course. No relation, I suppose? No." I shake my head, wondering how many minutes he had known the other Phillips before he shot him.

"Why have you come here, Mr. Phillips?" The tea mug jerks in my hand, and I try to meet his eyes as they survey me. They probe for the effect of his sudden question, to calculate the need for a *coup de grâce.*

"Here?" I wipe some tea from my chin.

"Yes, here. To this country, and especially to our little university. Ah, well," he forestalls my reply with a good-natured wave of the modified hand, "the mistake you made on the forms. Yes, yes, I had forgotten about that one." He pauses to give me what is supposed to be a mischievous wink, but on him it is menacing. The spires of the University of Alclair rise into the gray sky far across the city's roofs and chimneys. It is a distance to be measured in more than miles. "Actually, Mr. Phillips, whatever your reasons, whatever mistake you may have made," he pauses to draw out the sound of the verb, "the end result has been to give me a first-rate man that I might not have got in the first place. A man of your caliber with us for a year." He shakes his head in disbelief. "We have a saying in the Old Tongue, 'Every pot has its lid,' but I was only wondering, don't you know."

Suddenly, he is no longer talking and it is now my turn. I wonder what Crawford or Maxine Waters said in their interviews. He waits. "Naturally, your country is of interest to a historian," I begin, encouraged by the round head nodding. "You were the first to confront the Empire and break away." (Not completely true, but close enough and flattering.) "You were the first to practice successfully what we now term guerrilla warfare and to do so against a great power." Halfway through and words like dry wafers in my mouth for I sense there's no real approval in the nodding of the large head. I'm saying the expected; the standard runny rationale of any historian visiting here.

"Naturally, there are the great strides you have made, the development," I continue as he seems to give me marks for courage, "and . . . well, I don't mean to be insulting . . ."

"Tut-tut," he waves away the suggestion. "Speak your mind, Mr. Phillips."

"Well, because this is such a backward state and has been out of the drift of world circulation for so long, and is so poor. Naturally, the other university is a great institution but is it really you, if you know what I mean." His eyes seem to glow, as if the pig iron were heating up.

"This university, on the other hand, is about at the level of the working-class institutions in the post-Industrial Revolution period and I was just interested in seeing what that was like. In my country, we have isolated pockets of development where people still speak Elizabethan English and sing the old folk songs. We call them hillbillies and sociologists quite often go to live with them. The same reason I am here."

"Quite so," he says finally. I cannot tell whether he accepts my story or not, for he swings about and stands by the window. "We are indeed a strange lot," he begins in a soft voice. "A little more than forty years ago I had a price on my head, breathing or not; did you know that? I see you do. And now here I am today, the Dean of a fine, new university and all my credentials in order, thank you; Vienna, Oxford—even a year at your own Columbia. So this is not a political handout from the Great I Am. Do you understand that, Mr. Phillips?" There is not a hint of anger, and his voice is as melodious and even as it was at the beginning of the interview. "But I know where we stand, and I'm proud of it, knowing also where we stood. Do you follow me, Mr. Phillips? So I'm not at all insulted by your reasons for being here. I may not believe them," he smiles genially, resumes his chair, "do you understand, but I'm certainly not insulted by them. And it is graceless of me to even question our good fortune in having a man of your ability here with us. Never look the golden goose in the mouth, eh?"

"Dean Morraugh, there are two other Americans here as well . . ."

"Yes, of course," he jumps up to sit on the edge of the desk, small feet toe-tapping the floor, "and all very apt, dear fellow, all very apt. No confidence broken about

Crawford's little personal problem, have much of the same thing here among my countrymen. You are aware of it, but he's perfect here, and a fine man for Ancient History. And Mrs. R. L. Waters, Associate Professor, retired, well," he waves his hand as if it were unnecessary to continue, but does, "a little on the big side, wouldn't you say? Have you seen her eat? Experience, there. But really knows her p's and q's when it comes to grammar. Splendid for our business course. Oh, that American Lit. Yes, something to fill in with. After all, you fellows don't have much of it, do you, I mean compared to . . ." and his hand, the one intact, sweeps toward the bookcase surmounted by Burns and Swift.

"Speaking of that, let me lend you a book that might interest you." In a bound, he is at the shelves, rattles a glass-paned door and returns with a volume. "You know of Maureen nu Nailly?"

"Your patron saint?"

"Yes, St. Maureen," he sighs, thumbing through the book. "Here is the eyewitness account of her blessed martyrdom, put down in the ninth century by Friar Georgio just as he saw it from the roof of the monastery and translated only recently—the full text." He holds the book out to me and only then do I see that he is blushing.

"This is your translation," I guess.

"It is that, and a poor one beside the glorious tongue of the old friar, but he had the moment fresh in his mind." He goes on with the story. How the old orders built convents outside the monastery walls in the hopes that raiders, satisfied by what they found in the convent, would leave the treasures and books of the monastery alone. And it usually worked. But on this lamentable occasion in the ninth century it worked better than planned. For Maureen nu Nailly preferred not to wait her fate like a chicken in a coop, but walked down to the beach and her transcendental doom, where she was gang-raped by a boatload of Vikings.

"The helmsman was the worst, the blighter." Morraugh taps the book, knowingly.

And all of the facts of this "blessed martyrdom," all the details down to the last hair on a Norseman's buttocks, were recorded for posterity by the monk on the roof. This testament to sufferance for the sake of others and the deliverance thereby achieved is now placed in my hands.

"I can't thank you enough," I say. "But tell me, Dean Morraugh, for what was the monastery famous?"

"For this, old chap, for this." He taps the book in my hand.

"I know. But I mean before. Were there manuscripts or valuables, a sacred relic, that St. Maureen nu Nailly's sacrifice protected for the world?" I am at the door now, and he comes toward me, his eyes like ball bearings.

"This," he says through clenched teeth. "Only this," he taps the account of her martyrdom. "Don't you understand?"

Driving up to Providence that day, Pat talked about her foster parents. It was cool and bright and there were suggestions in the Connecticut countryside of the spring that was to come. Col. Edmond Gates I knew about, as any student of government or the reader of *Time* would. The Colonel was only a little to the left of Torquemada and he had made the newspaper he published the *Pravda* of the Republican Party; that is to say, the Democratic Party was never mentioned except in terms of its defeat in local elections. He enjoyed riding to the hounds, all the finery and ceremony, and was—according to Pat—a man of many costumes. Army-Navy Day was celebrated in her house with a festive solemnity second only to Memorial Day, and she amused me as we drove along with descriptions of the various retired admirals and generals staggering about the lawn in let-out dress blues. What I did not know, and what she told me, was the nature of her foster-father's death— from a stroke following Senator McCarthy's censure.

Happily, then, my wife's formative years were not influenced by this dull footnote to the contemporary scene, for she was only eight or nine when her foster-father died. Nor can I trace any of her opinions, mannerisms or habits back to her foster-mother, as little as I know the lady. The widow Gates is one of those attractive, seemingly practical, yet silly women one encounters at benefits for refugee pianists. I have met her but twice.

I say silly, for I regarded any of the parents who sent their daughters to Scott Junior College as silly. And her practicality was illusionary though made real enough by an adequate supply of money to paint over the errors. But there had not been enough paint to cover the mistake made with Patricia.

"I was about thirteen when she told me," Pat said, looking over a field with stone walls. Her face was filled with that same familiar haughty expression. "Until then I thought I was no different from anyone else—except for the Colonel, of course. He was certainly different from any other father," and her mouth pulled a droll grimace. She had fixed her hair this day in a way which has since become my favorite, pulled back over the ears and into a lustrous bun at the nape of the neck. She wore a becoming olive green suit and matching high heels—the first time I had ever seen her dressed so, and the transformation was startling. The appearance of a studious and very proper young lady was an appealing disguise.

"Edna Simpson," she referred to her foster-mother, "called me into the bedroom the day after my birthday party. She had had a very nice dance for me at the Club with all the others and this next day she called me into the bedroom and I steeled myself—steeled myself for all the gripping facts of life that I thought I would hear. Though I was curious to hear her version. Imagine my surprise when she told me that I had been adopted. Just like that."

"And your reactions?" We had just crossed from Connecticut into Rhode Island.

"Well, first I was relieved. I had never really liked the Colonel and always felt a little guilty because I didn't like him. He used to call me 'Kid' all the time." And her face turned to me with a smile, still registering some of the insult. "But it gets better. Edna Simpson also told me all about my illegitimacy. It seems my mother was a young girl from a very *good* family, Edna stressed that, who was having a thing with her English professor and got knocked up. Her parents prevented the marriage, there was the usual trip away and I was born in Rio. Then the Colonel and Edna got me."

"She told you nothing more."

"No, either she doesn't know any names or she won't tell me. She did say that she thought the college was either Vassar or Smith, but that doesn't mean anything because Edna just assumes that's where girls from the *very good* families went in those days."

"Like to Scott now."

"Right. Then, the week after I fell off the roof for the first time . . ."

"You what?"

"Came of age, got the curse, you know," and she made a bothersome gesture with her hands. "She hadn't told me much about that, Edna hadn't. So you see, *cher maestro*, the puberty rite in the Gates household was celebrated in a special way. Hometown, U.S.A." And she broke off and lit a cigarette.

I drove without speaking and she smoked. She held the cigarette inexpertly—I had noticed this before during our office talks—between two fingers and a thumb, scarcely inhaling and sometimes pursing her lips to blow out the smoke.

"But after a while, I also started wondering just who my real parents were." She fooled with the cigarette a bit longer, then threw it out the window. "I kept reading all the society notes in *The New York Times* looking for pictures of someone like me, only older. But that was hopeless. Then last year, when I came to Scott, I got this idea. He still might be teaching. So I got all the catalogues and made a list."

"But how can you tell?"

"Well, the fact that he teaches English narrows it down. Also his age, and where he might have been teaching about twenty years ago. All those things." Her sudden silence turned my attention from the road. She had removed the glasses, blew upon them and polished them with her skirt. Her eyes were deep and expressionless. "Also," she said finally, "I'd know him when I saw him."

We had just come over a rise and the towers of Providence swam before my eyes. Before I could stop myself, before the cool objectivity of my historical training could protect me, my imagination created the strange odyssey she had been living for the past two years. Her apparent promiscuity, her reputation on the Eastern seaboard, her complex availability had only been a way of seeking the true love that had conceived her. For two years she had been hopping from one bed and one campus to another in search of her long-lost father as surely as Telemachus had hopped from one island to another in search of his.

A sobering thought cut through my romanticism, perspective to the rescue. She was an engaging, attractive and spirited young woman with an abnormal preoccupation with sex, and I had only been looking for a reason to justify this preoccupation. My motive was all too clear, and it shocked me.

"But what about girls' colleges," I said quickly to cover my embarrassment. "How do you get invited to them? I mean," I continued, for she looked at me with quizzical eyes, a little contempt twisting her mouth, "there are English professors at them. I suppose that's a whole new field," and I was immediately sorry for the joke.

"They were the easiest," she said finally, sliding down in the seat. "It's easy to apply for a transfer and to interview the different teachers or to be interviewed. I have a whole drawerful of applications." She was smiling, the childish uper lip a bit more proffered than the lower. Her eyes glinted, sidled toward my face. "No, that's one sport I haven't the taste for," she continued, and then in almost a stagy, offhand manner, "and God knows, I've had my chances with all those crypto-lesboes at Scott."

"What? I don't believe it. Who?"

"Well, there's Sue Ellen Dryden for one," she said, flicking a scarlet fingernail.

"I don't believe it." I envisioned the principal stockholder-to-be of American Gulf Sugar, a dimpled, blond and blue-eyed darling with a sensuous drawl and perfect legs. "I don't believe it. Really?"

She began to laugh, her amusement wriggling up through her body as she pulled herself erect, kicked off her shoes and tucked the long legs beneath her. She looked at me with different eyes. "How do you think she made top sergeant on the drill team?" she said through gurgles and snorts. "The things I could tell you. Then, there's—"

"Okay, that's enough. I give up," I said and laughed too. We drove in silence, my mind now pondering where we would stay, for I could foresee complications.

"You're a square one, aren't you?" she said suddenly, but with a softness that mollified the gratuity of the remark. Her voice had been that of a child coming upon an unusual shell on the beach.

The What Cheer Motel was an enormous egg crate set upon magenta-colored girders, a few miles from downtown Providence. I picked it obviously for its distance from those chance meetings with colleagues which might compromise us both. Obviously, there could be questions raised at the more convenient and more staid hotels in the city. Obviously, there would be less opportunity for her to meet last year's frustrated freshman, his ticket to the Senior Chorus or whatever still unpunched. In fact, the real obviousness of why I had picked the What Cheer Motel made my bag heavy as we walked in to the reception desk. But Pat gave no indication she was aware of anything unusual, exhibiting that amazing dissemblance the female exudes when she senses she is desired.

And so with the full knowledge of what I was doing weighing upon me, with the alarm bells ringing full tilt and my sense of history and the cyclical theory reminding me of the student-teacher relationship of her natural parents—with all of this I managed to sign the register. We took separate rooms, and she nonchalantly questioned the desk man on whether her room came with a shower or bath, she preferring a bath. The ease with which she handled the conversation and the undeniable practice she exhibited with the situation made me grind my teeth. It was a mistake to ask, "Is the room to your liking?"

"It's all right with me, sir, if it's all right with you." The moue brought a grim smile from the desk clerk. I could have brained her on the spot.

At the top of the hill, I pulled over beneath the bell tower and let her out. We had not spoken on the way to the campus, except for a casual "Ready?" when I paused outside the door of her room at the motel. She assured me she would return to the motel by eleven o'clock—and I wondered if the curfew should not be advanced to six or seven—and left for her appointment. I watched her walk across the campus in that disjointed gait, just this side of grace, already too familiar, nor did I fail to notice the stares of the white-bucked bravos upon her.

But for the moment other matters attended me. With eager anticipation of the usual result, I threw myself into the atmosphere of the Brown campus. It could be any university. The substance and security of the halls and buildings, the perennial craft of the grounds keepers whose hedges, lawns and flower beds lend their scrupulous tidiness to one's sense of rightness. Moreover there is the seeming perpetuity of undergraduates strolling across these lawns or sitting upon the steps of these halls, for they all look alike, which grants an observer the illusion of athanasia. And in the timelessness of scholarship, of orderly inquiry and impersonal discusson, there is a hint of that congenial, spontaneous void wherein immortals live. Before my own interview, I strolled about the campus, throwing myself into this magic pool, but the magic had worn off if it had ever been there. I emerged from the attempt feeling a little foolish, as Ponce de León must have felt coming up out of the swamp water. For as I rounded the library steps I heard a laugh much like hers and turned quickly to see no one, just the door closing gently on itself. I found myself circling the red brick Victorian structure that housed the English department, imagining the tilted Valentine face with the questions upon it and the one big question within, and I sought refuge in the noisy clatter of the Blue Room. And even there, I suddenly overheard conversations—the one at the next table by a trio of beef-faced undergraduates comparing the weekend's conquests—and I jumped up, spilling coffee, and walked onto the terrace.

It was silly. I took great gulps of the New England spring air and leaned against the brick façade. She had become a particular in my timeless schema, an unreconcilable item in my carefully planned syllabus which dated it and therefore made it worthless. I was accustomed to working within a comfortable parenthesis of space into which dates were tumbled, in which events and personages came and went and wherein the geography never actually changed. And then Patricia Simpson Gates entered my office, apart and yet a part of all this, with her one-of-its-kind quest, her specific commencement in an unknown latitude, and ruined the theory. History would have to be rewritten.

Even during my interview with the chairman of the history department, a delightful and articulate longbean of a man, she interjected herself. While he commended my articles on the development of medieval guilds, his obvious knowledge of the subject enforcing the praise, the insane vision of the backs of her knees came into my mind.

And poor Gretchen, prettily golden in the candlelight of the Italian restaurant where we dined, chatted on and on, animated by the information the appointment was mine with the promise that I finish my doctorate. I could see behind her blue eyes a plan forming, one which included more intimate dinners, more skillful resolutions upon her studio couch and the eventual symbolic union of the departments of history and philosophy—a challenging, if not risky, synthesis. Indeed, it had been a plan to which I had been not opposed, which would have completely contented me until that day. But now no more.

And at the film, I could not concentrate; kept holding my watch aloft to see the time and trying in my imagination to place Patricia at some point within it. Nor did the film help. It was one of those dreary Italian numbers— Gretchen had announced this to be our "Italian night" and even insisted on using her Fulbright Italian at the restaurant. I remember passing some remark about going around the world with Columbus, the feebleness of it I repeat to demonstrate my state of mind—but the film had to do with a group of holiday excursionists who spent all their time looking for one of their number, a girl, who had wandered off by herself.

Finally, at ten o'clock, I used the phone in the rear of the theater and called the motel. Pat answered and she sounded half asleep, but the more we talked, it was depression I distinguished in her voice, not fatigue. Professor Owen McEdwards was definitely not her father.

Whether she was too absorbed in the aimlessness of the

film or too surprised by my abrupt change of plans, Gretchen merely nodded when I returned and whispered that I had to leave. I cannot remember what excuse I gave her, not that she seemed to want one, and I had none anyway. All the way back to the motel, I could not think of a single rational excuse, no logical justification for what I was about to do.

The gin in this country is of rare quality and though I cannot drink it as the natives do, straight and warm from the bottle, it makes a first-class martini. I prepare a second of these for the two of us, using the last four ice cubes from the one tray in the toylike refrigerator. Patricia bends over the stove, frying sausages, and it's just because we are having sausages and mashed potatoes for supper, and have had sausages and mashed potatoes for supper nearly every night this week, that I cannot tell her of the Thanksgiving festival spontaneously organized.

By now, the guest list has grown by one more, Professor Crawford, whom I met at the Red Dog on the way home. By the third ale I had felt sufficiently sorry for him to ask him also. He is, after all, an American clinging as we are to Mother Europe's bosom.

True, Mrs. Maxine Waters' husband's mother's genius with the cranberry would be reproduced, but this would be a negligible contribution compared with the remainder of the meal to which I had thoughtlessly committed my pregnant wife. The enormity of my deed sinks heavy within me as the oily aroma of the frying sausages rises in my head.

I sit on one of the two stools and contemplate her. Looking at her from behind, the four months' pregnancy is not apparent, and I see the same straight back gracefully curve into that swell of hip that is a classic fascination. She reaches for the saltcellar above the stove and the line of thigh is emphasized, the soft nook behind the knee exposed, and the muscles in the calf elongate and harden. Several ales and two martinis are all it takes to make a Viking of me, and in my stuporous imagination, the sausages burn to a fine, black crisp as my lust martyrs her on the cold linoleum.

"How has your day been?" I ask.

"Not bad," she answers. She picks up her drink from the counter and takes a good gulp. "Better now. You know, I could become an alcoholic. A couple of drinks and all the symptoms disappear."

"Nonsense. By the way, I discovered a small little shop today—on Fleebus Street—something on the order of a gourmet place. But anyway, they seemed to have a fair amount of spices and—"

"You don't like the chow in this place." She hammers the frying pan with the fork. The long hair swings about her shoulders when she turns. "You can go elsewhere."

"Not a bit, not a bit," I quickly assure her, "but it's just that . . ."

"Ah, Hamlet." She comes to me and leans against me, hugging my face to her bosom. "What have I done to you?"

"Whatever it is, I like it," I say. And I mean it. I put my ear to her belly and listen. There is only the crackle and pop of the sausages.

"You're a nice man," she says finally, patting my shoulder, and returns to the stove. "I'll try the store, but I won't promise anything. If I can just get this damn house cleaned up early enough to get downtown. If you only knew the things I dread doing every morning I wake up." She pulls the heavy sweater low over the mound of her belly, so obvious in profile, supports the growth and burps. "Oh, boy, that was a goodie."

To mention the gourmet shop is only one more of the not-so-delicate hints I have been making about her cooking. This was not always the case. When Patricia moved in, or rather took over my discreet bachelor apartment near Scott Junior College, she had stocked it with a shelf of seasonings and delicacies. Her approach to cooking was similar to her amatory genius; inventive, sometimes daring, but always completely satisfying. There had been no recipe she would not attempt nor any she failed. Her ability was self-taught, assisted by a natural curiosity to try what "sounded good."

So, I sit on one of two stools and eye the pair of salt and pepper shakers above the stove, the only seasonings to come into her hand for several months. I smell the sausages and recall the pâtés, the cacciatores, the sorrel soups, the endless gastronomic pleasures she once concocted. They sit above the stove, this pair of basic ingredients, in their plain containers like the stern portraits of puritanical grandparents.

"I'll give it a try," Patricia promises, spooning out the mashed potatoes. "But look at this stove. Why only three burners? Why not four?" And she points to the blank space at a front corner of the stove. It is a legitimate question. "What kind of a crazy country is this anyway? I sometimes think the Colonel was right." She spears two fat slugs of sausage. "Bomb them all!" And she slaps the plate down before me.

"That would play havoc with our balance of trade, wouldn't it?"

"Listen, the more I think about it, the more I think the

Colonel was right about a lot of things." She prepares her own plate.

"Yes, except for his sense of direction," I say, making a little canal of the potatoes for the sausage grease to run.

"Now what does that mean?" Her plate is beside mine but she still stands. "Look who's talking about sense of direction. Any man who would crash into the only hill in the state of Illinois." This allusion to the airplane crash that took my father's life is a standard gibe, but my martini-dulled reflexes rise to the bait.

"Charles Mound is not a mountain, it is true, but it is some twelve hundred feet above sea level and is the highest point in the state of Illinois." I speak with an authority to end the matter.

"And it's the only high point in Illinois, Prairie State I think it's called, but *your* father managed to find it."

"He died in the service of science. Had he perfected the radar he was working on—"

"Ha! Had *he* perfected it."

"Oh, listen," I say, beginning to lose my patience, but it is enough. She sits down quietly and we begin to eat. We perch side by side on the stools, eating from the kitchen counter like two strange commuters. It takes me several minutes to realize she is not eating. The tears pour from her eyes, roll halfway down her inclined cheeks and drop onto her plate. "Oh, Patricia, don't." She comes against me, my arm supports her.

"God, I've become such a bitch," she snuffles. A paper napkin pushes her glasses awry and she wipes her eyes. "Is this my real nature? Does having a baby make you act the way you really are?"

"Just the opposite, I'd say."

She becomes very quiet and I look down. The face is

that of a child concentrating and then suddenly it wrinkles up and the tears gush. "Oh, Hamlet. I want to go home. I don't like this place and this crummy old house and this dumpy country . . . and this lousy kitchen . . . and . . . this clammy . . . weather . . ." and boohooing is the only term to describe what follows.

All I can do is to hold her tight, for there is nothing I can say and less to do, so I hold her tight and let her cry it out. It passes as quickly as it came: a few sighs, a stabbing gasp, a sniffle and it is over. "Come now, eat your sausages, before they get cold," I say, and we both begin to laugh and I must hold her again to keep her from falling off the stool.

There is the usual choice after dinner of one of us reading while the other watches television or of both of us watching television. Patricia sometimes resolves this dilemma by falling asleep on the couch, which obligates me to turn off one reading lamp and retire to the Chippendale chair before the television. The programs here are usually the worst of the American reruns. Occasionally there will be a program from the BBC or German television, the latter being heavy-footed imitations of American musicals complete with hearty Fred Astaires.

There are also a few local programs, special events in our house, and all in the Old Tongue. Patricia and I made an attempt to try to learn the language when we first came and would lean forward on the hard Chippendale seats to catch a familiar phrase or the sense of the dialogue. But it all began to sound like a tobacco auctioneer played at slow speed and we usually ended up being more amused than educated.

I suggest going to a movie, perhaps the bright lights of the capital city and the extravagant nonsense of the current

Doris Day film, the most popular American import here,
might lift her from the doldrums that still dull her eyes,
but she shakes her head. Anxious as we were to dutifully
explore our first European capital together, we made
weekly pilgrimages along the main boulevards only to discover that we were doing the same thing each time. Dinner
at a Chinese restaurant and then off to Doris and Rock or
sometimes, if lucky, Debbie and Somebody.

Even the Chinese restaurant came to a bad end, for an
exposé by the morning paper revealed that health author-
ities discovered one of them serving cat meat in the *moo
goo gai pan.* It was not the restaurant we frequented, but
the knowledge that one of them was doing it lent a rather
smug malevolence to the inscrutability of our favorite
waiter, so we never returned.

So we take our places, she before the television and I
beneath the one reading lamp on the sofa. I open the account of St. Maureen's martyrdom, translated by Gilbert
Morraugh, L.L.D., PhD and Order of the Green Shield. I
expected nothing of what I found, but opening at random,
this is what I read.

Then down another Berserk came, followed
By a fifth. Two-horned monsters, jerkins
Open on a third, great pommels swollen
By the carnal hunt, to clip the tender prey
Furry nest and all—of late the long-oared oarsman's lock.
 Ah, poor creature, ah! Blessed be her torture!
 Would the sun were black and eyes plucked out,
 She's covered all over with glory.
Forgiveness smiles from Maureen's lips as
Nectar spills the upturned eyes. Mercy lipped, her
Dulcet privities exposed, a birth of blessings
'Nough to save a Christian nation, though not nu Nailly.

Sweet limbs cruelly strung, the saintly morsel served to
 heathen fork.
 Ah, poor creature, ah! Blessed be her torture.
 Would the sun were black and eyes plucked out,
 She's covered all over with glory.
Horny ram of Viking rends the supple gusset.
Maureen trembles 'neath the Norseman's mortal wound-
 ings,
Transcendent in her transfixed sanctity, suffers,
Wine of martyrdom atones the pagan spear effulgent;
Stone of suffering lust soft from her splendid sacrifice.
 Ah, poor creature, ah! Blessed be her torture.
 Would the sun were black and eyes plucked out,
 She's covered all over with glory.
Fifth to lift her 'bove mere mortal state, rudely
Turns the damsel's form, his mate enhalves the apple
Modest womanhood would die to show, vicious
Altar all exposed, where condemnation is said to worship.
Pierced to soul, she bears the swinish swiver of the
 sweetmeat there.
 Ah, poor creature, ah! Blessed . . ."

The euphemistic language and sense of poor Maureen
pulled this way and that by the two Vikings, as seen by
Friar Georgio on the roof, is enough to engage my own
yearnings. Moreover, a brief calculation reveals that this is
only Viking four and five; with the whole boatload to go,
not to mention the helmsman. And above my sensual gut
rises the admiration and respect for Gil Morraugh, the
Bloody Whip of the West. A man who can turn such a
phrase as "swinish swiver of the sweetmeat there" cannot
be all bad.

I rise and walk into the dining room. Patricia sits
hunched over on the Chippendale, engrossed in a Walt
Disney film featuring beavers. The moment I put my hand

upon her, she knows, for she stiffens and peers more intently through her glasses at the cavorting animals.

"How do you think they do it?" I say, trying to be offhand.

"None of your damn business," she replies and shrugs me off.

"Slipping through the water or in their furry nests?" I determinedly pursue the guise, though knowing it will come to nothing. She has even crossed her legs.

"Pick out one of those eight chairs and sit down and cool off. You might learn something," she says, still staring at the screen.

"You're a cruel woman, Patricia Gates," I say half mockingly, but with seriousness at heart. "I shall die of prostate cancer. There are more ways to season sausage and mash than with just salt and pepper." She turns from the television and looks at me. She merely looks at me, coolly and with all the disdain with which the Colonel must have regarded a Democrat. I confess it is all I deserve.

She had been watching a late movie on the television in her room. The What Cheer Motel had settled down to another night of salesmen's turnings and tossings, the parking lot arrayed with their sample-packed automobiles, ready for the morning assault. And on the highway, like great tanks going ahead to soften up resistance or perhaps following up, consolidating the day's gains, huge trailer trucks passed each other at breakneck speed. Pat seemed to have expected me, opening the door to my knock and returning to her chair before the set, all without a word— as if I belonged with her in that room. The long black hair lay loose upon her shoulders. And this alarmed me, this matter-of-fact acceptance. I had been thinking in terms of a contest, the one within myself already lost, but yet with victory over the situation still possible, only to arrive and find surrender already in progress. It was somehow not fair.

"They've got super cheeseburgers here. Are you hungry?" She had asked the image of Clark Gable, who did not look at all hungry. I was, but shook my head.

It is not unusual for a teacher to have an affair with a student; not especially acceptable either, but not unusual. The literature is full of many instances—there were her own parents, after all—and the thought depressed me all the more.

The study of history has left me unsentimental, but to be part of a pattern, to become a mark in the sequential accumulation called history, has been my one anathema and it has led me to make choices or decisions, some of them so "out of line" that they arouse the patient indignation of friends and colleagues. My decision to teach at Scott Junior College, for example, when both Duke and Chicago were competing for my services, lost me the respect and ultimately the association of the last few friends, those who had held on tolerantly to the end, finally giving me up because I had not realized their expectations.

And yet this unexpected decision to come to this mediocre finishing school for rich and weary girls was putting me into a pattern more formidable than any I had ever known, one which I could feel myself entering. The irony of it pressed upon me as I sat in the What Cheer Motel room and watched Patricia. She sat with knees drawn up beneath her chin, staring at the television. Her well-manicured fingernails traced the cuticles of her well-

manicured toes. I was but another in the succession of
warm male bodies she would cling to on a Saturday night
after a potential father had been interviewed in the afternoon. I was to be repaid, as all before me had been repaid,
for the opportunity given her to meet and inspect another
candidate for the position.

But I was not fooled by the gift and this set me apart
a little from the Harvard Harrys who had shared her bed.
When I imagined the fatuous, egotistical presumptions
they made for their irresistible charms, their delusion
washed out any jealousy, any envy I may have felt and
with a dark amusement. None of them had known that
she had used them and not the other way around, that she
was seeking to obliviate, for however momentary a caress,
the ultimate denial of love she had suffered long ago. She
had given herself to sustain the hope that this ideal love still
existed, and to protect the treasure of this invaluable faith.

"So he's not the one?" I said finally.

"What?" She turned her face, resting her left ear upon
her knees.

"Professor McEdwards, he's not the one."

"No. He was in Europe when it happened."

"What was he doing in Europe?"

"The war. He was a pilot."

"A pilot," I repeated. Professor McEdwards' war record
was suddenly very important. "A fighter pilot?"

"He didn't say." She looked almost sullen. Reflections
of the old movie flitted across her glasses. "I knew when
I saw him he wasn't the one. Too young."

"How old do you suppose he is?" I asked.

"Oh, I don't know." Her mouth pursed as she reck-
oned. "No special age, maybe fifty, maybe sixty."

"That old?"

"I have a feeling he was a bachelor or maybe a widower."

"Or maybe a respectable married don with a secret letch for schoolgirls," I said.

"Pish-tosh." She rejected the idea with a swirl of hair. Again, the expression was arrogant as she returned her attention to the screen. "No, I have a very real idea of what he looks like," she said after a moment.

"Wears tweeds, of course."

"Well, yes."

"Smokes a pipe, hair a little longish but neat, manly but gentle eyes—understanding, totally understanding eyes. And a small moustache perhaps, now white." She was smiling. "Look," I said, leaning forward, "Ronald Colman is dead."

She continued to sit, knees drawn up, continued to smile. Then she said softly, "That wasn't nice."

"Surgery is never nice," I answered. But I had nothing more to say and I worked around for another topic that wouldn't sound too inane. "My interview went well."

"Did it?"

"Yes. There's no problem. I only have to complete my doctorate, just a few credits. No problem. It's a very good department."

"How was your friend?"

"Who?" Poor Gretchen, I had forgotten her. The film must be over by now and she would be walking back to her apartment alone, reinterpreting the melancholy search of the film's plot by my sudden, unexplained disappearance. "Oh, she's fine. We went to a film."

"Which one?"

"I can't remember the name. It was Italian. We had dinner and went to a film. Have you eaten?"

She nodded her head toward an empty plate on the bedside table. "Yes, the cheeseburgers."

"They were good, were they?" She nodded, lighting a cigarette, holding it in that curiously inexpert way. "Look, Patricia," I said, not knowing what I would say next, nor did her turning toward me help. "This is not the ordinary way I . . ." That was no good. "This isn't the usual . . ." Nothing there either. "What I mean to say . . ." She waited and so did my tongue, "I want you to understand, after all, you are my pupil. I'm responsible for you—well, I know why you're doing this," I said triumphantly, though whatever seemed to be gained disappeared beneath her blank stare. She blinked those big eyes once, twice and then smiled.

"Why I'm doing what?"

"This insane pilgrimage of yours. You must bring it to an end, because it has no end of its own. You could go on looking for your father for the rest of your life. Take my own father, for instance." And here I told her about the circumstances of his death. "When they found the wreckage it had burned completely, incinerated, with nothing left but some metal fragments. I could imagine that he was still alive somewhere, simply because there was nothing left."

She began to shake her head, taking between her lips a gold religious device, or so I assumed, always worn around her throat. "It's not the same," she replied. "It's so boring not to know who you look like. I used to think I had the Colonel's nose and Edna's mouth, but the moment she told me—I remember I was looking at her mouth, really finked by what was coming out of it—anyway, I could see the difference right away. Funny." She continued to bite the medal.

"But this matter of going from one campus to another" —my voice assumed the pretentious tone of the faculty advisor, but I could not stop—"of being with all these boys. Well, it's . . ."

"Immoral," she supplied.

"I was going to say 'not wise.' " I tried to smile benignly.

"Yes, I thought of that." She rubbed a bare foot against the calf of one long leg. "The first time it was an accident." I tried to interrupt, for I immediately felt all my hypocrisy, all my ragtag moralism. She looked so defenseless and contrite, then with an abrupt shift of her body, now sitting tailor-fashion, she had become that Braggadocia which both moved and amused me. "Anyway," she had continued, "they were all so cute, and I liked it, so I said, 'What the hell.' You'd be surprised at the girls that don't like it."

"No, I wouldn't," I replied, sorry to have been trapped into the smallest implication of my personal life.

"Now that seems immoral to me," she said. "Just because it's expected of them. I think it's immoral to do anything you don't want to do only because it's expected of you. It's not honest. Is it?"

"No."

"For example, all those jujubes before World War I you're always talking about, they got into that mess because they all behaved the way people expected them to behave. None of them sat down and said, 'Now look, boys, honor and patriotism is one thing but a lot of buddy-boys are going to get fritzed if we behave like gentlemen.' Right?"

"Well, it was a little more complicated than that." As

she pulled the medallion back and forth on the chain around her neck, I recognized its shape, for I have one myself. It was a Phi Beta Kappa key.

"You should see Sue Ellen Dryden after a big weekend. She's either constipated or throwing up."

"That's no concern of mine," I said, unnerved by these dormitory revelations, "nor is it your concern. What other girls do—"

"Yes. I know. I'm different." She interrupted me with a mischievous laugh. "Edna always told me that and I never really understood what she meant until that day in her bedroom."

"You are different."

"How do you mean?" Her eyes widened but she regarded me calmly.

"Where did you get that?" I indicated the Phi Bete key.

"It was his," she replied. "Apparently he gave it to her as a sort of engagement deal, and she passed it on to me when I was born. Edna gave it to me that day in her bedroom. But the name was rubbed off." She turned it over and I could see the reverse side had been blanked by a jeweler's wheel.

The television was suddenly off and I was standing before her, lecturing. I don't remember what the words were, and like all pompous drivel that hides a genuine emotion they merely took up space and time. I talked about the impossibility of finding her father, of wasting herself in the search, of the damage it might do her as a person. I think I even mentioned something about reputation, immediately skewered by the mocking glance she threw me, and so I went on some other tangent. Her head had bowed beneath my tongue-lashing and I wondered if I was being too harsh. I talked about her own fulfillment as a person. I told her to forget her father, not to use him as a crutch, to look within herself for her own identity. On I went. My lecture paused. Her head remained bowed, she trembled as if weeping, but it was laughter. She looked up at me with a big grin on her face, took off her glasses and stretched. She had the grace not to yawn.

I grabbed her by the arms and pulled her to her feet as if she were a naughty child. I shook her so violently that a small mote of fear passed through the brown eyes. I shouted into her face, "You mustn't do this anymore. Do you understand, you must not do this anymore."

"Why not?" she managed to say during one of the lulls I permitted. The glasses were off, held in one hand, my grip preventing her from putting them on. Her eyes were like velvet, and she continued to smile up at me.

"Because."

"Because why?"

"Because I don't want . . . because you are . . . because . . ." and it seemed simpler and more honest to kiss her.

There will be no detailed exposition of what then followed; I am, after all, describing my wife. Moreover, there have been so many memoirs, novels and films of late which relate how a man and woman prepare for and maneuver in a bed that this episode would only be one more tedious diagraming of a basic geometric truth. But perhaps some general comment is important along with a few sketched momentos.

As I lay waiting for her to finish brushing her teeth, a rather childish endeavor under the circumstances and one which she seemed perversely to take a great deal of time doing, I wondered how she would be. I'm sorry to offend those who would prefer the term make love; an inaccurate phrase, for love is rarely made and it is certainly not made in a bed. Men and women do only two things in bed—they sleep or they fuck, and often, as Mark Twain noted, they die. But make love? Never.

I've always divided women into two categories; prewar and postwar, a qualification of attitudes rather than of time incidence. The prewar girl generally approaches a man with a questioning, sometimes utilitarian attitude. The good ones in this category have read all the books on the subject and set about the practical application with a mechanical cerebration that often makes them seem lewd.

The postwar girl, on the other hand, approaches a man with no reservations, but with all her heart, soul, body and mind. She is permanently "turned on," as is currently said, and needs no instructions, manual or anatomy to find her way. She instinctively knows where she should be and what she should be doing at all times, and there is a spontaneity and humor to her performance that can never be learned. I have made an allusion to cooking and sex before, so let me elaborate.

Good cooks are usually people who like to eat well, to eat interestingly. The same can be said for women and sex. Performance at the stove is directly related to performance in the bed. I have no sociological or psychological evidence to support these findings, only personal data. Indeed, I spent a whole afternoon and early evening one time trying to explain this theory to a sociologist friend of mine, including the effect of the war, jet travel, intraculturization and other errata, but I could see it made no sense to him at all. We ended up at his house, slightly drunk, where his wife served up frozen TV dinners.

All of this preamble to establish one thing about my wife—Patricia Simpson Gates Phillips is definitely postwar.

My own moments of pride and glory were not lacking

that first night either and it is with admitted immodest satisfaction, but in the truest sense of historical objectivity, that I report Patricia took a very deep breath at one point and sighed "Holy Mackerel!" The awe and the wonder in her voice obviously erased her memory of all those buttoned-down bunglers.

It was a wild night and with a few hazards; more than once, the golden key dangling from her neck nearly cost me an eye. There was also the moment when we were only able to rub noses and content to do so. We held each other at dawn and listened to the rush of trailer trucks outside the window, resembling the sound of crashing surf. Nor will I forget her laughter when she came to the door of my room just before we checked out and caught me mussing up the unused bed, thumping the pillow and rumpling a towel.

I could not take my eyes from her. As we drove back to Scott, our hands would meet on the seat between us, then part and then miles later meet again. After we passed through Hartford, she rummaged through her purse and pulled out the small notebook. She made a casual perusal, page by page, and then with a pencil drew a line through the name of Brown University. It was the last to be marked. I watched the small white pieces of paper swirl in the rearview mirror and disappear.

The breeze pulled them from her fingers, as she let them go one by one, with peaceful purpose. I gripped the wheel and pushed down the gas pedal. I began to sing.

I T IS SEVERAL DAYS SINCE MY IMPULSIVE INVITATIONS HAVE committed us to a Thanksgiving feast. Nor have I told Patricia about it yet, and wonder if I should as we dress to go out for dinner. She stands before the largest of the two bedroom mirrors, trying on dresses, disgustedly noting the way each has become too small. It is not the time and place to break the news.

Perhaps after this evening, when we have enjoyed the novelty of dining in one of the exclusive clubs, I can bring the matter up. For we have been invited by Dean Morraugh and his wife to a small dinner party at the Royal Hunt Club and maybe the night out in these unusual surroundings may bring her spirits up.

We enter the white stone Georgian edifice and I am again reminded of the strange way these people cherish the memory of their former masters. The Royal Hunt Club, like every other building and institution left behind by the British, is kept in a state of polished degeneration. The brass fixtures are cracked and thin yet shined to regimental luster. The carpets are worn, some with actual holes, but tacked down neatly and well brushed. Patricia looks even fresher and lovelier in these surroundings, an American college girl on tour, somehow pregnant, but still very new and young and unspoiled; the gray flannel jumper she finally chose to wear, the perfect choice as she always makes. Small diamond earrings twinkle in the pink lobes of her ears beneath the swept-back black hair.

Across the waxed parquet of the entrance hall, scars of dragoon spurs still in evidence, Patricia and I walk slowly in order to register the overwhelming remnants of the British Empire. There are miniature brass cannon to the left and right of us. Tattered guidons are grouped in the corners. Stern viceroys hang from the wall, their cheeks, above the crisp white whiskers, as red as the coats they wear. There are portraits of horses also, riderless and wise. And the rich tribute wrung from this colonial outpost, the treasure gleaned from this rule, is ranked in cases set against the wainscot. The trophies, the silver plates and cups glisten behind glass, glittering relics of the victories of hound and horse over fox. As Americans, we cannot take it seriously, though I pass a remark of how the Colonel would have enjoyed it; yet, as Americans we are also foreigners and forced on the defensive by this splendid array, we become gawky outlanders in these surroundings dedicated to a ritualized diversion beyond our ken.

I will admit that these observations may be very personal, for Patricia seems at ease, though obviously not a part of this heritage. But in any event, we are thrown a line of rescue; the harsh Midwestern voice of Mrs. Robert Lewis Waters is cast from an adjoining salon. We find our party standing by a small walnut service bar in the corner of the room.

"But, my dear," Mrs. Waters tells Dean Morraugh, "he is one of our great poets, and it is criminal—criminal, I tell you—for your people not to be able to read him." She holds a sherry in one hand and makes her point with a crumbling hors d'oeuvre in the other.

To her right stands Jack Crawford, elegant and manly

in his rumpled tweeds, his flushed face burned by the wind of the disease that has blown him from one faculty to the next. He talks with Mrs. Morraugh, a tall, handsome woman with the pale complexion and blue eyes of her Viking ancestors.

"There you are." Dean Morraugh swings round to us. "To you," he completes the greeting with the colloquial phrase. At one time it may have been "Hello to you" or "Health to you," but whatever prefix there was has long disappeared, substituted by a faint catch of the breath before the preposition and pronoun. "We are only waiting for another couple," he says genially. "The Smith-Royces; he's our shadow minister of education, a brilliant fellow," he adds casually, suggesting the quality is inherent to all members of the Dean's political party. The small band of rebels which seized independence split into the two major political parties of this country and Dean Morraugh's wing is temporarily out of power. "Here they are," he speaks over my shoulder, and I see another couple has followed behind us.

Smith-Royce is a stiff, pale young man of about my age and height, and his wife matches him in height, color and fierceness of eye. The drab simplicity of her maroon dress, cut square at the neck and with puffs at the sleeves, indicates that it is the gown worn on special occasions.

"To you."

"To you."

"To you."

"How do you do?"

"To you."

"Nice to meet you." The introductions go the round, more drinks are requested from the dairy maid behind the bar, as I try to place Smith-Royce, for he looks familiar.

"Music Hall," Pat helps me in a whispered moment, reminding me of the German variety show on television and, in turn, of the local panel program that usually precedes it and of which, I now recognize, he is the moderator. Conducting the program sometimes in English, sometimes in the Old Tongue, Smith-Royce cross-examines officials of the political party in power in the guise of public service.

"Well now," he says to me, sipping a gin and lime while his right hand poses against his vest, suit jacket thrown back, "another nasty flare in your racial problem, I see."

"Oh, really?" I answer, playing dumb. Remarkably, his sharp-featured face has little more color in the flesh than it has on the black and white television tube.

"Yes, in Chicago. Don't you know? Had it on the news this evening. Nasty business there. How will it effect the election?"

"It's hard to say."

"I hate Chicago, anyway," Mrs. Smith-Royce says. Her sparrowlike frame closes the gap to make us a foursome and cut off from the others.

"Yes," her husband agrees. "We spent a year there. Northwestern, don't you know. Fearful place, though the pay was good, I dare say."

"Oh, I hated it," Mrs. Smith-Royce shudders.

"Fine library though," he continues, as if beginning to remember a few good points, "the people there all very generous. Very generous indeed."

"Perfectly frightful place," his wife confides to Pat. She even arches her head back and nearly spits out the judgment.

"It gets very cold in the winter," Pat says.

"The weather was the least of it," Mrs. Smith-Royce answers. "It's all so materialistic, everyone out for his own end and damn the rest. Positively shocking. It's a wonder to me there are not riots every day."

"Yes, it's a pity you can't get this racial business fixed up," Smith-Royce says cordially. "You Americans are really such a generous people, it's a shame this has to happen."

"Yes, but Kermit," she turns upon her husband with the same suave penetration I had seen him use on some luckless minister, "why were they so generous with you? Did you ever ask yourself that?"

He is saved an answer by Maxine Waters, who joins us, sherry in one hand, the other at her throat, fingering some beads. "I hear the name of Chicago," she says, an uncertain smile upon her large, fleshy face. Her bearing is ladylike and gracious though a bit reserved, like someone first joining tablemates on a twelve-month cruise. I make the introductions, again.

"Yes, the Smith-Royces didn't care for it," Patricia explains.

"Ah, I quite agree," Mrs. Waters nods. "And I was born there. Always trying to keep up with New York." The mention of the Empire City seems to infuriate Mrs. Smith-Royce even more.

"All those people," she begins, but has no chance to elaborate.

"But you must see St. Louis." Mrs. Waters overcomes the dialogue. "My husband used to say that St. Louis had all the qualities of a great city. Yes, oh yes," she says, though no one was disagreeing, "St. Louis is a great city."

"And St. Francisco?" Smith-Royce asks after a moment's silence. I envision an evening testing Mrs. Water's opinion of American cities, one by one.

"Ye-e-es," she draws out her consideration of San

Francisco. "A lovely town. My husband and I spent some time there a number of years ago. He was a Southerner, really . . . really just a farm boy," she laughs and nods, "so he sometimes was a bit taken in by the big city." Mrs. Waters fingers her beads.

"Your husband is no longer alive, I take it," Smith-Royce says.

"No. My husband died in 1962." Mrs. Waters finishes her sherry and peers into the glass. "In October of 1962."

"You've no doubt heard of Robert Lewis Waters," Pat says after a moment. "Robert Lewis Waters," she repeats into the blank, thin face of Mrs. Royce-Smith, "one of our leading American poets. You know his ballads, of course." And she swirls her martini around the one ice cube in the glass and takes a swig.

"Yes, of course." Smith-Royce turns to Maxine Waters with a bewildered interest.

"Oh, indeed," chimes his wife with the same muffled recognition.

Down another corridor pictured with famous equestrians and their equally famous mounts and then into a large dining room where we take our places at a big round table by tall French windows. The deepening twilight plays upon the rolling hills outside. There are other diners, all looking like successful civil servants and their wives and we are served by awkward, thick-legged girls with rosy cheeks. Pat says later that she expected one of them to throw her white apron over her face and screech, "Oh, sirrah!"

In contrast to the thick napery and the cumbersome, ornate silver—all part of the spoils of the revolution, I suppose—service is family-style, beginning with a large tureen of tasteless, gray soup. Dean Morraugh portions out the bowls majestically, and we pass them around. There are several glasses at each plate and sherry is poured into the first.

White wine comes with the fish, some kind of flounder served up with a neutral dressing tasting like wet mittens. And with the roast, carved with manly precision by Dean Morraugh, red wine is poured, into a third goblet. There's a large bowl of creamed onions and something that looks like prehistoric celery which has fallen into an open fire. And upon a silver platter by themselves are boiled potatoes in a steaming pyramid. There is a really excellent cheese, followed by the announcement of dessert, whose name brings murmurs of delight from both Mrs. Smith-Royce and Mrs. Morraugh and which turns out to be vanilla pudding with a dab of raspberry jelly in the middle. Then comes a pale, scalding-hot liquid that resembles coffee, and some superb brandy.

So much for the menu, and I go into detail only to give a fair example of the cooking at the Royal Hunt Club, for it is about the same everywhere else here. Eating out in the several so-called foreign restaurants, one encounters the almost identical bill of fare with a few variations. In the Italian restaurants, spaghetti is substituted for potatoes, though it is not uncommon to see diners eating both potatoes and spaghetti, and in the French restaurants the potatoes are quartered and fried to a shiny black. A dish of red cabbage comes with the meal in those restaurants calling themselves German. The one exception is, of course, the Chinese restaurants with their weakness for pussycats.

Our dinner party plunges into this massive meal with courage and gusto, depending upon where you sit, all except Jack Crawford, who merely picks sufficiently at his plate to justify the refilling of the glasses before him. I note that he turns down a second sherry with a gesture of courteous surfeit that is subsequently falsified by replenishments of white and red.

Out host and hostess are redoubtable trenchermen and the Smith-Royces are not far behind, but it is Maxine Waters who outdoes them all. Her savoring of the soup, gobbling of the flounder and gristmilling of the roast is a performance all its own. Conversation is difficult though she herself manages between bites and swallows to utter such commendations as "Beautiful, beautiful food." Indeed, she repeats it so many times that I wonder if she is not being sarcastic, and in fact the Morraughs and the Smith-Royces fall into an embarrassed silence. I wonder if Maxine Waters judges food not so much by flavor as by poundage on the plate. "Lovely, beautiful food." She smacks her lips.

"Do let me help you to more meat, Mrs. Waters," Dean Morraugh says, "and here's a nice potato just for you." And over her halfhearted protests he piles her plate high again. It is then I become aware he is just as solicitous of Crawford's needs. "Professor Crawford requires more wine, I think," he mentions to the waitress, or, "Professor Crawford, do try another of the red, it's a special vineyard to us and the bouquet builds. Of course, you Americans have had more experience with wines than we, our peasant heritage you know, but this has a character of its own. Don't you agree, Professor?"

"How do you find our food stores, Mrs. Phillips?" the Dean's wife asks.

"Well, I just walk to those in the neighborhood, so far," Pat answers. "But I'll find the others as we get settled. Ham has already discovered a gourmet shop on Fleebus."

"A gourmet shop on Fleebus Street?" Mrs. Morraugh

says in wonderment. "Think of that," and she crosses a look with her husband, which has some special meaning.

"One thing, I do know," Patricia continues, her face flushed by the wine, "you do have excellent sausage in this country," and she looks at me. I ignore her and turn to the Smith-Royces.

"Chicago couldn't have been too bad as far as restaurants are concerned," I say.

"Yes," Mrs. Smith-Royce painfully acknowledges. "There was one restaurant that was quite good. What was that place we found so good, Kermit?"

"Yes, what was it called? Somebody's name. Simple name."

"Yes, that's right," she says, smiling with fond remembrance. "Something-something. Something Johnson."

"Howard Johnson," Patricia says flatly.

"Yes, you know it?" Mrs. Smith-Royce says eagerly.

"No, but I've heard of it," Patricia says and sips delicately at her wine.

"This is quite an impressive meal and surroundings," I say to Mrs. Morraugh. "Do you have many members here?"

"Oh, yes, many."

"My wife won several cups in her younger days," I say, ignoring the flash of jet eyes across the table. "Do you ride, Mrs. Morraugh?"

"Oh my, no." The Dean's wife nearly goes face down in her plate with the absurdity of the idea.

"What's that, Greta?" he notes her amusement.

"Mr. Phillips asks if we ride." His amusement is more controlled, almost patronizing.

"The only thing I ever rode," he says, "was a bicycle with a Lewis gun on my back. And that's no mean feat.

Ah, no, Mr. Phillips, we are only simple people and all this passion for the horse and hound belongs to another era, another class. Indeed, I doubt if there is anyone in this room," he gestured to the other diners, "who knows from which side you mount a horse."

"But I saw stables, I saw horses in the paddock."

"Ah, indeed, we have members who ride. That's true, but they are nonresidents, you might say. Some English, and a good deal of your Americans come here for the season. Yes, fly their mounts over and all. And they're most welcome. Yes, most welcome. But the resident membership, you might call us, no, we've kept the old place going just for old times' sake. Also, you can't get a better meal in town than here." I must nod in agreement. "We ride?" he repeats softly, and his moon of a face splits into a silent laugh, the leaden eyes roll.

Mrs. Dean Gil Morraugh gets to her full height and it is a signal for the ladies to leave us, adjourning to the small parlor where we first gathered. The port is served, Jack Crawford waving it away though letting himself be urged to a third brandy, and Dean Morraugh calls for cigars. Kermit Smith-Royce leans over the table and the conversation like a pasty-faced gargoyle. Morraugh leans back in his chair, puffing contentedly.

"Well, now look here," Smith-Royce says, "what are you chaps going to do about your racial problem?"

"Well, first of all," I say, "I don't think it is entirely our problem alone. Whatever happens, whatever we do will set the pattern for the rest of the world. So says Baldwin, and I agree."

"Baldwin?" Morraugh asks.

"Yes," Smith-Royce tells him, "that Negro chap that writes the dirty books."

"Ah, yes," Morraugh remembers.

"But we have no racial problem here," Smith-Royce says. "We have no blacks here."

"There's Africa," Jack Crawford says quietly.

"I beg your pardon."

"I said there's Africa," he repeats, smoothing his moustache.

"Yes, quite."

"Speaking of dirty books," I turn to Dean Morraugh, "Mrs. Waters is very upset because one of our authors is banned here. Apparently he's considered obscene."

"Yes, she's spoken to me about that," Dean Morraugh replies. "It is a bid lewd, don't you agree, young girls cohabiting with stallions. Rather impossible in any event, unrealistic. But there's no problem there, really. If she really wants to read it, we can easily arrange for the books to be imported—though we'll have to be careful about who gets his hands on it."

"There's no censorship here," Smith-Royce interjects. "I can acquire any book I wish. No problem to it."

"What about her?" I nod at one of the dumpy serving maids just as she hoists a heavy tray of dishes from a near table.

"Wouldn't understand it, would she now?" Dean Morraugh puffs his cigar. "We are a simple people, Mr. Phillips, with a lot of catching up to do, as you Americans say. You can't feed a starving man frogs' legs first off."

"Oatmeal," Crawford suggests.

"Quite so," Morraugh continues. "You see, you Americans have had your freedom from the very first, or for so very long, which is why I suppose you are so generous with it—why you want to give it to the rest of us. But

I'm not entirely sure we want it all, perhaps it doesn't suit us, you know."

"And indeed, you seem to deny it to some of your own citizens," Smith-Royce says. "This Chicago business, for example. It's a pity since you are so generous with the rest of us—all these loans and plans and foundations and so forth . . ."

"You seem to be impressed with our generosity, Mr. Smith-Royce," I say. I wonder how Patricia is making out with the ladies.

"And why not, dear fellow? It sticks out all over you. Our papers are always full of your Rockefellers, your Kennedys and the rest. You really are all millionaires, you know."

"The only effect the Sherman Anti-Trust Act had," Crawford says, "was to drive the wealth underground. No longer able to monopolize industry and the market, the money was turned to monopolize culture, politics, the arts. After all, that's really the best kind of monopoly to have —culture. Something very similar happened in the Fifth Kingdom, you know—except it was priests, not millionaires."

The three of us look at Professor Crawford, waiting for more, but he only sips at his brandy. Smith-Royce is bug-eyed with concentration; his forehead furrows once, twice and then again.

"By the way," I sense it's time for a change in subject, "is it possible to get a girl like one of these to work in a private home?"

"Nothing easier." Morraugh eagerly follows my lead. He literally jumps on the subject. "Why of course your wife will need a girl! You should have mentioned this before. I know the perfect girl! Just up from the country, she is, and I know her people. Simple folk but straight as a die. I'll send her over for your wife to interview. But don't spoil her now, be very business with her."

"Yes, and for God's sake," Smith-Royce says, "don't pay her any more than the going rate. It will ruin her."

"What's the standard rate?"

"Have your missus ask mine," he replies.

"There are the dreamers of the dream," Crawford says, "and there are those who buy the dream. There are more buyers than dreamers and only one dream." And with that he tosses off the rest of his brandy.

There seems to be nothing more to do but to join the ladies. On the way to the parlor, I step into the washroom. It is an ornate establishment, immortalizing in marble, brass and the intricate curlicues of exposed plumbing the Edwardian preoccupation with luxurious evacuation. Standing before the urinal, a magnificent slab of black marble supported on the shoulders of four alabaster nymphs, I make the usual inspection of the wall in front of me. There are five black circles all spaced within the area of a hand, two of them splintering the smooth gray surface of the stone. There is no doubt that they are bullet holes.

Dean Gil Morraugh stands alone beneath a large portrait in the foyer. From the parlor Mrs. Maxine Waters' voice rises above the rest. Dean Morraugh's short, round body is poised lightly on small feet, a comical dancer, and he holds a brandy in one hand and a cigar in the other as he inspects the painting. He is obviously having a moment to himself and I hesitate to join him but then come near.

"By the way," I say, "I've read a little bit of the book you loaned me." He remains looking up at the likeness on the wall. "The book on St. Maureen nu Nailly. Her martyrdom."

"Ah, yes," he sighs, continuing to stare into the painted eyes of the viceroy above. "A terrible trial it was but a splendid sacrifice."

"Yes, splendid. But it's a little hard going, isn't it? I mean, frogs' legs and all that—especially now that you've put it into English."

"Not a bit. Purely a personal indulgence of my own and privately printed at that. The text is fully known to us all. Taught in school, secondary of course, once they can grasp the Old Tongue."

"That book is read by students here?"

"After all, it's a sacred document. She is our patron saint." Waving the trivial matter away with his brandy, he points the cigar at the portrait. "Fine-looking man, wasn't he?"

I agree and read the brass plate at the bottom of the gold frame. Sir James Kilpatrick, Viceroy, 1908–. Sir James has a very poetic face and is perched on a tabletop, one glossy, black-booted leg swinging free. The brilliant red jacket is slung over a shoulder and secured by a golden chain across the chest. In the crook of the right arm rests a burnished helmet with a dark blue plume.

"We bagged him at the crossroads in Timpletown," Morraugh says. "And a bloody good sport he was, too."

It is easier to take Professor Jack Crawford home from a party than it is Mrs. R. L. Waters. It is also quieter. In any event, the Smith-Royces greedily seize the opportunity of escorting a semi-celebrity from the hated Chicago, and Patricia and I share a cab with the Egyptologist.

The streets are all but deserted when we enter the city, for the Royal Hunt Club is situated on the outskirts. The pavements glisten with the heavy dew of evening, and the air is thickened with the smoke of warming coal fires, thickened and scented by "the rich smell of the poor," as one of their contemporary poets puts down. The cab moves down the wide avenues and boulevards of the eighteenth-century planning and into the narrow byways of nineteenth-century expediency.

I sit beside Patricia and as we talk and laugh over the evening, Crawford stares out of the window. We round the curve and pass the domain of the University of Alclair, its main gate shut against the ignorant night though there are lights still on in the library. We become silent as we pass, all three staring through the iron portcullis into the shadowy quadrangle beyond.

Crawford's flat is on the third floor of a Georgian manor house. I leave him at the door, a ceremonious dignity to his fumbling with the lock, and rush back to the coziness of the cab, to the soft warmth of Patricia's side.

"Ballads of Robert Lewis Waters, indeed," I say. She laughs and leans against me. I tell her of the possibility of a maid and her spirits rise even higher. The wine, the brandy, the evening out with the cast of characters and all contribute to her good humor. I sense that we are turning a corner, that we have come through a trial period successfully.

In the enormous bedroom, she hums as she puts her things away. The wardrobe door swings open, but instead of cursing its delapidation, or wedging the matchbook cover we've fashioned to keep it shut, she lets it hang. She turns toward me as I lie in bed, nude but for her glasses, and approaches like a black-haired, nearsighted Botticelli.

"Well, here I am." She snuggles against me and pulls

the cover over her ear. But her self-depreciation is not justified, for I find her beautiful and it is like old times.

There was a bird outside my window all last spring, fluttering against the screen to rest upon the ledge to warble his morning song. I would awake, lazily listening to this unidentified herald, while checking off the items for that day; the conferences, the examinations, the telling of another chapter in the story of Man's flight from Divine Right and the subsequent chaos. And I would also wonder what she would wear that day, how she would look in the third row, fifth seat of European History Since Bismarck, sometimes reminding myself to tell her to take more notes and not stare at me so much.

On weekends, the trilling outside the window seemed gayer and I would awake to feel the long length of her wedged against me on the narrow bachelor's couch. Patricia slept on her back, head thrown back and her smooth neck trustingly bared to my scimitar lips. How often my kisses would cut her dream in two. Fretfully, she would cling to slumber, clutch at the fragments of her sleep's fantasy, sometimes even fending off my intrusive hands, and then, almost always, there would be a sound that resembled "Humph," or a deep-throated chuckle, and she would turn to answer the call of the bird. The eyes would slowly open, glimmering slits beneath the long black lashes, and then gradually grow into the lustrous dark pupils that would accommodate the morning light, then turn up toward me with a droll leer. More often, these deep brown eyes would thoughtfully inspect my face, as if there might be some change from the night before, and her hands would hold my head close, her myopia transmitting every detail, every crease and pore.

This was a season of games. There was first the hide-and-seek we were compelled to play by both community mores and college policy. Scott Junior College was very liberal with weekend permissions, the one underlying principle of the two-year course being adequate opportunity to sample potential suitors within a two-hundred-mile radius. Sometimes, I would meet the bus in Hartford, or Poughkeepsie or Great Barrington—depending on the cover story she had used—we would have dinner, maybe go to a movie, all consuming time so that we might arrive back at my apartment after dark.

"You don't know what you've done to my reputation," she said one Friday as we left the city limits of Pittsfield.

"How do you mean?" A cold sword pressed against my shoulder blades.

"Well, there's a big do at Harvard this weekend, and Cornell is having some kind of an egg roll, and here I am signing out for the Pittsfield School of Business." She waved the match out and puffed on a cigarette. "You should have heard the snorts and snickers over that one. My goodness," she observed nonchalantly, "we're across the state line already."

"Yes," I replied. "I intend to sell you at the first gas station."

An unspoken agreement kept us from New York or any other city after the one trip to Providence, for it would mean the disquieting, somehow smirching effect of a hotel. Moreover, we reveled in the coziness of my apartment, committing our unholy acts beneath the noses of the Student Union.

However, on one occasion, and without planning to, we found ourselves on the bed of a model home in a new development in Arthursburg. I posed as an IBM engineer and the woman who showed us through the split-level achievement of Orchard Estates, one blighted McIntosh justifying the name, was very taken with the young married couple we portrayed. Indeed, no one could not have believed and been moved by Patricia's performance.

She rushed through the house oohing and ahing over the conveniences, reverently touching the Nubian slave lamps by the sofa ("I've always wanted these!") and whirling rapturously in the kitchen like the key illustration in a woman's magazine.

"Oh, darling," she cooed from a small bedroom, "how perfect for the baby."

"How old is your child?" the lady agent asked eagerly.

"Not yet," Patricia replied, lashes lowered above a coy smile. "We've only discovered this week." I remember concentrating on the thermostat.

"We have a good school in our district," the agent persisted, and then to me, "Two-zone heating. You young folks take your time. I'm just going over to my place to start supper." And she left us. It had only been a lark, to pretend we were buying a house, but as soon as the front door closed, we looked at each other, our laughter subsided and the other idea arrived simultaneously and with a hot flash. Prudently, I tested the door lock as I heard Patricia sound the resiliency of the bed.

"Are you sure the cat is out?" she asked as I tumbled her over.

The routine and protocol of Scott Junior College enfolded us during the week. Our meetings were ordained and circumscribed by the standard student-teacher relationship, and I began attending the traditional Thursday formal nights at the college. Since the Civil War, the sweeping stairway of Main Hall would become a tableau featuring young American womanhood, marching two by two in all their finery, to the strains of Gounod or Chopin. Faculty and gentlemen guests would wait at the bottom as rank by rank stepped down from the floors above and on into the dining room where, in the candlelight, a chorus or two of the school song, having to do with "delicate friendships untrammeled by time" (Josephine Watson Byrnes—'97), was sung with delicate resolution. It was a production that reminded one of the "big number" in an early Warner Brothers musical, and I fully expected them all to break into a time step, especially when, looking higher, I saw the smirks of the upper floors become gracious smiles at the turn of the stairwell. Patricia always marched without her glasses, the long black hair coiled on top and looking piquantly old-fashioned, even though I knew that beneath the shimmering silk of her gown she was wearing toreador pants and an incredibly dirty pair of sneakers.

Reality could be suspended in that dining room of glowing, bare shoulders, aristocratic necks and exposures of breast, soft above the meat loaf and whipped potatoes on the plates below. Faculty members distributed themselves at various tables with a largesse made more touching by their reception, and the faculty wives endured the evening with a gray fortitude, their efforts at simple elegance on simple faculty pay courageous disasters. It was a dream world and if one could put aside the responsibilities and concerns of the day as one might put aside *The New York Times* with its detailing of those concerns and responsibilities, there was a certain disjointed charm to it all.

"Why don't you sit at my table?" Patricia said one Thursday night. We strolled among the ferns and potted geraniums of the glass-walled conservatory adjoining the dining room. Coffee had been served and was being sipped to the industrious bowing of the Cade County Community Chamber Orchestra. "Lack of attention can be just as obvious as too much."

"No more obvious than what I found this morning in my notes. I'm a little angry with you." She "pish-toshed" and turned with her demitasse to a fern. She had apparently read through my notes the previous weekend, for that morning as I delineated the power structure of the thirteen colonies, I turned a page and across the paragraphs describing the role of the Adams family in that earlier Establishment was an eyebrow pencil scrawl. "My America, my new-found world."

"You reject an honest expression of affection," she said.

"Not a bit, but there is a time and place for everything. You must not tamper with my notes again," I told her, immediately regretting my harshness. She appeared a primitive, a subject for Rousseau, with her large dark eyes, the olive skin against the yellow of her gown and the small jungle of the conservatory all around. "It was very sweet but very disquieting," I said, "that's all."

"You once said that you were responsible for me," she spoke without turning, "and you are, more than you know. You have overcome me."

"Oh, come on," I laughed. We had the place to ourselves, I noted.

"There, you see," she turned, "you are not serious. You do not really want to be responsible for what you have done to me. What did you have in mind when you began tampering with my life?"

"I tamper with you?" I replied. "My dear girl," I started, but was stoned to silence by her look.

"You see, you talk to me like Henry James or somebody, and I'm trying to tell you something important."

"Well, the surroundings are partly to blame."

"I believe," she continued, "in everything at all times and all places," and she sank down upon the oversized ottoman beneath a suspended pot of ivy. The toe of one worn sneaker poked out, then disappeared.

"I think I get your meaning, but that's a bit super-charged for a mere member of the academy."

"You're not that old."

"Of course not. I never said that."

"Also, if I see that Miller bitch gooing over you any-more, I'm going to make a scene." She was smiling, lean-ing back and with one arm on the ottoman's top, confident of the luscious picture she made. "I watched her at dinner, and if she had leaned over any farther you could have seen all the way to Georgia. You know, she puts a half a box of Kleenex in her B-cups."

"She only wanted to know more about the invasion of Poland," I said, laughing at the face Patricia made.

"I'll bet. You should hear her rendition of 'Down on the Delta.' It would curl your hair."

The squeaking of an unoiled hinge alerted us and we adopted our proper roles just as Miss Bryant approached on her artificial leg. In addition to this manmade limb, the elderly English teacher also wore a neatly marcelled black wig and there was a rumor that a breast had been removed. A further credential was the fact that she had been one of the first deans of Sarah Lawrence.

"May I join you?" Miss Bryant said, gimping across to the ottoman and sitting down beside Patricia. "Now then, what were you two talking about?"

"We were discussing the delta regions," I said, sipping my coffee. The Beethoven Trio in G swept to its con-clusion in the drawing room.

"Ah, yes, I spent a Christmas there one year. A lovely

girl, Mary Lee Fleming," Miss Bryant settled warmly in her reverie, hands clasped in her lap, "invited me down. Her father had an enormous cotton plantation. It was truly remarkable the use they put to that land, and how much they had done for that region."

"Yes," Patricia said "and them's that's plantin' is soon forgotten." She looked meaningfully in my direction, but I had put a large potted begonia between us.

Patricia's propensity for leaving me little notes of affection, scraps of faintly concealed erotica in iambic pentameter that she had gleaned somewhere, was one of the hazards of that bright spring. I would find them in my socks on a Monday morning, in my faculty mailbox or scrawled across my lecture notes as already described. Each was a reminder of the responsibility I had incurred. I took to inspecting my office at an early hour in order to collect this epistolary evidence of our affair from the chance perusal of a colleague. One morning I found pinned below the lithograph of Tom Jefferson

My hard and formal dreams will learn to ride you,
My destiny in its golden car shall guide you,
Holding as taut as madness reins: the rhymes
Written by me, all poet's paradigms.

"Who wrote this one?" I asked her that afternoon. She sprawled across from me dressed in the mannish ROTC uniform of the drill team, an institution at Scott. The black wool stockings, the lumpy navy blue skirt and blouse with the black Sam Browne belt—all circa 1917— made her into the heroine of a Soviet war film.

"Apollinaire," she replied, rolling some chewing gum around her molars.

"It's a pity you don't spend as much time researching

your real work as you do on this. Your term paper in American Government is overdue."

"Lucky for you, that's all that's overdue." She crossed long legs and cracked the gum.

"You mustn't let your work slide," I advised her, ignoring the jibe. "You still must finish here, regardless—regardless of us. You had a B average here and it's important when you go on"—her chewing had stopped—"well, if you decide to go, later, to get the marks."

"You're so depressingly fair," she said, the back of one hand against her forehead. "I don't suppose I could even blackmail you into an A, could I? Ah, well, flunk 'em and forget 'em—I know your type."

"Patricia," I nearly reached for her, to take her—open door, corporal chevrons and all—"you have a responsibility to me too, you know. Yours is not the only life that has been changed." She finally rose and walked to the window, back toward me. I unfolded the paper and reread the four lines of verse in the round hand. "To change is one thing," I continued, "it's good and I like it, but to wreck, tear down the whole structure, is something else."

"I'm sorry, Hamlet," she said, still facing out the window. "It's just that everything is so—well, I can't bear to look at the moon anymore, it hurts my eyes. . . . Do you know what I mean? Ah, *mon petit carré*, there is no need to worry about discovery." She returned to her chair, buffing the large belt buckle with the sleeve of her tunic. "The administration is so busy raising money for the new science complex and my schoolmates are so concerned with their contrived nuptials that no one important will ever notice us as long as we maintain the minimum decency."

And she was right, of course. So this was another game we played last spring. To fit ourselves into the pattern of

Scott Junior College, to become chameleons and adopt the protective configuration of our surroundings. The surroundings were hypocritical; not our sense of survival. I remember watching from my office window that afternoon the maneuvers and parade of the drill team on the field beside the tennis courts. Beyond the frightening aspect of militant females, squads right-and-lefting, shouldering arms, stepping smartly to the barked cadence of the Marine sergeant especially assigned by some political manipulation to the college for that purpose, there was a pathetically moving industry and determination demonstrated by every girl in the ranks. It was by far the most popular activity at Scott and the competition for non-com stripes or officer's buttons was as keen as it was sometimes vicious.

It had seemed paradoxical to me that the student body always voted unanimously to continue this activity, begun during the World War I years as a wholehearted but ineffectual gesture toward national mobilization. I could spot among the black-stockinged marchers girls born into huge fortunes, empires that claimed the vassalage of millions of people, and other girls who seemed destined to maintain the same frivolous traditions which had kept the family name in the gossip columns for two generations.

The squads of princesses of modern capital stepped off smartly across the field, breaking apart in moving hyphens, and then turning right, some left and others about face to magically regroup in the center into companies and then again into platoons, all moving as one without fault and in a precision which belied the almost comical, dumpy effect of their Liberty Bond garb. I saw Patricia striding several paces before Company C and carrying the unit's flag. She marched alone, just behind the company's officers, but she resembled the rest. Her face was a mask of undiluted attention, her ears—one jutted prettily above the edge of the blue overseas cap—her ears were nearly pointed with anticipation for the commands they received. And though she marched alone, she moved with all the others, step for step, her heel grinding into the turf at the instant thirty others did for a right oblique, her arm swung in the identical arc, her back straight and the bulky mass of the tunic pushed out by the marvelous breasts I knew were there. My guidon-bearer, whose destiny would guide me.

There was a more serious game that spring, one which brought my commitment to full term. Required reading for my class in American Democracy was the daily *New York Times*, and on the front pages were the horrible and proud accounts of the civil rights movement. We read and discussed the legal maneuvering of the Southern states or certain communities in those states. We reviewed the wanton lunacy of the shootings and bombings that ripped the carefully woven fabric of government so pleasurable to study at a leisured distance. The determination and devotion of the Negro demonstrators was both moving and frightening.

I will confess to taunting the composure of these wellborn young ladies, to playing upon the sense of outraged justice that is a part of the young, of even taking an agreeable, if not petty, delight in pinpointing their high position above the storm waters. My own complacency was showing, of course, and I would tuck it beneath the sardonic pattern of my tutorial robes. It was Patricia who delivered me.

> When they nailed him on the cross?
> Was you there, Charlie,

The message was typed, and left in my office typewriter,

one more reminder of my responsibility for her. The trip was organized with great speed, though she later admitted to a quiet hectoring among her classmates, and I could hardly refuse the earnest delegation that asked me to lead them through the streets of Selma during the spring recess.

The administration initially tabled the idea, the dangers inherent in a civil rights march being more than those encountered on the beaches of Bermuda. But when it was learned, from letters and a published notice, that there would also be contingents from Smith, Wellesley and Vassar, permission was granted.

A bus was chartered, and the two dozen of us were sent on our way one rainy morning in April, Miss Bryant standing in the forefront of the other faculty members, waving a pale yellow handkerchief and seemingly ready to hobble down the driveway after the bus on her wooden leg. We passed small groups of girls, waiting beside gay blocks of luggage, and they also waved to us, obviously self-conscious about their own trivial destinations, and roundly criticized inside the bus for their "amazing lack of social consciousness."

Cindy Miller had brought her guitar and led us in such dormitory standards as "Down on the Delta," which was indeed a hair curler. The poor bus driver hunched over the wheel, his ears becoming more crimson with each mile, and his vulnerability amusing and inciting them to greater exploitation. They even went through the show of drawing straws for him ("Who gets Dick tonight?"—unhappily his first name was Richard), and I finally mentioned to Sue Ellen Dryden, whose recent promotion to a platoon lieutenant on the drill team gave her some authority, that perhaps his initiation was over.

"Jesus, Mr. Phillips," he told me, "I'm a married man but I never heard anything like this." We had stopped for dinner on the Jersey turnpike and I followed the driver around as he morosely kicked the huge tires of the bus. It was tempting to ask what he had heard as a married man.

"These girls are just a little nervous, a little apprehensive —on edge at what they are going to do. They're just blowing off steam. Believe me, they are much different from the way they may sound."

"But why are they doing this anyway?" he asked me, his small face pinched. "Why are they going to mess into this business down there? What's in it for them?" And he looked at me suspiciously.

So from the beginning the motives and character of our expedition were misunderstood or purposely ignored and, more ominously, by one of our own group, or at least by one who would be intimately associated with us for the next ten days. There was a caucus that first night in one of the motel rooms about what to do with the driver. The charges brought against him were "being uncool," "Bourgeois" and "bad breath" though the real reasons for their dissatisfaction were not expressed. I pointed out the practical necessity of keeping him and suggested that he be just ignored. They reluctantly agreed but with some qualifications.

The next day, they jabbered about poor Richard in French, and I did begin to feel sorry for him in his own self-constructed hell.

"*Le chauffeur de ma tante, il a de grandes oreilles,*" a voice would say from the front.

"*Oui,*" the chorus answered, "*il a de grandes oreilles rouges.*"

"*Nous confions nous au voiturier?*"

"*Jamais vous confiez a un voiturier?*" the chorus would respond.

When we passed from Maryland into Virginia, a girl from Mississippi stood in the aisle in the front of the bus to lead us in dialect lessons. "Repeat after me. How'r *yew.*"

"How'r *yew.*"

"If I ha-ad mah druthers . . ."

"If I ha-ad mah druthers . . ."

"Ah'll have mo' beeskits, thenk *yew.*"

"Ah'll have mo' beeskits, thenk *yew.*"

"Emmy Lou," a voice corrected our teacher. "Down in Alabama they say, 'Haw '*r* yew,' not 'How '*r* *yew.*' "

"Well, I guess I ought to know how to say 'How '*r* *yew,*' " Emmy Lou spat out. "I've been saying 'How '*r* *yew*' all my life."

The debate, nearer an argument, never resolved the correct inflection, but it gradually subsided until nothing was heard for several hours above the steady throb of the bus's engine. But it was obvious that the tension and anxiety were entering their natures. There was another kind of tension between Patricia and me.

I had anticipated with some curiosity and some temerity the effect of these ten days upon our relationship. How would we treat each other in full view of the others, how could we guard our secret and, most important to me, how would we spend the nights? Unconsciously, we sat together that first day and before the first of many comfort station stops, I could feel the secret of our affair become general knowledge. It was something in their eyes, neither approval nor disapproval, but a rather bemused sliding glance over the two of us, as if to say, "So that's it," and the recognition somehow explaining a puzzlement that had arisen simultaneously with its solution.

Although Patricia joined in the songs, the jokes and the raillery with the rest—sometimes kneeling on the seat to face the rear—she had assumed a separateness more specific than the general cloak of her former role. She was with me, and we were together, and that's all there was to it.

I looked for hints of trouble but found none, and even Sue Ellen Dryden seemed not to mind, nor was there the slightest impulse to fawn over us as an idealized, romantic couple. They were a cool bunch, and I realized an appreciation for them never generated in class. So much for the days.

The nights were different, yet different from the way I had imagined or hoped. By the third day we had made Charlotte, North Carolina, and I was still sleeping alone. The first two nights I had showered and shaved, arranged the lighting low in the motel room and finally fallen asleep to the hissing blank of the television, gone off the air.

"What's the matter?" I asked her on the third day. She looked at me, her eyes curiously speculative, and then looked out the window at the passing tobacco fields. "What's the matter?"

"All right," she finally said. "Tonight." And I was struck by the joyless look on her face, lips pursed and eyes dull, as if her feelings were hurt.

She was waiting in the rain outside my door, wearing a tan coat over her jeans and shirt, sneakers wet and a rain hat pulled down over her face. She resembled a lost camper, and stood dripping before the television set, listening to the late news program which had so absorbed me that I had not immediately heard her soft scratching at the door. It was a local program and the broadcaster was reporting our arrival in the area, and that of other students converging upon the hapless Southern status quo. There was even a short film clip of our bus wheeling into the motel parking lot, Richard hunched glumly over the wheel, and several of the girls disembarking.

"We've become a part of the video-memory bank of Charlotte, North Carolina," I said, removing her coat. She let me pull the coat down her slack arms, followed by her hat, her interest in the program feigned. My hands shook and my breath choked me and there was that same tumbling in my stomach that I experienced the first night in Providence.

Our lips met. Her mouth seemed to scout the territory ahead, to explore the depth and field of passion before gradually the rest of her followed. Arms around my neck slowly constricted, laying first breast, then belly against me, the pelvis next finding its place and the long thighs lazily moving in with a maddening uncertainty as to the best place against mine. With a greed that only increased our hunger, we fed upon each other for several minutes.

"Elsewhere on the state scene," the newscaster rambled on behind us.

Leaning away from her in the circle of her arms I began undoing the damp shirt. "You'll get a cold with all this. How did you get so wet? Have you been walking in the rain?" And one by one the buttons slipped through their holes and her breasts, almost out of proportion to the lithe boniness of the rest of her, were in my hands, for she rarely wore a brassiere. The flesh pebbled as a slight shiver went through her, and the nipples were hard and cool within my palms. She hung about my shoulders, looking down, and watched my hands stroke her with a bemused detachment. I caressed the satin puff of belly above tight jeans, returned to weigh the now smooth breasts, their round volume freshly fascinating, and traced the hollow of her spine. Though freely giving herself to me, there was an unnerving distance between us. But I could feel her reacting to my touch.

"I almost didn't show up," she said finally, and pressed

herself against me. She gave me an almost desultory peck upon the chin and turned away.

"What's the matter?" Her back to me, she bent over to search through the pockets of the fallen raincoat, one hand trying to hold the shirt together. The failure of this attempt at modesty was absolutely stunning. "Is it the others?" I turned off the television.

"Oh, no—not really," she said, waving the match out and puffing on the cigarette. She went to the bed and folded her legs beneath her, sweeping the long fall of ebony around and down over the right shoulder. "I've gone out for pizza, as far as they're concerned."

"Do they believe it?"

"Maybe," she shrugged her shoulders. "But it doesn't matter. Girls are different. We don't talk about it and we only need a reasonable excuse."

"Well, then what is it?" I sat beside her on the bed. "Is it this motel room? I don't like it myself, but under the circumstances it's all we have."

"You know, you're funny about that," she said, looking around for an ashtray. "That sort of thing doesn't bother me at all. You must feel guilty about me or something. As a matter of fact, I rather think hotel rooms can be fun."

"Do you rather think so," I said, handing her an ashtray. "Look, Patricia, there's something on your mind and it's not the difference between the male and female psyche." I held her free hand.

"Well, you came close just now. It's the circumstances. It somehow wouldn't seem right in the circumstances," she said, nodding toward the television screen.

Her meaning was clear, but I avoided the cognizance of that meaning because of the throb of my body. But its rightness struck me and I groaned. Moreover, I was flabber-

gasted by this obvious dedication to the spirit of freedom
and justice that I had evidently inspired in her, and the
others, as a teacher. Flabbergasted, humbled and a bit
ashamed; I was all three at once and I wondered, suddenly,
about all the rich patrons of eccentric inventors down
through history who doled out the money and gave encouragement for their own secret amusement with their
protégé's obsession and how they must have felt, these
complacent lords, that day in the square when the damn
thing actually worked. It just took off and flew!

Swacked by conflicting emotion, my desire whooshed
out of sight and I could see more clearly and I understood
something else. If I had persisted, say if I had gently
pushed Patricia back on the bed and bared her amoral
breasts to my lips and hands, she would not have resisted.
On the contrary, it was certain that she would respond as
eagerly as always and that I would soon be wedged between her thighs and bringing from her those deep-
throated female cries of animalism. But then what? It was
the "then what" that disturbed me. For the first time, I
admitted to myself that there was a possibility of something more for us beyond May's commencement cere-
monies. It was a moment like that of General So-and-so
turning right or left on the Winchester turnpike, as pictured by popular historians; the maneuver deciding what
the army ate that evening, how the combatants felt the
next morning and down on the ladder of cause and effect
to Appomattox.

I fell back upon the bed, masochistically enjoying the
ache in my groin. "It would be a little like Bermuda,
wouldn't it?" I said momentarily. Patricia's mouth opened
into a marvelous smile, and I noted for the first time that
her eyes behind the glasses had been tight, a little wary

and speculative. They were no longer. She leaned over me and kissed me sweetly on the forehead, the nose and mouth, her rich hair falling over and tickling my face.

"You're a good man," she said.

"You're not helping matters," I said, for my hands had unconsciously lent support to her breasts.

"C'mon," she said, jumping up and tucking in her shirt. "Let's go get some pizza."

It is not fair to leave unqualified the dismal and dreary impression of this city given by earlier remarks. One's environment and how it appears is as much an object of a psychological inner eye, to be interpreted and thereby take shape accordingly, as contemporary sociologists would have it the other way around. What would have been the difference, for example, had the dour and humorless Pilgrims landed in lush Roanoke and Raleigh's cavaliers pulled up on the desertlike beaches of Cape Cod?

Patricia's exasperation with herself, the negativism of her personality caused by the pregnancy coupled with my own self-pity and disgust for mistaking one university for another prevented us from seeing the charm and small majesty of this country. But now, thanks to Dean Morraugh, we have Marie Therese bustling up and down our stairs, preparing supper and turning out dozens of hot, crusty scones at teatime.

She arrives every morning, rain or shine, in her black trench coat, black galoshes and clutching a black umbrella. With her crimson cheeks, she appears to be a monochrome print which some thoughtless doodler has defaced with red crayon. I hear Patricia singing in the bath the evening of Marie Therese's first day with us and the following week I am asked to mount a small spice rack above the stove.

Moreover, my wife is once again that playful, adventurous bedmate who, I had begun to wonder, was only a fiction of my frustration, the mist of her nausea dispersed by Marie Therese's sunny fervor for housework. Once again Pat brings her body to mine with an immolation that is also a self-indulgence, a paradox sometimes described by lady French novelists of dubious empiricism.

Patricia's changed disposition affects mine, and I am able to convince myself that my mistake on the foundation forms was a happy one. The University of Alclair, from its architecture down to the shabby gowns of the dons, is really no more than a rather hazy fifth or sixth impression struck from the original stone of Oxford. And though without reputation and despite the trade-school atmosphere of Alclair U., there is a vitality and a truthfulness, grubby as it is, which appeals to me now as man and historian. As for reputation, it has never been one of my requirements for survival.

So then, let me once again set down a few notes about this city which, thanks to our happier state of minds, appears somewhat differently. It is a Saturday morning and remarkably the sun is out. Indeed, the sun seems to be shining more often these days, not all day ever, but with brilliant appearances divinely timed, as it were, just as one tires of the gray drip-dripping from the leaves.

We leave Marie Therese happily humming as she rushes about her work—she never walks—and Patricia and I board the big double-decker bus at the corner for the trip downtown. We rush to the top deck to wheel and sway above the traffic, watch the cyclists who avoid being run down at the last minute. There are crowds of soccer fans wearing the paper hats of their team's colors milling like wind-tossed flowers. A right turn around Liberty Park and the broad expanse of Gonorah Street is before us; designed in the nineteenth century to maximize the effect of grape-shot, the great breadth now serves the proliferation of traffic that jams it.

"A lovely day," Patricia says. She stretches contentedly, hands clasped before her, and then polishes a patch of sweat from the window. "I love to ride up here, it makes the second-floor windows more useful." She peers at the passing fronts above the ground level. "Windows were meant to be looked into as well as out of."

"Perhaps there should be triple- and quadruple-decked buses for the higher buildings."

"Yes, why not?" she answers.

"Well, on the third floor there might be something one should not see or be sorry to see. I remember once riding on the Sixth Avenue El . . ."

"Sixth Avenue had an elevated?" She looked at me with feigned wonder.

"Yes," I reply wearily, "it used to."

"Oh, look at the flowers," she says. And in the bright sun there are masses of tulips, carnations and freesias sprouting from a battalion of pushcarts parked along the banks of the Livia. Like almost every European capital, a river divides Alclair into old and "new" portions and despite the efforts of patriots such as Dean Morraugh to rename it something else which sounds like "Cathrone," the river is still known by the name given to it by an un-known Roman cartographer in honor of Augustus's ambi-tious second wife.

"All straight from the hothouse," I say.

"But how beautiful," Patricia exclaims. "And what colors. We must stop and take some home on our way back."

Just now the sun emerges even more brilliantly from around a cloud ledge and the whole scene transcends reality like one of those colored prints on a lampshade, dully acceptable with the light off and unbelievable with it on. The amiable verdigrised roofs of the government buildings are a soft green against the blue sky, the limestone façades shimmer with a peachy velvet, the waters of the Livia roll smoothly as an olive green that borders the red, yellow, purple, orange and pink blossoms that actually are the spectral levee.

"It's great! Terrific," Patricia says and with a tone and squeeze of arm that makes me feel that I had something to do with it.

"With a wave of the hand," I say, matching my words, and—by chance, the sun momentarily moves behind a cloud and the scene is muted as if a great rheostat has reduced the power. "It's nothing," I manage to say.

"Golly!" Her eyes are huge within the harlequin frames, and then she touches me, with reverence.

We alight from the bus in the main section; we have come to buy sheets, for the venerable articles furnished by the landlord gave way beneath our venereal antics, and the smells of Alclair assail us. Over the basic scent of chimney smoke, that soft pungency which pervades every-thing here, are layers of fragrance, subtle drafts flowing from the doorways of shops and stores, and the smells identify the stores as clearly as do the signboards on the fronts.

"Wait," I say, closing my eyes and holding my hands before me. Patricia instantly knows the game and takes my arm. The tap-tapping of heels and slough of feet move around me.

"Here?" she asks.

"Obviously, Goram Tea and Coffee, Limited. That was easy."

"And now?"

"Ah, some kind of lunch counter. Fried fish. Also smells like popcorn balls. Is that right?"

"Yes, aren't they terrible?"

"They smell different today, not as soggy. Now what do we have here—stale suppositories?"

"Ugh."

"But a pharmacy, right?"

"Right. And now—here's a cinch." She presses my arm.

"Sunday morning breath. A saloon."

"Yes, but which one?"

"Oh, c'mon; well—The Cardinal. The Cardinal?"

"You know the area, that's all. Here, watch your step. There's a kind of manhole lid. Now here's one."

"Hmm." I take a deep breath. There is a faint suggestion of something. "I have it. A woman's store, lingerie and that sort of stuff."

"You're peeking." She jabs me.

"I swear I'm not."

"How can you smell anything like that? You're a filthy beast, do you know that, going around smelling lingerie counters."

"A harmless outlet. Now where are we?"

"It's your game."

"A theater." There's a whiff of body odors, muted perfumes, and of something else.

"No."

"Department store." An aroma of polished wood and metal wafts out.

"No."

Then again there is no identifiable smell, but a neutral odor that overpowers the others. Something very old. "How about a museum? No, wait a minute. A historic spot. The stables where the National Martyrs were slaughtered . . ."

"No, no." Patricia tugs my arm impatiently. "Give up?" I am stumped.

"Okay." And I open my eyes. "Why, of course." We are standing before a church.

The Cardinal Lounge is a duplex establishment that simultaneously hosts two divergent clienteles. The ground floor is a quietly elegant room of fine leather and discreet chrome with steeplechase prints on the wall and two waiters in black jackets who serve a horsey crowd of Americans and English. Upstairs, where we go, is entirely different. The roughhewn tables and chairs, the cracked leather of the settee and the threadbare carpet make for a cozy delapidation. A dumbwaiter by the Franklin stove, always with a smoldering fire even on a good day like this one, brings up the heavy glasses of ale and beer from the taps below to be distributed by Clark, the one attendant. This is a hangout for students, for those radicals dissatisfied with either of the two parties and for those writers who have not been summoned either by the BBC or by some American university.

"To you, Dr. Phillips and Missus," says Clark as we enter. "Saw you on the telly, the other P.M.," he smiles at me, polishing up the table we have chosen. "He comes here, Mr. Smith-Royce does. A fine gentleman and he gives them bureaucrats whatfor, doesn't he though?"

"He does," I answer. We order beer and some ham and cheese.

"Mr. Hamilton Phillips, a distinguished American member of the Alclair University faculty," Patricia mimics Smith-Royce's clipped enunciation, "was a recent participant in civil rights demonstrations in the American South. Now, Mr. Phillips, will you tell us, in the five minutes we have, the background for the disturbances in Chicago, what are the aims and hopes of the Negro in contemporary America and what are your estimates of the success of those aims and hopes with some clear-cut examples, based on your own experiences."

"Was it that bad?" I ask her.

"Well, let's say you didn't add to the confusion, and I suppose that's something."

"Say, when did you learn all about that sort of stuff," I ask, pointing to the package of sheets on the seat beside her. At the department store, Patricia had engaged the salesclerk in a lengthy discussion of weaves and fabrics that had fascinated me.

"You got a lot when you married me, more than you expected, I bet."

"That's for sure." The place fills up, young couples mostly; the girls wear the latest mod fashions from England, the short skirts exaggerating the length of legs, which are sheathed in very white hose. It resembles a giddy convention of nurses.

"There's a cute number over there," Patricia says, nodding toward the far corner. I saw the girl when she entered; Patricia had seen me look at her. Tall and spare, straight blond hair, in contrast to the brunette bouffants around her, the girl is the center of a noisy group that has taken possession of several tables as a flock of birds might suddenly alight upon a portion of a square.

"A little on the thin side," I say.

"I should think you'd appreciate that about now." She

looks down at her belly rising above the tabletop: "Say, you were telling me about seeing something on the sixth floor from the Third Avenue El."

"It was the third floor from the Sixth Avenue El."

"What was it?" Clark has served us and goes to the group in the corner. Patricia makes a sandwich of the ham and cheese.

"Oh, just one of the scenes you can't get out of your mind. It was only for a second, like a camera lens opening and closing. It was a kitchen and a woman sat at the table one hand to her forehead and the other in her lap. And a man stood behind her, his arms outspread, a pained question on his face. He was a charade for the word 'Why?' That's all there was. But I always wonder what he was asking."

"What do you suppose?"

"Oh, I don't know. Maybe, why with him? Or, why no biscuits? Or, why tomorrow?"

"Why not?" she says. I study her face as she peers at the foam around the lip of the glass.

"Yes, why not?" A swig of beer bolsters my resolve. "Speaking of why nots, why not celebrate Thankgiving with all the trimmings?" Almost dreamily her face meets mine, and a disturbing smile comes to her lips. "I mean we can get a turkey, we have Marie Therese to help you now, and we could ask a few people in—Americans, of course." Silent laughter rises from her throat; a giggle spills over her lips and she pushes it and a scrap of ham back in her mouth. "What's so funny?"

"That's what he was asking? Why not have the neighbors in for Thanksgiving? And the poor creature is just sitting there, sick to her stomach, wondering how she's going to do it all. Oh, I feel fine," she stops my question.

"Well, all right. How many? There's Mrs. Waters and Crawford."

"Yes."

"Sure, why not?"

"You're sure you don't mind?"

"Not a bit." She sips some beer. "No, in fact, I like the idea. Gives me something to do, to plan. It's funny being pregnant. I often wondered how I would feel. I felt so icky at first and I was so mad at myself for getting pregnant, and for changing things."

"It wasn't that bad?"

"No, I knew what you had planned for us, the mobility of it, and here I am, the big lump in the path. I knew what it meant to you."

"Well, you make too much of it." She is solemn and I stifle the impulse to reach out and touch her cheek, the line of jaw softened by what could almost be described as baby fat. "Admittedly, it was a surprise. After all, it's not as if we belonged to the Planned Parenthood League. But what worried me more was your reaction—you were so changed."

"That's all over now, I hope," Pat says, lighting a cigarette in that amateurish manner. "It's funny how it changed. Maybe it's Marie Therese, or maybe it was that night at the Royal Hunt—something about that night, wasn't there?—anyway, I feel very content now." And she pats the small hump of her belly.

"Mother earth."

"Yes, mother earth. I even want to read *Woman's Home Companion*. Isn't that the end? Little Mr. Zygote has turned me into Marjorie Morningstar. Maybe that's what upset me at first. I'd been so different, thought I was anyway, and then to find I was just the same mess of tubes and instincts as all the others."

"You seem to think you've got a boy there. What should we name him? How about Edna, after your mother?"

"Yes, I think it's a boy," she says, ignoring me.

"We could always name him after your father, whatever name that was." She makes a face. I watch her mouth close over the sandwich, the teeth choosing a delicate portion to be tasted and swallowed. "But all these changes you mention I like. I like them all, especially there. There's more of you."

"Yes, I must be almost a thirty-eight," she says proudly. "And have you noticed the tips?"

"Yes, I've noticed," I say.

"One thing worries me," she says offhandedly, "and that's the cranberries."

"Cranberries?"

"Yes, for our Thanksgiving feast. Do you think we can get cranberries over here? You know, I'm getting very excited about this meal. It's a great idea. Maybe the Embassy can help us with the cranberries. There must be other Americans with the same problem with cranberries."

"Why not parcel it out? Let Mrs. Waters worry about the cranberries, for example," I say casually.

"Good idea. Oh boy," she crosses her legs and wriggles with a comfortable anticipation. "I saw a marvelous recipe once for oyster stuffing. It's very moist and salty and I can really pack it into the turkey. Creamed onions and asparagus. Maybe I'll find some white asparagus, long and firm." There's a mischievous smile on her face, and in an offhand way she reaches up to pat the bun of hair on her head.

"Why don't we give Marie Therese the afternoon off and we can go over the menu," I say.

"Jolly good idea," Patricia says. She recrosses her legs. "How long would it take us to get back home?"

"About twenty minutes by bus. A taxi might take about fifteen."

"Let's take a taxi," she says; her eyes are like ripe plums. "That's something else that's changed too. I mean, I was never, well, inaccessible maybe is the word . . ."

"That's the word," I assure her.

"I'll overlook that because of my condition," she continues, "but now, I'm even more so. Have you noticed how quickly I . . ."

"Yes, I've noticed," I tell her, "and if you don't stop talking about it, there won't be much reason to go home." I'm frantically trying to get Clark's attention to pay our check. He's totaling up an account for the large group in the corner, some of its members already filing by our table and out.

"*Mon petit carré*," Patricia soothes me, her hand patting my knee under the table, and I nearly jerk from my skin. She leans back against the seat, laughing.

A harried Clark, hands full of currency, slams down our check on the tabletop on his way to the cash register. As I am checking the addition, mathematics not being a strong subject of the National schools, and counting out the money, Patricia sings with an exaggerated huskiness, "I can't give you anything but LOVE, BAY-bee."

"Hello, you must be the Americans." The girl's voice is behind me, just over my shoulder, and I feel cloth brush against my ear. It is the blonde we noticed earlier. "Do forgive me, but it is Mr. Phillips, isn't it? And Mrs. Phillips," she adds after a one-beat pause. "Frightful to bust in this way. May I sit down?" She sits down. "I've heard so much about you from my dad. Dean Morraugh, you know. I'm Iz Morraugh, short for Iseult. Oh, Perce," she calls to the group thronged at the top of the stairway, and a man, as blond as she but considerably older, turns around and comes back. Patricia's face is flushed, swollen with resentment.

"Do be a darling," she says, playing with the man's sleeve, "and get us a round."

"We were just leaving," I say.

"Ah, you can't do that," she says, drawing out the verb contraction in almost a parody of the way it's pronounced, for there is a different accent in her general speech. "We must get to know one another now that we've met. And tell him," she directs her escort, "none of that canned lime in the gin either. Well, now"—everything is settled, including the thigh-high skirt over white, clockwork hose—"it's absolutely *la crème* to meet you." She is a slimmer version of her mother, the same blue eyes and Nordic complexion but with a roundness of nose and chin attributable to the Dean's peasantry that saves the long face from being cold. The mouth is small.

"Here we are." Her escort has returned with the drinks. There's a deceiving ruddy youthfulness about the lines and creases of his middle-aged face. He's dressed in all the tweed dandys, including ascot. "Mr. and Mrs. Phillips—it's Hamilton, isn't it? And . . ."

"Patricia," I say, agreeing with the dismal signal in my wife's eyes.

"And Patricia meet Percy Browne—with an e—formerly Group Captain Percy Browne, VO, VD and all that sort of rot."

"All that sort of rot," he repeats, chuckling and exposing

a set of yellowed, broken teeth which put the final coup to the ravages of a once handsome face.

"Just flew over from London to give Dad and Mumsy a break," she tells us. "They get so worried about their little darling in the wicked city, don't you know. Have to pop back now and then to show them everything's okay." And she straightens up to show her flat stomach. "All top hole, don't you know."

"Top hole," repeats Group Captain Browne-with-an-e.

"I see you're in the family way," she tosses at Patricia, who visibly bristles. Her eyes are hard agates. "Who's your man, Patricia? Give me a cig, dear." She reaches across me, long fingers taking the cigarette Browne has offered.

"My man?"

"Yes, your doctor." I seem to have the matches and I hold a light for her. She slowly bends over it, holding back a fold of the straight blond hair. "Thanks awfully."

"Dr. Hewson."

"Oh, first class." The blue eyes roll. "Something special there, isn't he? He turns me on, he does."

"You never mentioned," I say to Patricia, "that your doctor is attractive." I figure we may as well make the best of the situation.

"If you consider a big moustache and hairy hands attractive," she snaps back. "Personally, I like everything clean-shaved."

"Everything?" Iseult asks, her face bemused.

Patricia brazens it out. She takes a deep swallow and holds a cigarette up. I light hers also.

"Ah, you Americans. You're so deliciously frank."

"Yes, frank. Quite so," echoes Browne.

"Are you attending school in England, Miss Morraugh?"

"Do call me Iz. Ah, no. I'm what you call a drop-in, no,

what is it, drop-out. Yes. I have a small concern, fashion and all that. Import the native woolens, give the British a swatch of the old home industry, don't you know. Designed this myself." And she stood to briefly model the short dress.

"It doesn't look as if it took long to design," I say.

"Oh, they're getting shorter," she sits down. "Just below the goodies, you might say. And I have some utterly divine ones for preggies," she tells Pat.

"Really?" Despite herself, Patricia is smiling now.

"Yes, you must let me whip some up for you."

"That may not be such a bad idea," Patricia answers. "I'd like to see them."

"But I hear your classes are marvelous." She launches herself toward me now. "Dad praises you *beaucoup*. You're bringing a bit of class to that dreary place."

"Oh, I don't know. It has been a very rewarding challenge for me." The slant of the sunlight on the wall tells the late hour. We are caught in the national custom of "rounds," a perpetual consumption of alcohol set in motion by anyone who joins a table and buys a round of drinks.

Iseult Morraugh nails us to the spot with her conversation, her escort occasionally driving home a phrase for her with a well-timed repetition. We learn that she is twenty-two and that living among the English puts her in a perpetual state of shock. ("Absolutely delicious, though.") We learn that Group Captain Browne has only known her for a few weeks and has accompanied her home to satisfy some kind of pilgrimage of his own. He is a designer, also, but of aircraft.

"Can we run you home?" she asks us, as we stand beside a Jaguar sedan at the curb. The day has become drab once again, a gray lid fitting tight over the building tops.

"No, we'll take a taxi," I say, looking hopefully at Patricia. She stands sulkily to one side, her pregnancy obvious. She seems to be deliberately sticking out her stomach. And then, for a reason only to be found in the series of beers and whiskies I had consumed, I spread my arms and look up. "Oh, great Sun God, let down your mantle upon us and give us light for our campfire, warm us with your great fire."

"Why, that's blasphemy," Iz Morraugh says seriously, standing straight and narrow. And then not so seriously, almost lewdly, if that is possible. "Delicious blasphemy."

"Not a bit," I say. "It's an old Indian prayer, a legitimate prayer and no irreverence intended."

"Really?" She seems disappointed.

"Do you know any of those war whoops?" Group Captain Browne asks, suddenly alive.

"Boola-boola," says Patricia and pulls at my arm.

In the taxi home, the bunches of daffodils and tulips we bought by the Livia lie between us on the seat. We say nothing, and stare out our respective windows at the colorless façades that pass, set pieces drawn by a practiced though unimaginative hand.

Finally, I say, "She's a funny girl, isn't she?" Patricia slides her eyes toward me and says nothing, but hugs herself and makes a soft grunt like "humpf." And we say nothing more until we are home.

Marie Therese has left us a note, propped against the teapot on the dining-room table. "Missus—scones in the oven, sausages as well. Boil water for tea." But the oven is cold and so are the scones. I start a fire in the grate, for the house is damp and chilly. Patricia and I move around the rooms on our different missions; she picking up clothes, putting away the new linens, and I to assemble coal and

kindling and fix the flowers. I reread some articles by
Walter Lippmann on American foreign policy, hearing
her, now, in the kitchen, methodically putting dinner together. And in this way, we prepare for evening.

Let me stick in here more of a description of Marie
Therese, Emtie as we call her, as she has become stuck in
our lives. I've already mentioned that she proceeds about
the house at a trot and even in those stationary pursuits
such as peeling potatoes or cleaning out fire grates there's
a faint trembling of the flanks, a twitch of the limbs, as if
it is all she can do but break into a jog in place.

"To you, Mr. Phillips. How's the Missus this morning?"
is her usual greeting to me as I'm having my toast and
coffee in the kitchen.

Pat sleeps late, long legs tucked up protectively under
her gathering charge, embryo around embryo. As Emtie
fixes a breakfast tray for her, we invariably have a few
words on the weather.

"A fine morning," she says if there is the faintest hint
of sunlight, or if not, if the rain runs down the spouts onto
cement runoffs in the back garden, she will say, "A bit of
the wet this morning, Mr. Phillips," in an offhand manner
clearly meant to belittle the storm.

She is about fifty, yet has that wide-eyed, rain-freshened
look about the face, a girlish spinsterhood enforced upon
her, as it is upon many here, by the care of two very aged
parents. Indeed, one sees married women single-filing two
and three or four children down the street who wear their
much younger years with a dulled and faded mien beside
Emtie's chaste sparkle. And she is very devout, not that
virginity is a concomitant to religiosity, a theory certainly
blasted in the holy personage of St. Maureen nu Nailly,
but there is a schoolgirl fervor, the same childlike devotion

that can be seen in the faces of nuns playing kickball in the churchyard on the corner.

"How are your folks?" I might ask.

"Ah, God preserve them, they had a poor night," she will answer. "It's the catarrh in their blessed passages that kept them awake the night long. I've purchased a bottle of Formula 44, and I shall say a prayer to St. Joseph for them this evening." And she turns to her work, with full confidence in the success of this one-two punch on her parents' mucous membranes.

Patricia, in her dark moods, sometimes complains of being treated as if she were the Virgin Mary, although I find Emtie's reverence, almost awe, of the state of pregnancy touching. But when she mentions that she is crocheting "a fine do for the ba's christening," neither of us has the heart to tell her the ritual will not take place.

"You've got a fine strapping lad in there," she proudly tells Patricia, who is standing full-blown in a tentlike housecoat.

"Oh, yeah," my wife answers dully and is about to say something else when I catch her eye.

There's always a merry "God bless" as she bundles out the door at the end of the day, and invariably a cheerful "in Jesus' name, long life" hallows the light supper she sets for us before she leaves. We are wrapped in the cozy cocoon of her homely faith.

There is no trouble finding her in this large house, for whether she is hanging laundry in the basement or running the sweeper in the dining room or neatening up the marble mantel in the bedroom we use for a dresser top, her voice croons a continuous medley of music-hall favorites. "A Bird in a Gilded Cage"; "I'll Take You Home

Again, Kathleen"; "Another Jar of Porter, Mary Dear"—
her repertoire seems endless and is rendered with a fluttery,
ladies' club contralto sometimes interspersed with pants
as she skips up the stairs or lugs in the box of groceries just
delivered.

"For God's sake, shut up a minute," I hear Patricia say
occasionally. And Emtie pauses, good-naturedly, but in
another minute or two another selection is trilled out,
"The Look in His Eye Brought a Rose to Her Cheek."

In addition to her adoration of Patricia's condition,
Marie Therese seems overcome with my wife's belongings;
her clothes, sweaters and lingerie, her blouses, and also
with the bottles of cologne and lotions and the other
knickknacks on the marble mantel of the bedroom. Emtie
spends the first hour of every morning folding and refold-
ing and stacking these articles in the armoire, which inci-
dentally she has fixed with a clasp so that we no longer
need the folded match cover to wedge the door shut. Next,
she removes everything from the mantel for an unnecessary dusting and then solemnly replaces each item. There
is a curious reverence in her handling of these things, as
material objects, which is almost embarrassing to us, for
though Patricia is not extravagant in her tastes, the sweaters
and the like are of a difference that cannot be acquired
here. It is almost like holding up glass beads to the Indians.

And what jewelry my wife possesses—a few family
pieces, the diamond earrings, and a brooch in the shape of
a rabbit—I gave her in a whimsical moment; every piece is
carefully itemized and aligned each day in the velvet lining
of the case.

"Shall I polish up your holy medal?" Emtie asks one
morning. "It's a bit tarnished."

"My what?" Patricia turns from the far mirror where I am helping her with her coat. We are joining Maxine Waters in an assault upon the library.

"Your holy medal," Emtie repeats, and dangling from her hand on its gold chain is the Phi Beta Kappa key.

"No. No, thank you, Marie Therese," Patricia says evenly, "I don't wear it anymore."

One more note on Emtie and I'll leave her for the moment. One Saturday afternoon, I'm riding downtown to fill a prescription for Pat's continual nausea, and I see Emtie walking along the street. She's dressed the same as always, black raincoat, umbrella rolled and at the ready, but there is a calm possession about her that is new. She is walking slowly, so slowly and with a serene detachment that I imagine she has just come from church. There's nothing more to it than this, the bus lurches around a corner and she is gone, but I remember being caught up by the sight of her.

It was true. Even had Kermit Smith-Royce's program gone on for five hours and if I had been able to put down the sensation of being a fatuous "five-minute authority," I still could not have explained the racial problem. After all, we have not been able to explain it to each other after two centuries.

The general description of the civil rights marches has been ably reported in numerous journals and I will not attempt to add a dated version here. It is history and not a history that concerns us now, but if that Eden, so reverently re-created by some Southern novelists, ever existed, that garden where white and black lived in purity and harmony, we saw the closing of the gates.

We were prepared for the hostility of the whites but

not for their initial reaction when they saw us in the line of march.

"I'm beginning to feel sorry for them," Patricia said one evening. "They look so hurt, almost like they could cry when they see us." And it was true almost every time we rounded a corner or passed through a village; we would be looked at with disbelief, then a wound would open in the perplexed expressions to become a running sore of hatred.

We were not entirely defenseless and I remember one of the girls turning on a young deputy who had made some remark to her, perhaps jostled her almost playfully in a big-brotherly way. From the black velvet hair band in her hair down to the fine bones of her sandaled feet, she was obviously of a class he could not relate to the other demonstrators. Perhaps she had maybe made a mistake and got into the wrong line. The cold, calculated obscenities she used, remarkable in their variety and ingenuity, left him white and shaken, and his nice-boy, rather chubby face, not unlike the ones seen lolling around the campus on spring weekends, crumpled like the image on the back of a discarded Wheaties box. White or black, segregationist or no, he had trespassed, he had touched her without her consent.

There were quiet evenings when it had been arranged that we have supper and stay with black families along the route. Some were tenant-farm shacks where the faith and purpose of what we were doing, or what we thought we were doing, was personalized for us in such a way that made us doubt our own motives.

Picture a flat crossroads, the treeless fields stretching out in all four quadrants endlessly, and, set back from one corner, a frame church. The front and one side has been recently painted a glistening white, though the one coat

was not thick enough to smooth over the peeling crenella-
tions of old paint jobs. Inside, in the basement, the tables
are set, neatly covered with long sheets of brown parcel
paper, and there are plates of ham and chicken, yams and
greens. There are biscuits.

It is a plentiful meal and the girls sit among the con-
gregation subdued, feeling out conversational ground in
the weather or on the different ways of frying chicken.
There's an overabundance of compliments on the biscuits.
Several children in the corner, dressed in stiff party dresses,
push and play and dance and sing in what can only be described as a performance, because it is just for our benefit, and it is somehow disturbing. There had been much
discussion among the girls, Patricia told me, on what to
wear to the church supper. Should they dress modestly?
Finally, it was decided to wear the best clothes they had
with them, since our hosts would be wearing theirs and to
do otherwise would not seem right.

"And we thank you, Lord, for these witnesses to our
effort." He is an old farmer, an elder of the church, who
stands for the benediction beneath a wall calendar from a
feed firm that pictured a lean, ascetic, pink and white
Jesus bearing the cross. "These fine young ladies who have
come down here, who have left their lovely homes, the
premises of peace and plenty, to join with us and be witness to our righteous cause."

"I'm ashamed," Patricia said later. We walked about
the play yard of the school where a dormitory had been
set up for us and others. "It's really no different from
Bermuda, after all. We will go back when vacation's over
and nothing will be any different."

"Well, you didn't really expect to change anything, did
you? There is an alternative," I told her. "We could stay

on and become professionals." We had encountered that new breed of cultural drop-out, the white students who skipped and hopped from one area to the next, almost sporting the list of their participations—Memphis, Jackson, Mobile, etc.—on their luggage like hotel labels. "Or if you really feel guilty, each of you could take a nice black boy into the bushes." We had seen this happen also.

"Don't be piggish."

"Well, what do you want out of this?" I asked. "Isn't it enough in the personal—well, shock maybe's the word. When you read the accounts you'll think of these people. You know them now. You've seen them."

"But is it all only personal experience? I had expected more than that." She shuffled in the dust of the school yard, her shoulders rounded. There was a thread of grime encircling her neck.

"What?"

"Oh, I don't know. Involvement, I guess."

"Like the man said, you are witnesses, nothing more and nothing less. You served your time, you've done your jury duty, you've paid some of your dues. However you want to put it."

I did not convince her because I did not entirely convince myself. There was something missing, a span lacking in the construction that would have completed the bridge, and though the span was sometimes sought in sex or in a curious debasement that dishonors both sides, the structure was not entirely sound. There was an occasional flash of recognition, of extraordinary mutuality, but so brief and fragile as the passing of butter from white to black and back to white hands at the church supper as to be pretentious and once again embarrassing.

The feeling was not helped by others in the black community we met. There was a party given by a dentist. The house was a comfortable, brick split-level in a middle-class Negro development, and over cocktails we discussed the latest Broadway plays or the new fashions. Sammy Davis, Jr., was mentioned—ha-ha-ha. Lena Horne—ha-ha-ha. The girls babbled like idiots, then suddenly there was nothing more to talk about except what was happening, and our hosts apparently did not want to talk about that. This is the way it was then. In a crazy way, their efforts to demonstrate how much like us they were, how we shared the same interests, made them somehow more out of the picture than we were. Guilelessly, the girls oohed and ahed over the steaks broiling on the patio.

As I said, we were prepared for the hostility from the whites, but it was the reaction of some of the Negroes that unsettled the girls, the typecasting. It could be seen in the faces of the organizers and managers of the march, sharp young men with quick smiles and dark glasses that hid their eyes but reflected ours. There was the casual calculation in their regard, an insouciant questioning of purpose made more pertinent in the hard-eyed inspection given by their wives and girls.

"Cindy Miller heard one of them call us 'the rich white bitches,'" Patricia told me.

"Well, is that an incorrect description?" I asked, but I knew what she meant and her morose expression moved me. At one point, I nearly made a ludicrous gesture of my own. One day I was seized with the urge to approach one of our leaders and say, "Look, do you see that mill there? The management of that mill controls this town, right? Change the thinking of that management and you can change the whole social-political pattern of this town, right?" As I plodded along, I imagined the speculative look grow on his brown face. He was ready for the clincher and I would deliver it calmly, almost offhand. "Well, that mill just happens to be a subsidiary of a corporation in which that little redhead over there will someday manage the controlling stock. Now, forget for the moment the empty-headed designs she may have on your chastity—just go over and make friends and be practical, be realistic about this thing in bread-and-butter terms."

But I stifled the urge and probably fortunately stifled it, for I had a second image of the suspicion that might come to his face and of the suppressed distrust, the growing hatred of this representative of white management where now he looked upon Elizabeth Rollins as only a silly college girl from up North. So we trudged on through and out of the town limits, leaving the status quo intact. I laughed at myself.

We walked on down the road, singing the songs which now sound strangely quaint and old-fashioned, and our feet became blistered and callused. A tough shell grew around the girls as well, a protective covering against the insults, the obscenities shouted at them from the crowds of whites with much self-congratulations on their originality. They bore it well, almost good-humoredly for the most part, occasionally someone like Sue Ellen Dryden sweetly answering a jibe with a string of oaths that gagged the Yahoos open-mouthed, astounded and shocked as the lower classes have always been astounded and shocked by the upper. But it was too much for poor Richard, the last straw being the morning he awoke—he always slept in the bus—to find his cherished vehicle decorated with house paint and with the usual words. He left us without saying goodbye, but no one considered it a desertion.

Of course, we were finally all arrested and lodged in a

remarkably neat and odorless jail, and were it not for this
final happening, the whole trip, superficially at least, would
have been a complete failure. It *was*, after all, and we only
realized it when the keys turned in the locks, maybe what
we really came down here for—to do time. White and
black really together, segregated for once only by sex, we
spent two days and a night in perfect harmony, a completely shoeless, beltless and tieless equality. We sang,
kidded our distressed jailers and joyously ignored the time
when we would have to return to the distinctions of the
dreadful freedom outside our prison. The sheriff's office,
with all its brutal efficiency, had supplied the missing span,
had made the connection.

But like all events in history, a small flattery perhaps
only to employ the parallel, the practical soon interfered
with idealism. We had to get out of jail. I toyed, but only
for a moment, with calling an old classmate of mine now in
the Attorney General's office; then, imagining the conversation with this hard-nosed realist, I dismissed the idea.
Suddenly and unaccountably, Cindy Miller's father showed
up, a middle-aged Ivy Leaguer still wearing button-down
shirts and regimental tie.

"What are you, Phillips, some kind of a communist?"
he snapped through the bars. He was immediately booed
and Cindy, she of "Down on the Delta" fame, could be
heard saying, "Oh, Daddy!"

But his anger and especially his inability to understand
our motive formed a common bond between him and our
jailers, and from that grew a sympathy for him that led
the sheriff to relent. Bail was to be waived with the understanding that we would go home. Patricia instigated a
hurried conference in the corner with many nods and
whispered yeses.

"What do you mean, everybody or nobody?" the poor man shouted. A solid rank of soiled Brooks Brothers shirts and wrinkled shirtwaists confronted him. "What do these —these colored people mean to you anyway?" The ranks did not stir before the open cell gates and I half expected Sue Ellen Dryden, in her best platoon commander's voice, to order, "Backstep, march!"

"Well, what about it, Sheriff?" Mr. Miller finally pleaded.

"Okeh," the official finally said. "I'm gettin' tired of stinkin' up this place 'nyway."

It was something, perhaps a victory, and we slipped on our shoes, put on our belts and neckties and emerged into the freedom of a hot, muggy afternoon to separate on the courthouse steps, parting with genial handshakes and eyes already a little averted.

Our group returned to the Scott campus, singly or in pairs, the remnants of a battered patrol. Patricia had even left me to spend the last few days of the recess with Edna Gates, and I returned alone. This serious game we had played put a chill on all the others, the silly ones. We were not sorry for our pilgrimage, yet we could not but regret the effect it had upon us.

We did not meet except in class in the week following the resumption of the term, and made no arrangement for the weekend. We seemed to avoid each other, fearful of what might be a failure if we did meet. On Saturday, I spent a terrible day mulling about the apartment, putting away her clutter; a bag holding the sweater she was knitting for me still sleeveless, three knee socks hanging from the shower curtain rod and the bottles of lotion and cosmetics crammed into the medicine cabinet. And to one side, the spare brown bottle she kept at my place containing the pills which medical knowledge of the day had not provided her mother; happily, had denied her, I reminded myself.

On Sunday morning, I returned with the papers to find her making an omelet, some croissants already warming in the oven. Her hair was piled and pinned on top of her head, and she wore slacks and a shapeless sweater. A book-bag spilled its contents of library volumes in the corner, obviously the cover for the day. She looked up as I entered, and smiled, her eyes squinting, then went back to whipping the eggs.

Just as I reached her, the papers thrown onto a chair, she put down the mixing bowl and turned to me, as if she had planned and timed the distance, my movement from door to stove. There was some trouble with her glasses; and she finally took them off to blink owlishly at me, crinkles at the corners. Her mouth was soft and opened as her eyes closed, and I felt her reach out and turn off the stove.

We tore the clothes from each other, as her hair came down, a silky eclipse in the midmorning light. Strange sounds wracked us as we took handfuls and mouthfuls of each other, still standing, reluctant to move. It was almost painful, and I did hurt her as I pushed my hand over her belly and through the soft, black pelt below. We finally made it to the couch and I stood over her, weaving, dizzy with the rippling, the olive tones of that long, rolling body, the arms held out and up to me, fingers wriggling.

And then we were on the couch, my hands holding the hard muffin of a butt, my face bruising the heavy breasts while her hands reached down to do something exactly right to both of us.

"You—you know what?" she asked. Her mouth moved across my shoulder.

"What?"

"I said . . . I said to myself . . . what the . . . what the hell. It's all personal experience, personal . . . personal knowledge. Right?" I was too busy to answer. "I said it's . . . it's all personal experience so . . . fuck . . . fuckall. Right?"

"Right."

"Fuckall! Nothing . . . personal . . . exper-IENCE!"

"Fuckall!"

It would be neat if the episode ended with this timely climax, but there is an unfortunate raggety tail-end that must be included. I left her lying on the floor—the couch had become much too small for us—a rivulet of perspiration winding down the arroyo of her breasts, the dark hair wetly plastered over her face. She appeared as a woman who had just passed through labor, one long leg raised and the other lying flat and out, the arms by her side, her face drawn, serene.

I washed off in the bathroom, and, returning, saw the bookbag. If I had not paused to look at it there would be no other episode and, indeed, the whole story might be different. There would be no story. But I reached down and, with a curiosity that had a built-in knowledge of what would kill it, picked up a small brown spiral-leaf notebook from among the other books. Certain of what it contained, I opened the cover and read the new list. "Vanderbilt—Sewanee—Duke—etc."

"What the hell is this?"

She did not look at me, she knew what I had found, but turned on her side into a luxurious odalisque pose, one hand supporting her head. Her face had assumed that sullen none-of-your-damn-business look.

"What the hell is this?" I repeated. "We're not going through this again, are we?"

She sat up, primly closing her thighs, hands around her knees. "Well, it's just a list of colleges," she said, her voice getting very thin and high. "I get out of this place next month and I've got to go somewhere. I've got to go somewhere!" she said heatedly, but her voice cracked.

I knew what I was going to say, had known I was going to say it for some time, so when the words came out they had an odd familiarity. "You're going to go with me. With me, do you understand?" I repeated as a gesture toward originality.

She put her head against her knees and the long black hair fell over her shoulders. A heavy strand dropped between her breasts. "I must say, it's a hell of a way to ask a girl," she finally said. And then later, almost to herself, a sniffle in the sound, "And I want a proper ring, too."

"I'll get you a proper ring," I promised softly. Two tears glistened in her eyes and then spilled down her cheeks, and there was the urge to go to her, to hold her. But I turned on the oven to reheat the croissants. After all, one of us crying was enough.

3

"AND SO WE SEE THAT THE AMERICAN CONSTITU-
tion, contrary to what has been said elsewhere,
was not an agreement between slave states and free." The
faces above and partially around me are stiff with tense
attention, more attributable to the imminence of the dis-
missal bell than to the drama of 1787.

"Indeed, it was only two or three Southern states that
argued for the continuance of the slave trade, and it was
the threat of the delegates from Georgia and South
Carolina to withdraw from the convention that forced
the New Englanders to seek a compromise." I am nearly
to the bottom of the page. If I can only hold them. They
sit in the high tiers, a colosseum crowd ready to dispatch
me at the slightest alarm.

"There is evidence to support the belief that some of
the New England states were just as anxious to continue
slave importation for mercantile reasons. They were in the
business. However, the general truth is that there was a
feeling, shared by almost all the delegates, that slavery
would eventually die out on its own. Consequently, not
wishing to disrupt the convention and ruin the chance of
a Constitution on this one issue, they finally came to the
compromise that would not prohibit the importation of

slaves until 1808. . . . Within twenty years, they all told themselves, the institution of slavery would disappear on its own. But the best principles of man are often undone by the unexpected flash of his genius, for in less than ten years from the time of that compromise, the cotton gin was invented by Eli Whitney. Rather than slavery disappearing on its own, more and more slaves were demanded to raise more and more cotton to feed the insatiable machine that would make cotton king, and make the South prominent in every aspect of American life for half a century."

Books and belongings are being gathered together along the top row. I can almost hear the coils within knees compress, ready to spring. There are a handful who continue to take notes. There's only one more paragraph. "Let's look for comment, for judgment, in a contemporary. George Mason. Do you remember him?" The pale faces with coal-hunks of eyes lean over me. I search for a nod, a glimmer of recognition, a reward. "Author of the Virginia Bill of Rights. That curious paradox of the eighteenth century, an aristocratic egalitarian." There is a slight shift of recurrence on the adjective, a relation to the word "aristocratic" but only as a generic—one of them bloody bastards. ". . . a large slaveholder himself and yet a most articulate spokesman for the anti-slavery position held by many of the Southern delegates, especially those from Virginia. These are his words." I can feel the vibration begin in the lower shaft of the hammer, the surface of the bell plate draw in on itself with anticipation.

" 'Every master of slaves is born a petty tyrant. They bring the judgment of heaven on a country. As nations cannot be rewarded or punished in the next world they

must be in this. By an inevitable chain of causes and
effects providence punishes national sins' "—there it goes;
a shrill treble jerking their spines, separating their behinds
from the chairs—" 'by national calamities.' "

I stand by the rostrum, the cascade of students pouring
down the steep rapids of the auditorium and out into the
noisy swirl of the corridor, and then I am alone, a gladiator
too weary to care which way the thumb goes. My hand
shakes as I close the loose-leaf binder, and I am winded,
spent. The first ragamuffin rush is over and the hall is
relatively free of book-hugging undergraduates. Couples
break off their tease and chatter as I pass, in respect for
the American professor, a mental tug of the forelock for
the foreigner. Beside a glass case containing several examples of the Red Phlarope *(Phlaropus Fulicarius)*, Crawford's office door is open and I see him fussing with the
hot plate by the window.

"Ah, good," he greets me. "Just in time for tea." He
rubs his hands together before the electric heater and puts
out two china mugs, a teapot, a small carton of cream
and a box of sugar cubes. "This country owes a lot to
Marco Polo," he says. "Tea's about all they have worth
drinking. Yes, well, almost all." With the second finger,
he smoothes the yellowish gray moustache. "Why the
gloom, Phillips? Is the wet getting to you?"

I slouch in the armchair across from his desk, read the
titles of the books on the shelf above. "Oh, just one of
those mornings," I answer. "I'm not getting to them."

"Where are you?"

"The convention of '87."

"Ah, well, you ask the difficult, perhaps impossible.
Revolution over here is one class against another, down
with the King and up the Gil Morraughs. It's all they've

been used to. The fact that Washington and those chaps all wore wigs and silk hose immediately puts them on the 'other side.' Then how," he pours hot water into the teapot, "how do you explain a man who owns slaves, and continues to own slaves, arguing against slavery? I dare say, I'm happy I don't have your period. Give me all those merry Romans grinding down the barbarous Jew to build their monuments. That's something they can grasp."

I am depressed for other reasons, for the hiatus in the classroom is a temporary matter, something every teacher experiences. It is Patricia. She is down in the dumps again, going from tears to indifference. For several days she has not bothered to dress, but goes about the house in pajamas and housecoat, her hair in coarse straggles, a slovenly arrangement that is almost deliberate. She snaps at poor Emtie, growls at me and kicks at the stove. She spends most of her time sitting in bed reading American and English movie magazines, while greedily consuming chocolates and mints. Indeed, the only time the old light comes into her eyes is when I plunk down a fresh supply on the counterpane.

"Once you get past the Civil War, you'll be all right," Crawford is saying. "Monopolies, high tariffs and the rest of that grubby business." His disdainful smile exposes large horse teeth, as yellowed as the moustache above them. "They'll understand that."

"I don't suppose it would be any different over at the other place," I say.

"No. The same." Midway in pouring the tea, he looks out the window. The needle spires of the University of Alclair embellish the gray mist. "All those third and fourth sons who didn't make it to Cambridge would be just as puzzled, though for different reasons." He hands me a mug of tea.

"Are you sorry you made the mistake, Jack? About the schools, I mean." He sits down and his ruddy face becomes pinker. There is a clear, gay light in his blue eyes; the look of a thief caught so many times that his guilt has become funny.

"I made no mistake, Phillips," he says, sipping his tea. "Oh?"

"Yes, it was a happy idea of yours—and I don't doubt it a bit—but when you told us about it, well, I just thought I'd use it myself. Only for a little while, of course. I suppose Waters did the same."

"Then you chose this place."

"Well, if there was a choice, yes, I did." I'm sorry I asked, sorry about what I am to hear, for my own problems are already playing to standing room in my head. "I was never at ease in the classroom. The problem you had this morning is nothing to what I face every morning, have faced for every morning for too long. I've never been able to adopt the 'good guy' pose—not that you do, let me say—but it's a wonderful facility. How I used to envy those professors of English—and perhaps it's a prejudice that I can only relate them to the English department—but how I would envy the way they could talk out of the corner of their mouths and intersperse World Series records with Pope's couplets. They always seemed to be grabbing at their crotch; regular fellows, and all that."

"Showmanship is all part of the trade," I say. The man's weaknesses have become gaping faults. It surprises me.

"Quite so, and I'm not being critical. Not a bit. Perhaps I should have been a museum curator. I used to think

so. Who really cares why and how the Hyksos were over-
thrown? What meaning does the Memphite Dynasty have
for the Pepsi-Cola generation? Yes, hmmm."

"What meaning does any of it have?"

"Yes, a good teacher. Yes, a good teacher could give it
meaning. I quite agree. So it was nerve, courage I required.
Of course, the first time it happened—that is, my first
resignation, sounds something like communion, doesn't it—
it had nothing to do, nothing to do with . . ." and his
hand waves to complete the sentence. "No, I dare say it
only hurried the matter, but had no relationship. Quite
different, though not unusual. You've had a similar experience though you were luckier than I in the outcome."

His words are going click-clack through my ears, into
my brain, but I am not really listening. Then like the
tumblers in a combination they fall into place, the door
swings open and the stuff inside knocks me over.

"You mean, an involvement with a student?" The edge
in my voice startles him, and—as I alone know—for the
wrong reasons.

"Good mornin', gentlemen. Ah, a fine mornin' it is,
with just enough of the wet to bring the bloom to the
cheeks." Dean Morraugh stands in the doorway, laying
it on thick. It is, I determine, one of the most unneeded,
superfluous and gratuitous entrances of all time. "Mr.
Phillips, when you have a minute."

"What?"

"Nothing urgent, but if you have a minute, won't you
come by?" And he's gone.

Jack Crawford sips at his tea and I try to rephrase the
question pinwheeling in my head. The whiskey-aged face
is solemnly regretful. He's obviously sorry to have revealed
so much.

"How long ago was this?" I venture.

"Some years ago, when I was younger. Well, a little younger," and he gives that horsey laugh. "I don't want to talk about it."

"These things happen all the time," I say, trying to ease him back onto the subject. "Look at me," though I avoid his eyes. "I can imagine you must have been a very dashing character, graying moustache, tweedy and . . ."

"Please, Phillips, please." He sets down the mug on the desk. There is a twitch in his lips and the moustache points jerk. It is obvious that his class on the Roman Empire will have the afternoon off. "I really don't wish to burden you with it all."

"No burden."

"No, please. I've no right to put any part of the responsibility for my little omissions, commissions, upon you."

"It wouldn't . . ."

"Please," he holds up a hand and laughs halfheartedly. "I really only wanted to tell you that I chose; well, that's not the right word—I came here knowing which university was which." With a good deal of sorting and resorting of papers, alignment of cup with blotter edge, a brief review of pen and pencils, he gradually, almost painfully, puts himself back into the familiar character. He smiles at me, the humorous superiority of the Harvard man sparkling the eyes. "Probably, if the sun were out, I would not have even bothered to tell you anything," he says.

Melodramatic. Circumstantial. I do not dismiss these probabilities lightly, for history is a post-factum science in which one is constantly dealing with melodramatic circumstances or circumstantial melodramas. "What would happen if" is a forbidden game open only to those who wish to rewrite ordinary human melodrama into tragedy or comedy. Jack Crawford's words have me balancing on this dangerous edge as I go to Dean Morraugh's office. To take today's lesson, what would have happened had the threat of South Carolina and Georgia been ignored and the Constitution had forbidden slavery? Would the bloody melodrama of Gettysburg have been replaced by a genuine tragedy? Would we be any happier? Who is the man I have just talked with? Do the circumstances of his life make him a part of my wife's melodrama? Will young Lieutenant Bravehead deliver the message in time? Will the horses get out of the burning barn in time? Will they forget to tell Romeo that Juliet is only drugged? The answer is yes, yes, yes. Yes!

The small wall tablet outside Dean Morraugh's office identifies the interior as the place where the English, tired of being hunted down like fox, weary of snipers attending their cricket matches and almost bored with the whole matter of exploding constabularies, finally came to terms and gave this country independence. One can imagine the determined grace in that impatient, initial gesture, which, as the century progressed, became a helpless shrug.

He is standing by one of the tall, narrow windows that appear to be huge inlays of mother of pearl in the darkened finish of the room. His back is to me and I stand for a few moments in the center of the room, beside the "treaty table" with its small brass plate screwed into the top, exchanging a silent greeting with the ghostly figures above the bookcase.

"There you are, Phillips," he finally acknowledges my entrance. "Well, now, how are you getting on? I've had splendid reports about you. You're giving us a fine tone, you know, don't you?" He comes to his desk and sits down in the chair with an expression that indicates his complete lack of interest. But I try again.

"I'm not so sure about it," I say.

"Oh?"

"Well, it's a different sort of history." One of the three fingers on his left hand directs me to an armchair. "I mean, your own history is so recent, the beginnings of American democracy don't seem to have much relevance." I smile and he smiles.

"Yes, American democracy." He ponders the whole concept for a moment. "It may be more than a difference of time. You see," and he leans back, hands across his plump middle, his feet just touching the floor, "Europeans have always had the comfort of a class structure. There's a security, you know, in having someone either above or below you. And in our case, well, for centuries we were made to believe that everyone was above us. We lay beneath a large comforter, snug but not always very warm."

"The snobbery of the lower classes."

"Yes, quite. But you Americans come along with the belief that no one is any better than you are. A dangerous concept, Mr. Phillips."

"The belief is extended to all men," I say.

"There goes that generosity of yours again," the gray eyes wink wryly. "Oh, I've no doubt you want to believe that all men are equal, but do you really believe it, Mr. Phillips? I mean, you Americans. I've seen your tourists in our cathedrals and I've seen them in our back streets, slums you call them, and it seems to me they show no preference, they admit no difference—it's all one big, quaint junkpile to them."

"Well, all tourists are the same, I would guess."

"There you go again. You see?" His smile is almost patronizing. "In America," and he floats the word upon the full flavor of the Latin as if he were describing one of the Archbishop's birds, "in my stay in America, I noticed one very different thing. All those porches."

"Porches?"

"Yes, all those front porches," and a mystification veils his words. "I would take side trips from New York and I remember passing through neighborhoods with house after house on which there were these front porches, and the families all sitting on them, practically touching elbows. You won't find anything like that over here, no front porches like that. We take the air in our backyard gardens, all enclosed, separated by walls."

"Well, we have nothing to hide," I say.

"Is that it? I remember the word 'public' came to my mind. You all are so bloody public with everything. It's almost, or so I thought, that you were trying to prove to each other that you were all the same. Why they even rigged up some sort of arrangement of glass to use the porches in the winter, all like display cases, shopwindows and the like with the democratic merchandise on exhibit."

"Open covenants, openly arrived at." He nods agreeably and points a finger as if I have just made a most profound point. "Well, that's all changed now. Front porches aren't built anymore. There's something called split-levels these days." As I see the sage look come into his eyes I grow even more impatient with this yin and yan. "You wanted to see me," I say.

"Quite." His mouth tightens prudently. There is a noticeable constricting of his entire person, a steeling-up before an unpleasant task. "You've met my daughter," he says finally, the wind escaping from his lungs. "She was quite taken with the two of you. Being American, I suppose." He hunches over his desk and speaks to the blotter. A paper clip is toyed with. "I've had two roles in my life, Mr. Phillips, a soldier and a scholar, and neither has been helpful as a father. You saw her, you know what I mean."

"We both thought she was very bright and very . . ."

"Cute is the word, isn't it? Yes, you were about to say she was cute. All those miles in the slime along the hedges, all that blood—I am a religious man, Mr. Phillips, and would you believe that I see the men I killed in my sleep sometimes? Handsome, boyish faces they are, with the wide look of coming death upon them, the surprise that it's about to happen to them—and all that to have a cute generation. All that to raise an irrelevant brood."

"Dean Morraugh, I think you're being a little harsh. Young people . . ." But he waves me to silence.

"You met the man she's with. One of those few so many of us are supposed to owe so much to." He is very grim, the chubby face mysteriously losing its softness.

"I'm sure it's harmless," I say, not at all convincingly. "Equivalent to a bracelet or a new hair style."

"She thinks so, I'm sure. But it's not—it's not equivalent. A bracelet is worth more." He throws the paper clip down and looks up at the ceiling. The silence stretches on. He finally finds the words but does not look at me. "Would you and Mrs. Philips take a hand for me? Oh, I don't mean chaperones, do you understand, but she obviously was enormously impressed by the two of you and maybe just by being with you from time to time, it would give her an idea of how it should be, don't you know."

"I'm not sure that we are the prototype you want, Dean

Morraugh." I rise and go to the window, mainly to save him from meeting my eyes.

"I'll be the best judge of that," he says behind me. His voice is almost military.

"Well, what of her dress shop in London? How can she leave it?"

"Ah, that. The partnership will go along, I'm sure. I can get her to stay here well enough if . . . if you two are open to the idea."

I look down on the commons below, the traffic on the glistening streets and the stone figure of the national hero. But I am envisioning our Thanksgiving table being set for two more places. I wonder if the group captain will wear his medals. Dimly, I hear Dean Morraugh continue talking:

"Mrs. Morraugh and I would be immensely grateful if . . ."

"Very well," I cut him off. "I don't know what we are supposed to do, but we'll try . . ." And I never finish, for I see below a tall figure in a black Astrakhan hat walking quickly toward the main gate. Fleeing is more the word to describe Jack Crawford's pace, his thin legs and frame almost moving sideways like a dog whose rear legs are catching up with the front.

Returning home late in the afternoon, I let myself in the dark house, still uncertain of what I should tell Patricia. Should I walk in and merrily say, "Well, guess who your father really is? How about Jack Crawford?" And then follow it up by saying, "Oh, by the way, we've become sort of foster parents for that miniskirted delinquent we met the other day." I could have at least brought flowers.

It might mean the termination of all those wild guesses, the end of those proddings in the night with the whispered

"Maybe I'm Jewish" or "Maybe he was a Negro." I once came upon her nude before a mirror, closely inspecting herself. "Lombrosa says that the labia majora in Negro women are of a magenta hue," she said.

"Let me see," I asked, undertaking the examination with various interpolations while marveling at the depth of the sociology reading list at Scott.

So maybe a final explanation would be given, the original defined, and what would be the gain? She might even be worse off. And as I come up to the bedroom, I sense this is not the time anyway.

Patricia sits up against the pillows, hair loose upon her neck and pale hands resting on the hill of covers beneath her breasts. There are no lights on, Emtie has gone for the day. The floor by the bed is strewn with magazines and candy wrappers.

"How are you?" She makes a disgusted face, tongue curling out and back. "Would you like some Amphojel?" Her head rolls against the headboard weakly.

"Don't turn on the lights," she says, stopping me at the switch. "I look so dreadful. I've just thrown up again, just before you came. Come sit by me, if you can stand it." I sit down on the bed and she takes my hand. She seems feverish.

"Are you all right?"

"Of course I'm not all right. No, you know what I mean." She is without her glasses, and her eyes seem sunken. "How was your day?"

"A day like all days. Nothing unusual. How about here?" She shrugs and regards the bottom of the bed.

"Emtie was all over me again."

"She's only trying to help. I guess the mystery of the womb always inspires maiden ladies."

"Balls," she says.

"Them, too," I reply, gladdened by the smile that briefly lights her features.

"Oh, we had a phone call from that silly creature—Iseult Morraugh."

"Really?"

"Yes, she asked us to go on a picnic with her and Battle of Britain."

"What did you say?" I ask.

"I said no, of course."

"Maybe we ought to go along. I mean, it would be a chance to take a drive in the country—get out of this house for a while. It would do you good." She isn't persuaded. "We could both use a little outing. What's the matter?" Her eyes are becoming wet.

"Oh, I don't know." She pumps my hand a few times and then discards it, almost. "It's just ridiculous to come six thousand miles and to end up going on picnics. Pretty damn ridiculous. Where are all the little trips to Paris and London, the cruises down the Rhine, the afternoons in the sunny cafés—she begins to gasp and gag, she takes a breath —"this isn't the way the travel folder was."

"Well, we can do all that later, after the baby comes."

"Sure, big deal," she sulks. "Mamma and Papa and kiddo, all sharing a Pernod. Changing his pants in a gondola, I can see us now. The Bedermyers on tour."

"It won't be like that," I say, smoothing her arm.

"It will too. Here I am in one of the great capitals of the world"—I turn into the shadows to hide my smile—"four months before my twenty-first birthday—that's what's driving me nuts, I'm not even twenty-one yet—I'm still a girl—and I've got all the fun and everything of

Europe to see and here I am like this, sick as a dog, waddling around five months pregnant!"

"Well, it's not your fault," I say, patting her hand. She sniffs, finds a Kleenex in the bedclothes and uses it.

"But it is my fault," she says after a moment. Her voice is lusterless.

"Of course not. We're just part of that two per cent the statistics warn about." I try to joke, and suddenly it is not easy for me to joke about it. "After all, when they developed those pills, they didn't consider the Phillips sperm count." My words alarm her even more, perhaps the word sperm has sickened her. Anyway, her eyes roll as if stricken, her mouth opens and she groans. She stares at me with obvious effort and says very slowly:

"I wasn't using them."

It is a moment before I sort everything out in my mind. "What do you mean, you weren't using them? The pills, you mean you weren't using the pills?" Her face is now hidden behind her hands and she is crying quietly. "Patricia, you mean you weren't using the pills?"

"Yes," she shouts through her tears. "Do you want me to send you a telegram?"

"Now, don't be funny." I'm off the bed, standing at the foot. "Do you mean to say last year you were not using any, not any protection?"

"Oh, not that." She flops sideways, one arm over her face. "I wouldn't do that to you—give me at least that!"

"Then what do you mean?" Unaccountably, the dark room is suddenly flooded with light from somewhere.

"I mean . . . I mean,"—she struggles up to a sitting position—"I mean I stopped taking them the day before we got married." Her words clang in my ears, clang and reecho like a crazy carillon. And, coincidentally, the delicate chimes of the church on the corner begin their vesper run.

"But why?" She only falls back into the bed, her shoulders trembling. She even tries to pull the sheet over her face. But I jerk it down. "Why, goddamn it, why? Don't you think I had a right to know about it? To say yes or no? I probably would have said yes, if you want the truth. You had no right to do that on your own." She continues to sob.

"I had a reason," she finally says.

"Try me!"

"Well." In fits and starts, she pulls herself up against the pillows, wiping at her eyes. She motions me to her, but I remain where I am. "Well," and then she starts to laugh a little. "Well, it was something I just thought out for myself. Something personal, I guess. Oh, God, Hamlet, I don't know. There had been those others. You didn't seem to mind . . ."

"I didn't. I don't."

"I believe you. But—it's funny—all of a sudden I minded. It was like marrying you I should be different. I should bring something different to it, that's badly put, but it seemed like it shouldn't be the same as it was before— even with you before. Oh, God," she laughs and then gives half a sob, "what a mess." She wipes at her eyes again. "I just wanted to make it as new as I could."

I find no words for her and no comfort for myself in the view from the bedroom window. The street is quite dark now. The lamps are on, and one or two scarfed and capped pedestrians walk by the iron railings that border the sidewalk. They are hurrying home, I tell myself, to cozy fires, to tea and cakes, to gaiety and sympathy, if not understanding. To radiant trust they move also, over-shoes left at the door, and then into the illuminated parlor where a place is waiting for them, where their opinion is asked. And there may be children gathering at the knee, reading the evening paper and asking, "What would have happened if . . . ?"

"Emtie has left something for us in the oven," my wife says. I hear her move on the bed, hear her feet search and push into slippers.

"I'll fix it," I say, though I don't turn.

"No, I'll do it," she answers quickly. "I feel much better. In fact, I'm starving." And she slips from the room.

"We're planning a June wedding," I told the president of Scott Junior College. His desk was a triumph of steel and laminated walnut as were the paneled walls of his office. There was only softness in the thick carpet and the muffled clacking of typewriters outside the door. He was one of those tall, blond men who often have a gray look about them, the new breed of college administrators ac-quired from the chemistry department of some larger uni-versity, a smoker of long, thin cigars and more at ease with bankers and politicians than with a teacher of history. The recently poured foundation of the new science com-plex testified to his abilities as a fund raiser, and, to con-tinue his qualities, he was also a fair tennis player, as was demonstrated every spring by the singles he and his wife, a taller, stringier version of Jacqueline Kennedy, would play on the campus courts. In the long twilights of April, they would be seen lunging and swooping at each other with an abandon qualified in its fierceness only by the sprinkling of "Good shot," or "Sorry," or "Love," like a pair of sporting cranes.

"This June," he repeated. "Well, congratulations!" And he smiled easily and leaned back in his chair to unbutton the double-breasted jacket of his suit. For him it was tantamount to loosening his tie and kicking off his shoes. Then he became very serious, a great worry, a terrible problem had suddenly arisen. "There just might be some little trouble with the trustees," he said, his face thoughtful and concerned.

"I've already made other arrangements," I told him. The relief, the genuine appreciation and gratitude to me for recognizing his problem flooded his face. And I was angry with myself for giving him this help, suddenly realizing one of the attributes of his success. "That is, if you think it's best."

He paused for a moment, his eyes going to the print of a Maine coast schooner on the walnut-paneled wall, paused long enough to assure me he was being fair, that, in a matter of seconds, he was reviewing all of the evidence and considerations which had led him to the final decision that had called me to his office. Then, "Yes, I think it's for the best, Hamilton. Where will you be?"

"There are several possibilities," I said, trying to think of them. "There's an opening at Brown that looks good."

"Wonderful. Their gain is our loss," he said and laughed, pleased with the apt phrase. His use of the cliché, invariably followed by a grin or laugh, conveyed the ironic sense that he knew it was trite, while it defended the charge that he could think of nothing more original. "She's a grand girl," he said.

The death penalty for murder had only recently been abolished and I was tempted to take advantage of it, quietly to spend the rest of my life in a state-supported monastery completing my studies of medieval guilds. The words were foul in his Presbyterian mouth. But there's the difference between the scholar and the man of action, why one develops ulcers as the other makes history. Instead, with a timidity that shamed me, I said, "Your recommendation will be useful."

"Delighted. You can count on it," he said, again smiling, but only with his mouth.

"*Prendre la lune avec les dents*," Patricia says in the dark. I translate the phrase literally, watching the shadows of the tree limbs silently scrape the high ceiling of the bedroom. In the several days since her outburst, she has driven herself in a fit of expiation, I suppose, meals and sex elaborately ritualized. Passively, coldly I accept it all as I selfishly receive her now, kneeling on my thighs, her hair a tent over my belly.

"Yes, careful with the teeth," I say. "Burton, in his journals, describes how Arabian women would castrate British soldiers that way." There's something whorish about this prattle while the rest of me is lovingly caressed. "Ah, well," I shift to a better position, "nationalism sometimes takes curious forms."

"That's not what it means at all," Patricia says. She is sitting up, looking toward me in the darkness. Her voice is heavy and a little sad. "It's a colloquial phrase. It means 'to do the impossible.'"

I do not ask why she has thought of this phrase, put these words in relation to what she is doing. But there is an impossibility to what she has been attempting the last few days, an impossibility for which I am mostly to blame. My body is here, automatically responding to the tactile, to the cutaneous sensation, but in all of its rigidity there is not a fiber of joy.

The fact that I am able to simultaneously think rationally, so withdrawn, reveals the dichotomy within me, the division that is now between us. I think of those poor creatures who feverishly stand in bookstores looking for accounts of ultimate caresses in the dog-eared marriage manuals on display, and who return to their homes like incredible and somewhat suspicious Marco Polos, promoting the taste of bean sprouts.

For the fault is entirely with me, I realize, yet I cannot or will not do anything about it. Coolly, I review her technique and find it no different from the way it has ever been, deriving a satisfaction, only passing, and an appreciation, not stingy, of what our sex life has been up until now. Remarkable is the word for it. And normal, too, in the fullest sense of the spectrum the bright light of love can make of sex. But now all I can think of is the word pornography.

I realize that her use of my body to work off the guilt that she feels could be transcended if I but cooperate, participate in some small way. Instead I meet use with use, a utilitarian object based on a mechanical truth to which she is giving lip service. Perhaps pornography is obscene because it objectifies, reveals to us how very awkward, how ugly or ridiculous we actually are when we believe we are being beautiful. When the gods handed down their pleasures to us they withheld their dignity, and love must be our fragile substitute.

All this while I lie in bed, Patricia twined about my legs like a growing vine. She has become tired and is resting, a cool cheek against my groin, her silky hair encircling, enveloping me like a mermaid's. And with disgust, I recognize pity entering my awareness, and with a magniloquence of reasoning that ordinarily would have shamed me, I decide to help her.

"Go on," I say.

I let my mind project an obscene film, a festival of hits and misses from the past, excerpts of great or middling performances by lovers I rarely recall. Their faces, their turn of arm, lift of thigh, bend of waist, shape of breast are unreeled. It is helping a bit. I concentrate on the humid junctions, the soft pummelings of hands and knees. There are close-ups: eyes closing, eyes suddenly opening, rolling back. Mouths. Lips parting, pursuing. Tongues. Lips distended, gorged. Patricia senses the change and becomes anxious as a mother cat worrying her young.

But I am at a plateau—I recognize it with dread—a bleak, cold mesa from which the final ascent may be impossible. And then, a new figure joins the dirty extravaganza. I saw her only yesterday, watched her from the window of a bar as she walked down Gonorah Street, her blond hair falling straight down to splay upon the black leather of a short coat. All the refinements advertised in the back pages of seedy magazines suddenly in style, suddenly acceptable. The high black boots, the mid-thigh skirt and the clanking assortment of jewelry reminiscent of fetters. And so terribly thin, the almost bony assertion of the basic feminine. Iseult. A mechanical girl, made of imitation leather and metal and bone, and within it all, in the center of this glossy artificial creation: a close-up of that small, soft mouth. And this does it.

Patricia's determination, her courage comes through the vapors of my selfish pleasure. I feel her stomach quaking, a spasm, but she waits and waits with an iron will that speaks for her depth of guilt, describes her love with an eloquence that makes my mouth dry. And then she can wait no longer. She staggers, gagging, to the sink in the corner and throws up. I move to go to her and then lie back, guessing it better not to act out, to verbalize what has happened. And I wonder if we have not both become infected, that her sickness is caused by the appalling image I have somehow transmitted to her.

When I am forty, it occurred to me one day, she will be twenty-five. At forty-five, she will be thirty. Up until that point, everything would go well. There would be a fillip of pleasure from the admiration, the envy of all those graying colleagues with their slack-armed wives, those trim dumplings of co-eds with whom they had shared the exciting discovery of parthenogenesis in Biology 101, but who with the years and from the non-apogamous structure of their own egg-laying had become chubby good sports and den mothers. Phillips and his young wife, I could hear them saying, gritting their teeth with the thought of me lying upon that flat, taut belly to play the dolphin between firm, unwaffled thighs.

But then at the mid-century mark with so few years left to go, and these quieting years intended for calm reflection and the small savoring of those nuances overrun if not overlooked in youth's rampage, I would have a lusty, hot-blooded wench of thirty-five on my hands. Firsthand knowledge tells me a woman, and especially the best kind of American woman, does not really come into her own until she's thirty-five. All of her inherent mystique, that curious blend of conservative nature and irrational yen resolved into what is best, what "works" for her, is put together then with what she has observed and experienced with men and the world. At thirty-five, women are like great athletes who reach that peak in their careers where innate ability is combined with a fully learned expertise of the game, and it is then that they begin to play like champions. Phillips and his young wife, indeed. Ha!

I was out of my mind, I told myself on a gorgeous spring day. There was a zephyr sifting through the windows, playing with the papers on the desk in my apartment as I alternately fitted horns upon my head or sank into the spittled fantasy of a dirty old man. Patricia hummed about the place, playing at housewife, thumping cushions, sweeping and generally finding an astonishing amount of straightening up to do in a one-room-with-bath digs. She was barefoot, wearing the habitual jeans and one of my shirts, tail hanging out, open to the navel. The sleeves were rolled up high on her smooth arms.

"There's something I've been meaning to talk to you about," I said.

"What?" She turned, the swing of the ponytail revealing a small alarm, a little tension.

"The next time you wear my bathrobe, don't roll the sleeves up. I put it on the other morning and the sleeves were up above my elbow. I felt like a goddamned circus freak." I received a stuck-out tongue for a reply.

And that was another thing, I told myself. I was too old for this rearranging, this constant cleaning-up, the rolled-up sleeves, not to mention the inevitable laundry on the shower rod. Man was never really meant for marriage. Man was the hunter. The sower of seed. The maker and builder. It was a ridiculous idea, marriage. Absolutely ridiculous. Why couldn't we go on as we were? We could enter that golden period of life where

I could be of so much more value to her as a teacher, a
wise and noble counselor, a tolerant listener if nothing
more—all this denied by that absurd contract. And there
would be a mutual dependence based on, indeed nourished
by, a prideful independence. Her freedom I was thinking
of, her freedom when I was fifty-five and she only forty.

"You better get dressed," she said, while unzipping and
squirming out of the jeans. Long, brown legs kicked out
of the pants like trout leaping from a pond, and with
them leaped a sudden ache.

But it would be the same, worse, in fact. I watched her
unbutton a print blouse and then lay out skirt and jacket.
What kind of a toothless nanny would I have to become
in order to sit quietly, to sympathize with her on some
broken amour which she had brought to me as the hurt
child she still would be. Better to take the middle road.
Better to join the tribal ritual and suffer one's suspicions
than to sit numbly in the shade and hear them con-
firmed.

"What's the matter with you?" She asked. "You look
so glum." She was standing in bra and panties, holding
an atomizer of perfume, and as she spoke, she gave a squirt
under each arm, pulled out the waistband of the panties
for a shot down the crotch and then a general wisping
around her thighs and over her butt. It was almost disgusting.

Now a man would have taken a shower, certainly put
soap and water to a washcloth. But she used Balenciaga,
overlaying the sweat in her armpits and the aromas—mine
included—that rose from her groin with a veneer of
essence I had given her on Shakespeare's birthday. Twenty
years from now, I could envision her standing by some
bed on which lolled a weary, muscled clod—spraying her-

self. "Yes, Hamilton"—hiist!—"gave me this"—hiist—"for *Shakespeare's* birthday"—hiist. Well, that's all there was to it, I told myself, I'm marrying a whore.

"What's the matter with you?" she asked, buttoning up the blouse. The predominant color was orange and it glowed upon the skin of her neck and cheeks like a tropical sunset. "You're not worried about meeting Edna, are you? You mustn't be. I can handle her. Emotional blackmail."

"Well, a little," I lied to her and got up to dress. As I washed up and shaved, I changed the subject in my mind. Edna Gates I had seen in photographs, but I still did not know what to expect. I tried to compare her with my own mother, also a small, birdlike woman but with great style. I had only just received one of my mother's strangely formal though very personal letters, telling me how pleased she was at my marriage though regretting she could not come to the wedding. The postmark was French Somaliland and after the usual amenities had been observed, to acknowledge the marriage announcement, the rest of the letter was a report on the redoing of her house in Tangiers, all told with a co-ed's enthusiasm. But she had added as a postscript, as if to break out somehow from the pat formality that had gone before, "Patricia is a handsome young woman—and, Ham, I'm *so* glad she is tall for you." We had sent her a picture taken together with a class-mate's Polaroid.

It was curious—I paused, seesawing the tie around my neck—curious that she should mention that. My father had been tall, over six feet, I'm not sure how much, and my mother very petite. Had this been a problem for them, something that had bothered her all these years, had caused them some maladjustment? For a moment, I thought of that tall, gangling figure that was to disappear in a flash of flame, on a hill in Illinois, leaving me with a small income but without cause. Disappearing overnight, as it were, and with him seemingly went the marriage, as if it had never existed. I will say for my mother that she never made me feel an embarrassment, an encumbrance, for we shared a number of good years together, warm and confidence-sharing years. It was and is rare and impossible to explain.

But afterward, when I had tried out my wings, it was then I realized she had been elegantly champing at the bit to pull up stakes and to obliterate from the surface of the earth the most minute evidence of that marriage, from the house in Exeter down to the smallest wedding gift—a set of silver champagne swizzle sticks. They all went at auction one day, she writing me at boot camp in Parris Island to see if I wanted anything special and I didn't, everything disbursed and scattered over the terrain as completely as my father's ashes had been blown across the plains.

So much for their marriage, one which, despite its finale or perhaps because of its finale, made more sense to me than others. With the television boom, the one or two gadgets I remember my father tinkering with, as a form of relaxation from his complete absorption with radar, became the nuts from which a hardy royalty tree grew, and the checks floated down with timely bounteousness. My mother took to traveling, several times around the world, a winter in Jamaica, another in Mexico, and then, finding northern Africa suiting her income and temperament, she sold the last bone as it were, and bought a small house in Tangiers. I was touched when she asked my permission to cash the bonds, and gave it to her happily and with pleasure. From his experiments with radar, my father's dream of sightless vision so obviously faulty, there were no royalties.

And from my mother I turned to the thought of Edna Gates and all Patricia had told me of that loveless marriage. There must have been something between Edna and the Colonel in the beginning—but how much? And there was the shrine she keeps to the great man's memory: the house outside Rochester, as if he had only just walked out of it to kick a dog off the lawn, complete even to the framed photographs, the awards, the medals and pair of pressed "pinks" in the closet. I was discouraged and at a loss, and out of tune with the fineness of the day. There was another "hiist" behind me, this one coming from a can of hair spray, I judged.

While I had been dressing, I had not noticed Patricia, in fact had almost forgotten her, my mind wandering from Illinois to Exeter, to the Mediterranean, to Rochester, and so when I turned it was like looking at her all over again. The blouse I've described, the suit was a vanilla-colored linen, but it was the way she stood there, fixing a final roll in the ebony hair, a glance through the harlequin glasses, and the set bow of the lips. There was just the slightest question in that glance through the mirror, as if to ask if she were all right, but of course she knew she was.

I am not sentimental, or try not to be, but I was in danger at that moment of losing all my hard-earned reality. If someone had asked me at that moment to name the ten great artists of the world, I would have commenced the list with Charles Dana Gibson. Patricia was so clearly mine, she was so clearly for me, with me and about me that the whole day turned back again, the breeze blew the mind clean and fresh, and there was even a bird singing outside the window.

"Onward to Edna," I said.

"You betcha," Patricia replied, happily clucking, and we descended the stairs together.

I expected the bones in Edna Gates's wrist to shatter under the strain of breaking through the pastry shell holding the creamed chicken *aux champignons.* The delicacy of her construction and of how she moved and positioned herself set awry the hearty atmosphere of the Bird and Bottle Restaurant. And beside Patricia, the woman's pretty diminutiveness was even more exaggerated. I caught her stealing glances at this tall, lusty child who was certainly no issue from her loins, certainly did not resemble anyone in her family. Awe is not exactly the right word to describe her regard, but it is close enough.

This is not to say that Edna Gates was without reserve or an inner sense of security of place or position. Quite the contrary. I was made aware of that immediately when we met—a gloved hand offered with the minimum amount of pressure—and I sat through their home-town talk fully expecting her to ask me eventually about Patricia's grades, rather than about our coming marriage. I guess it must have been difficult for her to meet me for the first time in my dual role of history instructor and future son-in-law.

"Well, now, when should I ask Mr. Tate to reserve St. James?" she finally asked Patricia. They had come to the end of their social chatter.

"St. James?" I asked.

"Yes, Mr. Phillips—Hamilton," and she smiled slightly, as if she had a very funny though unmentionable thought.

"It's our family church," she told me. "Colonel Gates was instrumental in having it restored and it's a fine example of . . ."

"We're planning to get married on the Cape, Mummy,"

Patricia interrupted, and I nearly laughed at the childish appellation. "Aren't we, Ham?"

"Yes," I answered, hearing the plan for the first time.

"Ah, I see," Edna Gates said. "And the date?"

"Sometime in June," Patricia shrugged. "We haven't picked it yet."

"You will continue to teach, of course?" Edna Gates asked.

"Yes—you know we ought to start a new organization— Parent-Teacher-Suitor Association. P.T.S.A." There was a dark scowl from Pat, a pained looking away, and my attempt was further rewarded by a quick, silent laugh from Edna; a sort of "how very clever" expression. "Yes, I have several offers that are interesting." And then I found myself saying, "I also have a little income from my father's estate. Not very large, but it comes in handy."

"Of course." Her attention turned to Patricia. "Did I tell you that Suky York is marrying that nice young man from Princeton—what was his name? Oh, you know who I mean." A deepening flush rose in Pat's face, but she couldn't remember his name. Then to me she said, "One of Patricia's old beaus is marrying the daughter of my closest friend. I think he's going to go into politics, and he'll do very well too, I wager. Colonel Gates was county chairman of the Republican Party," she told me, "and he worked very hard for Eisenhower's nomination, the first time. I suppose you voted for Stevenson." Her smile was almost roguish.

"Not the first time," I answered. "I wasn't old enough."

"Really? I would have thought you were."

"No, I lacked one year. But I did the second time around. Also, for Kennedy."

"Yes, him."

"Mummy, we want you to come to the wedding."

"Why, of course. Just tell me when and where, dear, and I'll be there. Will your mother be there, Hamilton? I would enjoy meeting her."

"No, I'm afraid not. She's abroad," I said, not trying to explain our particular relationship.

"Did you know a family in Exeter by the name of Jones? They had something to do with a mill."

"Yes, they ran the brass mill."

And on it went through the salad, dessert and coffee. Edna Gates did not disapprove of me, mainly because she knew it would be a wasted effort to do so, and she obviously had more important things on which to expend her frail energies. Aside from a remark here and there, it was Patricia who was the dominant person, exercising the leverage of her birth, the lack of blood between them.

But as we were leaving, after almost a struggle over who would pay the check, with my finally giving in and letting her "treat" us because of the genuine anger, even hatred, growing in the pale blue eyes, she reached over and plucked at the Phi Bete key hanging around Pat's throat.

"Do you still wear that?" she asked, a little amused.

There will be one more place at our Thanksgiving table and it will be set for Mary Abbey. I'm familiar with her work, the sparse adaption of classic French verse form used for even drier introspections of her sex making her an outstanding exponent of the Feminine Hygiene School of American poetry. But when Maxine Waters introduces us, I see how much she physically resembles her poetry. There's a bleached, bone-white look about her, resembling the skulls one might see on the plains of the poet's native

Nebraska, and with her short-cropped reddish hair and scraps of eyebrows, she gives the likeness of Joan of Arc, after the fire.

"One of my star pupils," Maxine Waters tells us, spooning more *gai pan* onto her plate. There's a new Chinese restaurant just opened and we are trying it out. "My husband spotted her work at once and sent some of her things on to Conrad Aiken. Didn't he?"

Mary Abbey nods, not too happily it seems, and continues to smoke over her dinner. Her fingers are stained a dark yellow. "I've been in Rome on a fellowship," she answers Pat in a toneless but surprisingly throaty voice. "I'm on my way back now to the States, to do some readings, but I thought I would stop off here to do some research. And to see Mrs. Waters," she adds.

"Wasn't it lucky, my dear, wasn't it lucky," Maxine Waters nearly carols, "that I came across your name in the arrivals. I immediately called the Embassy and I said, 'Look here, we have one of our finest young poets just in town, and you *must* give her a platform.' Well, you know that cultural attaché they have there, he was a car dealer in Cleveland." She leans toward Mary Abbey. Maxine Waters sits on one banquette by herself, and the rest of us on chairs around the table. "Who's for the rest of this shrimp?" she asks, spoon poised above the dish. "Well, we mustn't hurt the chef's feelings," and she scrapes the last of it up.

"Well, what did they say?" Patricia asks.

"Who?" Maxine asks.

"The Embassy."

"Well, my dear, they never heard of Mary Abbey, the ignoramuses." Mary Abbey attempts to smile and tentatively picks up her fork. "Ignoramuses," Maxine continues.

"No wonder we have the problems we have with idiots like that representing us. Why, they only barely heard of my husband when I first went there. Now, eat up, Mary —you'll need your strength for the reading."

The poet picks at her food, bending submissively to the forceful counseling of her former teacher. It is not easy to refuse Maxine Waters, or rather it is easier to give in. She has become an ex officio cultural ambassador. When the IBM chorus made an appearance as part of their world-wide tour of cultural exchange, she even managed to rearrange their program, replacing "Smoke Gets in Your Eyes" with "The Banks of the Wabash." ("After all— Dreiser wrote the lyrics!") But her great triumph, until this evening, was the poetry reading which she gave herself, a two-hour program with the first half composed of works by Frost, Sandburg, Lindsay, Masters, Ransom, Jeffers, Cummings and Williams and the last half composed of the works of Robert Lewis Waters.

("The thing about minor poets," Jack Crawford had said, as we sat over an ale after Maxine's reading, "is that there is so much of them.")

"The tea is cold. We need more tea," Maxine says. "Here, boy." A waiter comes near. "May we have some more tea, please?"

"How are the medical services here?" Mary Abbey asks Pat.

"Fine. That's one of the good things about this country, the doctors."

"Do you like your doctor?" she persists.

"Yes. He's very nice. Why?" Pat asks.

"Well, I thought I might have a checkup . . ."

"You're not ill, my dear?" Maxine leans forward with great anticipation.

"Oh, no." Mary Abbey puts down her fork and lights another cigarette. "I like to have a checkup occasionally. Heavy smoker and all," and she shrugs away Maxine's interest in her health. "How long of a program do they want this evening?"

"As long as you want. Are you going to read some of your new things? I'm anxious to hear them."

"Yes, I thought I'd read from my new book. It will be out in the spring. Actually, this is really a good idea. It will give me a bit more practice before I get to the YMHA."

"You mentioned some research," I say. "How long do you plan to be here?"

"I don't know really," she answers through a heavy cloud of smoke.

"Well, if you're here for Thanksgiving, we're having a turkey and all the trimmings and you're certainly welcome." Patricia stiffens but smiles bravely.

"That would be fun," Mary Abbey says, an elfish grin lighting the bleak features. "Yes, that would be fun. I've been away over a year and something like that would be fun. Thank you." She is unaccountably overwhelmed with the invitation. "If I'm here, I'll certainly take you up on it."

"And there's another thing," Maxine Waters says, pointing her fork at me. Her eyes narrow, sighting down the tines. "Do you know when I asked them out at the Embassy about getting cranberries, they just looked at me as if I was crazy. It had never occurred to them to get cranberries before—they've had turkey without cranberries up until now."

"And now?" Patricia asks, almost giggling.

"Well, my dear, I wish you could have seen their faces

when I told them how they could fly them in from any PX in England. Oh my, then there were regulations about duties and importing foreign products. Well, I said, what are diplomatic pouches for? It had never occurred to them."

"Mrs. Waters is going to make the cranberry sauce," I tell Mary Abbey as an inducement.

"Yes, my husband's mother's recipe," she amplifies, cleaning up the rest of her plate. "What's your research, Mary dear? —Oh, you just don't know how wonderful it is to see this girl again," she tells us, gripping the poet's shoulders, shaking her like a doll. "Something on one of their people? I would think there'd be little left to research."

"Yes, you're right," Mary Abbey says. "No, there's a rather old manuscript having to do with one of their very early martyrs. I ran across a reference to it in the Vatican Library and I just thought I'd look it up."

"You're going to translate it?"

"Well, it's in the Old Tongue, so I would have to find someone to help me with that. I really don't know much about it except the theme appeals to me."

"Which is?" I ask, a tingle up my neck.

"Oh, well," she shrugs almost in apology, "it concerns a woman who sacrifices herself so that others may survive. Not survival of life, but a whole cultural survival. For no one survives," she adds thoughtfully. "But a civilization is more . . . well, specifically, she somehow saved a monastery here during the Dark Ages, some place with a library where a lot of the classics supposedly had been deposited, as it were"—she was warming to the subject—"in this country—the whole treasure of Western Man."

"You wouldn't know it today," Maxine Waters snorted behind a napkin.

"Was there much detail in this reference you saw?" I ask. Mary Abbey looks at me quizzically, then lights another cigarette.

"No, very little—just enough to interest me," she says finally. "But enough to get me interested in the theme—I suppose it's a theme I'm overly fond of," she smiles at Patricia, "woman's sacrifice for the survival of the race."

"That lovely poem on your mother," Maxine Waters says with dramatic reverence. "I'll never forget it." Mary Abbey smiles her appreciation and looks away, blushing.

As I stand in the rain hailing a taxi, the three women wait beneath the pagoda-shaped portico of the restaurant. I overhear Patricia tell the poet the name of Dr. Hewson, and Maxine Waters also briefs her on the names of the various officials she is about to meet at the Embassy. If information is power, as some of the modern political scientists believe, then I have suddenly been handed a package of it. I think of the small volume so tenderly given to me by Dean Morraugh and of the effect it would have upon the likes of Mary Abbey. And what would she do with it? For with power goes responsibility and, finally gaining a cab driver's attention, I recognize that my responsibilities are multi-leveled: to Dean Morraugh, to the people of this country and to those of my own, not to mention the blessed memory of St. Maureen herself.

"Was all this really necessary?" I asked Patricia.

"What?" she asked, coming to me and looking over my shoulder at the society page of the Sunday Times. "My goodness, why did Edna use that picture?" The picture, admittedly not a very good likeness but one of the usual airbrushed, nuptial passport facsimiles, the picture was not my concern.

PATRICIA SIMPSON GATES
AND HISTORY TEACHER

"Why didn't she say 'And *Her* History Teacher'?"
"Don't be dorf," Pat nudged me, "she didn't write the headline."

> Patricia Simpson Gates, daughter of Mrs. Edmund Gates and the late Colonel Gates, will be married in June to Mr. Hamilton B. Phillips, a teacher of history at Scott Junior College and an eminent scholar in the Middle Ages. Mr. Phillips is the son of the late John B. and Mrs. Phillips of Exeter, N.H., and Tangiers.
>
> Miss Gates, who is to be a May graduate of Scott Junior College, is the daughter of the noted New York State publisher and the granddaughter of Vice Admiral Pierce Gates who, as a young officer, was a member of Admiral Dewey's staff at Manila Bay. On her maternal side, the bride is the granddaughter of Flora Hanson Mapes, an associate of Susan B. Anthony. Through her great-great-grandfather, again on the maternal side, Judson Mapes, an undersecretary in Lincoln's first cabinet, Miss Gates traces her ancestry back to John James Audubon.
>
> The bridegroom graduated *cum laude* from Bowdoin College and received a Master of Arts from Harvard University. The couple plan a Cape Cod wedding trip.

"That's a pretty long pedigree for a mongrel like you," I said.

"Go jump," Patricia snapped, returning to the bed and book section. "You're just mad because you see it in print. It nails it down."

"But do we have to go through all this formal crap?"

"Sneak away in the night, eh? Nothing doing," she said, hiding behind the magazine.

I could only sigh and pick up another section, the travel one it was, and began to look at the pictures of beaches, of byways in Greece and bistros in Paris.

Great white tankers and freighters of clouds move in the blue harbor of the sky. The hedges, preparing for winter, are blackish green, and animals in the road stand smoking their own breath. The gray leather upholstery of the Jaguar sighs beneath us as Group Captain Percy Browne drives the car with a polished abandon, substituting horn for brakes. We pass through a village and it is a blur of textured whites and browns, patches of red or green representing door fronts like pieces of broken glass on a beach.

"I haven't been down this way in ages," Iseult Morraugh says, turning back to us. She is wearing a purple tweed slack suit, and her eyes are suitably made up. The small-lipped mouth is white. "Not so fast, Perce. There's a lovely ruin around the bend!"

Patricia shifts her bulk beside me to a more comfortable position and I look at her apprehensively; the jogging, the rapid twists and turns of the road may be making her sick. But she seems serene, observing the countryside. For some reason, I think of all the time we have spent together sitting side by side in some vehicle, looking at the scenery. She recrosses her legs, one of the heavy walking shoes she wears these days striking the picnic basket on the floor between us.

"Ooh, don't crush the grape," Iseult says, leaning way over to inspect the basket. A sudden flood of sunlight illuminates her hair. "What have you brought?"

"Some chicken and cheese," Patricia tells her. The reserve that was between them, or rather Patricia's earlier diffidence, seems to have disappeared.

"Oh, lovely," Iseult coos, straightening up. "I'm bags about your American fried chicken. There's a spot on Piccadilly that makes up American fried chicken and yellow corn bread—what's the place called, Perce?"

"What's that?" Group Captain Browne asks. Capped, gloved and ascoted, he drives with a cool concentration.

"That place on Piccadilly that has the American cooking?" she repeats. He shakes his head.

"I didn't feel like doing any cooking today," Patricia says. "Marie Therese made this up for us."

"And quite right, too," Iseult agrees, lighting a cigarette. "What's a holiday if you have to cook?" We ride on for several more miles, Iseult continuing to look at us. It is not a stare but rather a friendly inspection. She is sitting entirely backward in her seat and suddenly bends low to peer through the rear window. "Oooh, stop, Perce. Stop!" He stops, throwing us against the front seat. "Now back up." He backs up.

To our right is the rubbled remains of an old castle. Half of a Norman tower rises on one side, the rear wall stands intact though punctured by the gape of a large window, the elliptical tracery of stone framing the blue sky. The shape of this window is repeated in the stone squinch of an entranceway standing in the field all by itself before the fallen castle, like a set piece. Sheep pass through grazing.

"Let's look at it," Iseult says gaily. Browne pulls off the road and Patricia groans under her breath, but once she has pushed and pulled herself through the small door she seems pleased enough to be there. In fact, she is a bit overcome.

"Gosh," she says.

"What?"

And she laughs. "Just look at that."

"Come, you two," Iseult cries to us. She has Browne in hand and is leading him across the spongy field toward the ruin. The intense purple of her costume brings out the faded green of the turf and shrubbery.

"Gosh," Patricia says again as the old walls rise higher and higher on our approach. "It really was like this," she says with an astonished giggle.

"It really was," I say. "I would say it's a bastard combination. The Normans didn't appear until quite late. They brought the round towers and those pointed windows. You can see on that wall"—I point to the tumbled one to the right—"the older, square type of window."

Iseult and Browne have passed through the arch of the old entrance, and we follow them, though two steps to either right or left would have passed us around the remains. The archivolt is a series of small heads, a row of doglike faces. Patricia wonderingly passes her hand over their noses.

There are more sheep inside, nibbling at the grass of what may have been the main hall. Iseult runs ahead of Browne, hair streaming in the wind, and leaps up several steps at the end, turns and thrusts her arms above her head. "Fuck England!" she cries. The sheep give startled baas and skip a few steps.

"Up yours," answers Browne. He huffs up the two or three steps and they begin to wrestle playfully.

"Save me, America," Iseult pleads, an arm beckoning to me. I continue to walk beside Patricia, conscious of her slow, ponderous step. The sun rounds a fortlike cumulus and the scene is brilliant. Patricia stretches, in the warming light her arms shortened, put out of proportion to the rest of her swollen body. "You beast," we hear Iseult say to Browne. He continues to wool her about, his face close to hers. "Dirty beast," she says in reply to something, but there's no anger.

"Now what was this, actually?" Pat asks, turning full round to survey the place. "I mean, was it a place just for soldiers or a family, or what?"

"All of those things," I answer. "It probably belonged to some minor noble, a knight who in turn owed his loyalty to someone else."

"It must have been pretty grim in the winter," she says.

"Well, some had glass in the windows—the big ones— and, of course, we only have the foundation walls here. But some of them had very elaborate interior finishes. The wealthier ones had tapestries on the walls. I can't see where the fireplace was, probably up where Browne is." Browne casually slumps upon a piece of masonry that juts from the foundation. His weathered face is to the sky as if looking for something. Iseult is on the far side of the dais, hoo-hooing through a small aperture in the wall. We take the steps to their level.

"So nice of you chaps to drop over for dinner," Browne says affably, his arm hoisting us into the ruins. "As you see, the last raid has left us a little indisposed."

"Oh, rot," Izzy snaps back. "Get the drinks, Perce. We can at least toss a few while we're here."

"What's the history of this place?" Pat asks her. "Does it have any special meaning?"

"Meaning?" Izzy repeats, and her small mouth draws to one side. "There were no knights of the Round Table, if that's what you want." The purple stick of her is stiff, and her face is diffident. "This was nothing more than a bank, built by the bloody bastards to deposit what they had robbed from the poor creatures around here. We were slaves in our own native land."

"But the walls came tumbling down," Pat says.

"They did that," Iseult sniffs. "Here we go," she signals to Percy Browne, who comes back from the car with a shaker and four glasses. It is a tarnished silver cocktail pitcher with spout and cap, one of those I've always associated with old Joan Crawford movies. He pours the martinis. "Up the revolution," Iseult toasts and we drink. A small cyclone of leaves whirls in the corner as the wind prowls about the broken walls. "I see you are impressed," Iseult says, blotting the gin on her linden-leaf mouth.

"Well, yes," Pat answers. "After all, it's my first castle, and I guess I've never gotten over *Ivanhoe*. Are there any castles left that are livable?"

"Sure. You'll see them. I've no doubt the Beverleys will have you to theirs before you've done."

"Who are they?" Pat asks.

"Beverley Biscuits Are Better For You!" I quote the slogan seen on every wall and bus placard in Alclair, and Pat remembers.

The gaiety that had marked our trip so far is gone. A solemn caesura marks the day. Iseult kicks about the stone terrace, apparently depressed by something, and takes a final swig of her drink to hold out the glass for a refill. Browne lifts the silver shaker to her glass, a fixed smile on his weathered face. Patricia and I wander about the place, tourists without a guidebook. We come upon a large stone crypt within the rear wall. The heavy stone lid is aslant, broken and the sarcophagus is empty.

"Why not eat here?" we hear Iseult ask Browne. "No? You want to go to the other place?"

"Where are we going?" I ask.

"You'll see," Iseult answers, a sparkle returning to the gray eyes. "Oh, say," she nearly seizes me, "do one of those outrageous prayers of yours."

"Oh, I don't know . . ." I protest.

"Please do, it's just the place for it," she urges, walking to the center of the stone court, beneath the tracery of the large window.

"Don't encourage him," Pat says behind me.

"Well, all right," I hear myself say. "Let's see . . ."

"Wait, wait," Browne interrupts. "All must be full," and he passes among us with the last of the martinis.

"Oh, great Sun God who lights our campfires and warms our feet, fill our hearts. Tote that barge, lift that bale. Buffalo, buffalo, buffalo."

Browne begins to chant "Boola, boola, boola," and Iseult scurries below the steps, turns and begins a majestic ascent, the martini held in both hands and aloft.

"We come as brothers to offer this maiden. Give her a place in your bed of stars. Give her cooling waters. Give her Cayuga Far Above, Pluto and Saratoga Vichy. Mississippi—Kanawha and Kaw—Platte—Susquehanna." Iseult is before me, eyes lifted, and sinks on her knees after draining the goblet. The glass splinters against the stone floor. "Allegheny—Cheyenne—Missouri." Browne continues to chant, and there's an eerie whine at my feet. "Give us purple mountain majesties, fields of golden grain. We look for a sign."

The breeze from the meadow continues to play the stone lyre of the great, empty window. Izzy rolls over on the mortised floor and lies silently, eyes staring at the sky. But Patricia stands to one side, chewing on the inside of her cheek with an amused though speculative flash in the dark eyes. It's enough of an alarm to make me step back quickly like a blind man suddenly alerted to the dangers of a cliff. And it is only then that I see the boy.

He probably came to herd his sheep, a boy of about fifteen, rough and lumpy jacket open, shirt buttoned at the collar but tieless, a cap low over his eyes. His eyes are enormous as he stands near the remains of the old entrance, his mouth hangs slack. With visible effort, one foot is picked up and then the other, each step easier and faster until he is running pell-mell across the meadow, looking back at us, tripping over a stone, and scrambling up capless to flee over the hill—and gone.

In the car and on our way, we are quiet, subdued. Patricia avoids my look, the whites of her eyes luminous and enlarged around the brown pupils, a distance in them. The road begins to rise through some hills and then into small mountains. Looking back we can see the floor of the valley, patterned by the hedged fields and the slow-moving shadows of clouds. The sky has clabbered and the sun makes rarer appearances through the overcast.

"You're an aeronautical engineer?" I ask Browne. Iseult snickers as he cocks his head and shrugs.

"Plastics really is my field now," he says, peering intently through the windshield. He is driving slowly now, looking for something.

"It's a way yet," Iseult tells him. She turns back to us. "He makes models."

"Models?"

"Yes," he says crisply. "Big field in models, you know. Everyone builds them. Nostalgia and all that."

"Airplane models?" I ask.

"Yes. First War planes."

"You mean like Spads and Fokkers and that?"

"Quite. Just finished retooling for one of those big

Gotha bombers. Wonderful detail. It should go very well."
He pulls up at a side road.

"Not here," Iseult tells him, "there's a sign." We are
nearly at the top of the mountain and it is barren and
rocky. She is half turned around. "But it's better than the
dirty dollies he used to make," she says disdainfully.

"Dirty dollies?" Patricia exclaims, laughing.

"Yes," Iseult tells her, "pornographic dolls."

"Not at all," Browne chides her, then speaks over his
shoulder to us. "They were plastic figures for artists,
moved to any position, you know, just as good as live
models but cheaper. They were for art students."

"Art students, my eye," Iseult says, her mouth curled
up. "They were for dirty old men, that's what they were
for. There was the wonderful detail for you, never mind
your old bomber, down to the last hole and rivet," she
tells Pat with a girlish secrecy. "Everything," and she cups
her bosom.

"Ah, well," sighs Browne, "they didn't go, anyway."

"My goodness," Patricia says, "I would think they
would have been very successful." Her elbow slips between my ribs, intentionally or not I cannot tell.

"They would have been," Browne says, "but you Americans brought out a set of male and female dolls about the
same time, almost the same . . ."

". . . Not quite the same," Iseult says with a significant
eyebrow.

"Well, close enough. Anyway, we couldn't meet your
production," Browne says matter-of-factly.

"Here!" Iseult says suddenly, and he turns sharply into
a side road. There's a sign with a black cross pattée upon
it and the word "Cemetery." We jerk and roll down the

dirt road until after half a mile it becomes impassable. So we get out and with picnic baskets in hand walk the rest of the way. The wind strums the low-lying shrubs. There is a faintly acrid smell upon it, like that of rotting stone and vegetation, an organic odor not unpleasant. The elements have apparently tended the cemetery, blowing it clean of debris, and neatened the ground around the two dozen or more headstones, assisted by the altitude and the rocky soil with the weeding. The headstones are all white, all about the same, and each one bears, above the chiseled name, the same cross as on the sign. There are one or two that, except for this cross, are blank. The names are German.

"I flew Hurricanes out of a small field in Worcester," Browne tells me as we walk among the graves. The girls are setting the picnic, Patricia stopping to listen occasionally. Iseult apparently has heard the story before. "And we would try to meet them before they got to Birmingham." His old boyish face is lifted to the sky, toward the east, and the attitude, the expectancy in his look firms up the flesh around the jaw. "They were awfully good, really. Some of them had been in the Condor Legion. We were hardly a match for them."

"How old were you?" I ask.

"Just eighteen, I think," he squints into the overcast. "Yes, just eighteen. But the difference was we were fighting over our bloody soil, I guess that was the difference. Some of them tried to make it here, where they would be interned for the duration, maybe even get back into the fight. Of course there were some that were too far gone, all but dead at the stick. A long power glide away from the clatter straight into one of these hills."

The breeze moans through the scrubby vegetation, sheep move noiselessly in the valleys below and, though only a few graves over, the rattle of utensils and the girls' chatter fight upwind to us as if from a great distance.

"Do you think any of these are yours?" I finally ask Browne.

"For sure, can't say really." A cordovan toe pokes at a mound. "The natives buried them first and then the government here made it official. I heard about this place and thought I'd come to see it. To pay my respects, you might say." His yellowed teeth are revealed in a smile that once held great charm. "Any of them mine?" He repeats my phrase with an amused wonder.

"Well, I mean. . ."

"No, you're quite right. You Americans say things so directly. I suppose there may be one here that is mine." He looks over the graveyard. "But, of course, we were never formally introduced," and he laughs.

"Come, you two," Iseult cries, "it's time to open the wine."

The girls have placed a cloth on the ground among the headstones, and the picnic is appetizing. I am suddenly famished. "We thought we'd use Leutnant Heinz Hoffman," Iseult says, referring to the marble tablet nearby. "It has such a cozy sound."

"Like fifty-seven varieties," I say, uncorking the wine.

"Varieties of what?" Iseult says, sweeping back a heavy lock of hair to stare at me wide-eyed.

"He means pickles," Patricia tells her, and then starts to laugh uproariously. Her amusement roses the olive complexion, her eyes squint merrily behind the glasses and she looks very pretty.

"Well, here's to dead heroes," Browne says, raising his

glass of wine. We solemnly copy the gesture. And then we eat.

We are all hungry, it seems, and we devote ourselves to the chicken, cheese and cold potato salad made by Emtie under Pat's supervision and the mushroom tarts and fruits contributed by Iseult. The wine is fresh and clear, and on the second bottle we are surfeited and more silent. Iseult leans against Leutnant Hoffman's tablet, smoking, her thin purple legs pulled up under her chin. Pat sits queenly, legs tucked under the great mound of her ballast, a prim but solid bulwark against the breeze stirring her black hair. Browne lolls on his side, an arm and hand supporting his head.

"Pity we didn't bring a game with us," Iseult says after a long moment. "Something we could all play."

"Quite," agrees Browne, who sounds half asleep.

It has become overcast, almost all color gone from the hills and the stones, and the wind goes about its impersonal caretaking of the grounds. It has grown chilly as well. Patricia shivers, shrugs her shoulders and, with some effort, gets up.

"Well, I'm going to take a walk," she says above me. I rise and take her hand. The others remain, positions unchanged, almost in a stupor.

"You bloody Americans are so athletic," Iseult finally says a bit sullenly, but it is a means of discharging us, and we leave them.

We find a small path at the edge of the graveyard winding down the face of the hill in gradual curves, and I wonder what being, what human or animal, has worn this way to the cemetery and for what reason. Patricia steps heavily beside me, her brogans kicking loose a small stone that rattles down ahead. She has become very large of late and all the chocolates have had their punitive effect. Her face is still prettily childlike, but there is a grossness about the rest of her, thick of arm, massive of breast and a pronounced waddle in her walk. She coot-foots before me, the path only wide enough for one, as I mourn the neatness of her in my memory.

There's a small plateau, a natural landing halfway down the incline, where we pause to look out over the dark valley. A pile of rocks has been set in the shape of a pedestal and charred wood indicates a fire has burned here.

"Let's sit," Patricia says breathlessly. They are the first words spoken since we left the others. Beside her, I look out at the scene, at a white stuccoed farmhouse far down, a crocheted flume of smoke spinning from the chimney. Patricia takes my hand in both of hers. "You mustn't be this way," she says.

"What way?"

"You know. You're all inside. How much longer are you going to keep me in exile?" Her eyes screw up.

"Don't be foolish," I answer, though I feel my face flushing.

"After all, it's not as if you had to marry me—I mean, at least I waited until after . . . no, that's not what I mean." I had looked at her sarcastically. "Now listen to me, Hamlet," she begins again, her voice controlled. "I've gone through all the guilt about this I'm going to. The hair shirt is off. Starting today it's just me and the boyo. If you're going to put me down, then I have no other alternative. Don't do this to me."

"It was just the shock of it," I finally say. "The fact you didn't tell me." Her face lightens, my words encourage her. The simple fact of my speaking.

"Yes, that was wrong, I know. But if you can't forget, can you forgive? Jiminy, whatever we have must be able to get over this. Won't it?"

"Yes, of course."

"You don't sound convincing. Oh, Hamlet, tell me I wasn't wrong about you. Tell me you have the stuff to accept me, to hold me, warm it, make it all new. So I have changed our life, made it different from what you wanted. It was you who really is responsible. Yes, it was. It was you, because of you, I did it. Why are you being so selfish?"

"I'm not being selfish."

"Then childish."

"I'm not being . . ."

"Yes, you are. You're just like a kid that's had his ice cream taken away. You're better than that, you're bigger than that." She has been holding my hand in hers throughout and now with a final grip, a final push and pull, she lets go. "Well, as I've said, I'm through beating my breast. If you want to cry at the wall, it's your business."

She is right. Her profile is serene though there is a grim clench of muscle along her cheek. The gift she gave me in those nights and long afternoons following our marriage had been much more than she had given me before, had given any other before. And though it had been unasked for, been bestowed without my knowledge, did this make it any the less of value? Much more than any physical act, she had reasoned for herself a gratuitous act of love, a sign of her self, and I had failed that self. A gust of pure joy overcomes me and I feel silly, then content. I laugh out loud. Patricia is startled, smiles and then also laughs. I try to put my arm around her but her awkward bulk intervenes, makes the gesture ridiculous, sailing our amusement higher to the wind. She contents herself by leaning against me, her head on my shoulder.

"Mom and Dad out with the kids," I say. She sighs, pressing her swollen shapelessness against me.

"I'm terribly thirsty all of a sudden," she says.

"There's more wine left. Do you want some?" She nods.

Halfway up the hill toward the cemetery, I look back at her as she gazes out over the landscape. She seems to be a composite of the picture, as if the fields, the wandering sheep and lambs and the seemingly abandoned farms would not hold together were she removed from the composition. Almost at the top, my ears vaguely hear something over the sound of the wind. It is like oarsmen straining at their posts, and were my mind not filled with the memories of those nights in Wellfleet and all they produced, I probably would have recognized the sound and turned back, never made the crest of the graveyard.

But there they are. Neither sees me. In fact, Iseult's head is hidden by the tombstone over which she bends. Her purple trousers are down around her ankles, and the slim legs and thighs rise startlingly white, almost bluish white, to support the thrust-out bowl of buttocks. Browne, still capped and ascot in place—and for a wild second I even wonder why he's not wearing his driving gloves—leans over her, a steadying hand gripping the headstone.

Seconds, maybe, is all it takes before I quickly step back and down below the crest and away from this image that burns my vision. But it seems like years, enough time for me to be incorporated, woven into a picture similar to those tapestries featuring an amorous couple being spied upon by an innocuous face at the window. Not so innocuous at that, perhaps.

"No more wine?" Patricia asks as I return.

"No."

"What were they doing? Asleep?"

"Yes." She looks at me closely, speculatively. I look down in the valley, away from her.

"But there was wine," she says softly.

"There might have been, I don't know," I say.

"Oh my." Her hand goes to her face as she laughs. "Well, there's no better use for a cemetery, is there?" I look at her. "What's the matter with you? You look—you look mad about something." She is suddenly embarrassed, shifts awkwardly on the pedestal. "I don't know exactly how we can manage, but . . ."

"Don't be silly," I interrupt her, immediately sorry for the look on her face—the look of failure I have just put there. "I'm happy the way we are. I really am." She is not convinced, though she lets my arm go around her shoulder and finally puts her head upon me. So we wait, marooned on our ledge, unable to go higher and no purpose in descending.

"Hey, you two. Want a ride home?" Iseult's voice finally calls from the top. Patricia has fallen asleep and I had been measuring her breath against my neck.

The girls pack up the picnic things, gossiping and giggling between themselves over something that escapes me. I try to be useful, chasing down paper napkins, corking the leftover wine. Browne sits upon a headstone, face to the eastern sky. "It looks like rain," he says.

And it does rain, all the way back, the swishing windshield wipers keeping time to the silence within the car. Patricia rests, eyes closed, and Iseult faces forward. Her mouth looks more natural, a pinkish luster upon the lips.

"When are you back to London?" I ask.

"Me?" She turns in her seat. I nod, though realizing the question was meant for them both. "I'm staying on for a while, keep the old folks happy, don't you know. But Perce is leaving—when do you go, Perce?"

"Tomorrow," Browne says, driving carefully and easily over the wet road. "Back to the old grind. Mission accomplished," he adds, chuckling.

"Yes, paid your respects, is it," Iseult says sharply, though her small mouth is smiling, "then back to the humdrum?" He merely shrugs. "Different for me though," she says over the front seat. Her blue eyes are clear, untroubled. I look past her shoulder. "But it's better to smooth things out here a bit so that I can go back later."

"You really like London?" I say.

"It's the most," she says, tossing her hair. "It's a whole new world, don't you know. Oh, I'm not putting the old sod down. Warm chimneys and a pot of tea and all that. It's nice enough for later. I'll be back for good, no doubt, when it's time. To have me babies." She looks at Patricia. "It's super for that. No, I'll be back when I'm getting cozy. But right now," and she stretches her arms before her, fingers laced together, "me heart's in London."

"And more," I say, meaning to be funny, to share her banter, but it falls short. I am conscious of Patricia's look beneath heavy lids and I sense the image of Browne's eyes slowly evaporating upon the rearview mirror. Iseult's gaze is questioning, thorough, and the pink mouth twists to one side.

"Oh, yes," she says, "there's much more."

COMMENCEMENTS ARE PRETTY MUCH ALIKE AND I SUP-
pose it is this perennial and charming ceremony that
is one of the main contributions to the timelessness, alluded
to earlier, that makes academic life so attractive. There
were a few features of the rite as celebrated at Scott Junior
College in late May which made for minor distinctions but
which also emphasized the universality of the main program—the conferring of diplomas and awards to graduates
who would never again look so comely in the presence of
parents who would never again feel so graceful.

In the morning there was the customary Maypole Dance,
each member of the class circling about a stone needle, the
gift of a nineteenth-century maiden who had married well,
and each holding a strand of black-eyed Susans suspended
from the glans-like tip. As they sang the Scott anthem, the
flowered canopy of streamers revolved over the Maypole
Queen in the center; Sue Ellen Dryden, a hyperbolic
choice perhaps, though in view of her rumored partiality
not without some justice.

Before the president's luncheon, served cannily on the
lawn near the partially constructed forms of the new
science complex, the drill team passed in final review.
Smartly, the blue-jacketed squads and companies moved

163

across the field, shoulder to shoulder for the last time; the eyes snapped right, salutes given and guidons dipped before the reviewing stand, Patricia solemn and steadily holding out the staff with the pennant of Company C upon it, her black-stockinged legs resolutely making the last track in long strides. How enriched Napoleon's last years would have been had he been able to take the memory of this militant adieu into exile. There were few dry eyes at Scott.

The parents were the same as are found on other campuses in May or June with the exception of one type, and these were the mothers of the one or two "scholarships" Scott always had—intense, usually rather pretty women who smoked and drank too much but with quick eyes and marmotlike hands held chest-high, ready to thrust their offspring into the sweaty crotch of the rich. Edna Gates was certainly not in this category; in fact, she was not a part of any group of parents at that commencement, for she did not come.

"It's my Aunt Mary," Patricia said, reading the letter. "She's my great-aunt, and Edna was her favorite niece. She has to go to the funeral. She was very big with the DAR. Well, that's that," she said, folding up the letter and looking away.

There were any number of funny things I might have said, but I chose to remain silent, surprised by the genuine disappointment in Patricia's eyes. So we were alone during commencement week. The official announcement of our marriage set us off even more from the others and we enjoyed a rather perverse celebrity at the different functions. Parents of my students, especially fathers, tended to talk a little too loudly, as if I were deaf or had some other defect they were humanely trying to overlook. And I

cannot be sure, but there seemed to be a little more applause than necessary when the name of Patricia Simpson
Gates was called from the platform and she stepped forward in black gown and mortarboard, a handsome, serious-
looking girl who might go on to study animal husbandry
or archaeology or maybe become the perpetual chairman
of some Junior League's Hospital Cheer Committee. Of
course, I knew better.

"Come help me with my bags," she said, as the last
ceremony ended.

I followed her up the stairs of the main building into
the upper floors where no man sets foot until this perennial
moment but where now the masculine voices of fathers or
brothers exclaimed over the amount and weight of luggage
to be hefted down to the family cars. There was a frenetic
gaiety in the halls and in the open rooms we passed, a quick
hurry-up, hurry-up pace as if all were trying to get out
before whatever buoyed their spirits gave way.

"Good luck, Simp," a girl said, passing us. Her parents
and I gravely nodded to each other.

"Simp?" I asked.

"Yes, that's my nickname," Patricia explained. "Didn't
you know?"

I did not know and this new side of her, the unfamiliar
name and the strange surroundings of these upper floors,
made me very uneasy. Her room was toward the end of
the hall, and I was not prepared for the very prim, almost
sparse tone which not even the Cedar Rapids version of
pickled white Louis XV furniture could warm. I sat down
on the narrow bed, stripped to its mattress, and leaned
against the caned headboard.

"I'll have to drop this off at the office," she said. The
gown had been removed, folded and with the mortarboard

placed in a box.

"We can do it as we leave," I said. Girls and their parents passed the open door. Some paused to say goodbye, cheerily offhand.

"All the best, Simp."

"Thank you."

"Y'all come and see us, hear?"

"Let's keep in touch, Simp."

"You bet," she answered each over her shoulder or aside as she checked the closet, went through the drawers of the bureau and the boudoir table. There was a stuffed animal on the bureau, recognizable as Snoopy and covered with the usual buttons and rosettes, campaign medals from football weekends. But basically it was a child's, a young girl's doll and I looked at her again as if she were a stranger.

"Well, you're all packed anyhow," I said. Two suit-cases were in the middle of the room. A wardrobe trunk stood in one corner, locked, tagged and ready for the pickup service.

"Yes," she said distantly, looking about several times, making sure nothing was left behind, looking everywhere but at me, with a pout of concentration. So involved was she with her search and I with the pretension that it was several moments before we noticed the group at the door. If it was not the entire roll call of Company C, it was enough of them wedged tensely into the doorway and out into the hall to make it seem so.

"We just wanted you to know," Sue Ellen Dryden said in her disarming, fluttery contralto, "well . . ." she held out a large package, silvery and with pink ribbon. "I think it's . . . we think it's just great, Simp. Just great!"

She stepped forward and there was an awkward almost formal handshake; one pump, another, and then suddenly she and Patricia were embracing and the others were all around them, hugging and kissing, wild-eyed and teary with happiness and squealing.

I stood to one side, wondering when my turn would come and too astounded to be immediately moved. Patricia was nearly crimson and she took each one, almost in turn, for a cheek-to-cheek embrace, speechless save for an endless "thank you, thank you."

I heard Sue Ellen saying, "It's only a pissy cookbook— oops, 'cuse me, Mr. Phillips—but anyway, all of our names are in the flyleaf." She led the bunch to me and they single-filed past, a touching formality, hands out and with words of congratulations. "I've really enjoyed your classes, Mr. Phillips," Sue Ellen said to me, "and I'm certainly going to put what you teach to practice. Well, you know what I mean," she laughed. I thanked her and wondered if there were not some way I could sneak into the registrar's office and change her grade in Europe Since Bismarck to a straight A.

At the railroad station, bags checked through, Patricia excused herself and went to the rest room. When she finally returned I could see she had been weeping, her eyes were red-rimmed and the stub of her nose had a quivery softness. She seemed to have trouble keeping on her glasses. I did not like putting her on the train in this condition, subjecting her to the long ride back to Edna, busily framing Aunt Mary's DAR medals; Patricia vulnerable in this mood, too weak and softened for the jolts of the trip.

"What's all this between Sue Ellen Dryden and you?" I asked. A poor remedy, but I saw it was working. "Something very cozy between the two of you."

"You're a clod, do you know that?" Patricia sniffed. She took a deep breath. "You're an unremitting, square, phony-liberal clod. But I'm going to marry you on June fifteenth in Wellfleet."

"Sex is the curse of life," I sighed.

When I put her on the train, the fine luster of bravado was restored, the sheen of composure repaired, an uncontrollable joy breaking through and expressed by a spontaneous frug on the coach's platform. True, she was leaving me, temporarily, but in some way she returned to me then, completely, and her reappearance in a couple of weeks would almost be anti-climactic. I could not tell her then of the news I had had the day before, of the letter I carried in my jacket pocket. Thanks no doubt to the recommendation from the president of Scott Junior College, Brown University determined that the opening in the history department needed someone with a more general background than mine, though my own "estimable scholarship and potential reputation in the medieval period certainly dictates the application will be kept on file."

Singing "A Broken Heart Is a Rich Man's Toy," Marie Therese bears down the narrow front hallway holding the tea tray bosom-high. I fully expect her to run me down, the glistening and steaming apparition passing over me and out the open front door. But she swings to the right, the tray making a left bank through the air on the right hand while the other opens the living-room door. She zooms inside and out of sight.

Tentatively, I peek around the open door. Patricia stands in the center of the room, arms up, her thickened upper body bare save for the brassiere supporting swollen breasts. At her feet, pinning the hem of the skirt that clothes the rest of her, is Iseult Morraugh and in the chair by the glowing grate of the fireplace sits Mary Abbey, a cigarette held before her face, studiously observing the other two through the smoke.

"There you are, *chéri*," Patricia says. "Come see my new wardrobe." Iseult turns her head to me, her small mouth full of pins. She wears a short white skirt, a dark middy blouse and there is an enormous blue silk bow in her hair.

I kiss my wife, conscious of leaning forward a little far so as not to touch the rest of her. "What's all this?" I ask.

"It's the grandest thing," Pat says gaily. She pushes the glasses against her nose. "Izzy shows up with boxes and boxes of clothes and Mary shows up with a bottle of genuine bourbon." Mary Abbey holds up a bottle of Old Grandad, the level halfway down the label.

"Help yourself," she says to me. But I turn to the tea things, deposited on the end table by the sofa—the lamp on the floor—and fix myself a cup, munching one of the hot, crusty scones rich with melted butter.

"Isn't it lovely," Emtie sighs, hands clasped and standing to one side to watch. A blouse with full sleeves has been slipped over Pat by Izzy, and my wife turns this way and that, modeling the costume, an inane joy on her face.

"Wait until you see some of the others," Pat says to me, slipping out of the blouse and skirt to stand in her skivvies. The immense hump juts out from her loins, an unbelievable shelf of flesh, and she resembles an illustration in *National Geographic*. I fuss with my tea, and she senses my embarrassment. "Here"—she moves with surprising agility, gathering up the clothes—"I'll put them on in the dining room and show you, then you'll get the full effect."

Mary Abbey and I are alone, Emtie tripping out of the room to her duties, and I serve tea to the poet. The mantel above her head holds several books, one of them Gil Morraugh's translation of Maureen nu Nailly's martyrdom on the beach. "I didn't get a chance to tell you the other evening how much we enjoyed your reading."

"Thank you," she says, seemingly bored with the compliment. "One wonders sometimes, how much is performance and how much is the work." She takes a sip of tea, obviously the only one she plans to take, and sets the cup down on the floor by her chair. "They were very kind, I thought," she says.

Mystified would be a more correct description of the Embassy audience at Mary Abbey's reading. Certainly the flowery introduction by Maxine Waters did not prepare them for the complex allusions and sparse construction of her poems. And the major work of the evening, a long narrative ostensibly about her mother's hysterectomy but actually about love, left them stunned.

"How's this?" Patricia asks, waltzing out from the dining room. She wears an orange shift of myriad pleats that strikes her just at the knee and gives her the appearance of being in midair, as if she had just jumped off a roof.

"The whole point," Iseult says to me, "is actually to use the shape at hand. That is, to make the babe a functional part of the line."

"Do you like it?" Patricia asks me, expectantly.

"It's very nice," I tell her.

"Wait until you see the others," she says, encouraged, and leaves the room, Iseult behind her.

"Well, are you getting ready to return?" I ask Mary Abbey. The hot blaze in the grate is taking the November chill off my legs and back.

"No, I may hang around for a while," she shrugs. "This place is getting to me a little—a sort of small version of the way I remember Omaha on a Saturday afternoon. The hats the women wear; I can remember my mother wearing the same sort of hat in the thirties, going downtown to shop."

"How's your research going?" I ask, eyeing the volume above her head.

"Oh, so-so. I saw sections of the manuscript the other day. Beautifully illuminated. Like Tiffany glass. Have you seen it?" I shake my head.

"This one's a little more formal," Patricia announces and parades before us. It is a two-piece suit, again with a miniskirt, and the material is navy blue with neon green polka dots of various diameters, the largest green sphere, no doubt intentionally, positioned smack around the apex of the massive belly.

"Wow," I say.

"Do you see what I mean about following the line?" Iseult says, her long, narrow hand sweeping over Patricia's front as if to mold the convexity. My wife stands smiling placidly, allows Iseult to turn her around, even raise an arm. "And this is a nice line down through here and out," Iseult demonstrates. "Just a min," she says, "the back of the skirt needs a pin." And she squats down to make the adjustment. The white material of her own skirt tightens around the compact roundness of a seemingly impenetrable behind. Of course, I know better. "There." She rises. "That does it."

I pour myself some of Mary Abbey's bourbon, refilling her glass as well. The poet lights a cigarette from the stub of another. "Were you able to make any sense out of the story—the manuscript?" I remind her.

"No, nothing. It's in that peculiar pig Latin of theirs, old pig Latin, you might say. However, there was a summation of the story pasted onto the case that contained the manuscript."

"Really?"

"Yes, apparently she was a young nun—her name was Maureen something or other—and she was murdered by pirates outside the walls of the convent. I expect they did terrible things to her."

"Yes, probably," I say, looking into my drink. "They have a story about one of their saints here who was being grilled alive by some heathen bunch and—so the story goes —he raised up at one point and said, 'Turn me over, boys, I'm done on this side.' "

"Do you like this?" Patricia asks, hesitantly walking into the room wearing a pants suit of yellow tweed.

"That's the best so far," I tell her honestly, for strange as it may seem, the ensemble, the pants cut away in front for her bump and overlapped by a type of bush-jacket design of coat, is very becoming.

"D'you see what we're doing here?" Iseult says and for the first time looks directly at me. "There's no point in being ashamed of it, is there? So the new idea is to exploit the pregnancy, make it part of the ensemble."

Patricia saunters around the room like a deformed Edwardian newsboy, but strangely attractive. At the table, she picks up a glass and sips some whiskey. She supports her belly and burps. "That's better," she says. "Well, we have one more and then I'll see about supper. You all will stay for supper, won't you?" Iseult accepts quickly and Mary Abbey makes a few ineffectual excuses. "Of course you will," Pat says and leaves for the dining room again.

Mary Abbey leans forward to squash out the cigarette in the ashtray on the floor and then remains in that position, hanging over her knees, studying the rug. She did not seem too interested in the sacred manuscript after all and with nearly a shrug had dismissed it. Through the tall windows, facing the street, I see the lights coming on and realize it has grown rather dark inside.

"Here's the last one," Patricia says behind me just as I turn on the lamp on the floor. The little-girl image is clearly enhanced inversely by her pregnancy. The silky shift comes just above the knees, is straight-cut, and is devoid of any embellishment save for several inserts of lace around a prim collar. Her legs, appearing even longer and still with a golden residue of the sun that browned them last summer, move nakedly and pause, one knee canted against the other. She appears to be a twelve-year-old who, dressing up in her mother's high-heels and other accouterments of a false maturity, has obviously suffered at the hands of some transient brute. And I confess to being aroused by the perverse idea.

"Aie, that's got to him," Iseult says with a knowing mockery and lights a cigarette.

Patricia laughs good-humoredly and comes to me and we kiss, she standing almost sideways. One finger presses the glasses against the bridge of her nose and she looks down at her legs, holding them out in order to see them over the hump. "I've always liked my legs," she muses.

"Me too," I say, catching in the corner of my eye a swirl of yellow as Iseult tosses her hair.

"Well, now, I'll get supper ready." She kisses me on the chin. "Fix us some drinks." And she disappears into the dining room once again.

I move around the darkened living room, the one lamp on the floor casting long shadows upon the wall and ceiling. Mary Abbey continues to sit, her round face bleakly composed, as if she expects to be ravaged by a rabbit. And I wonder, as I pour the bourbon into our glasses, at the peculiar gathering this afternoon. There is one of them, singing to herself as she prepares supper for us, happily content with her natural state as she is obviously delighted with her new wardrobe, or perhaps because of the new wardrobe. There is the second one, morosely slouched in the chair by the fireplace, whose place in contemporary literature might be affected if I merely reached a book down from the mantelpiece. And there is the third one, who nervously takes up different positions behind me, each motion accompanied by the rattle and scrape of beads and bracelets. Or is it the feathery brush of femur and pelvic bones I hear? So I turn, handing each a fresh drink, and move to the sofa with the sure and satisfied tread of a sultan.

Iseult leans against the mantel and looks into the mirror, repairing mascara with the tip of a small finger, holding a drink and burning a cigarette in the other hand. I look at Mary Abbey, so different in her shapeless woolens, though her body is also slight, and in the haze of a couple of drinks I even begin to be curious about that spare body. And with an alcoholic irresponsibility, the scene changes again, and I am pondering which one I shall choose to take upstairs after settling the price with the madam in the kitchen.

There is a child's game, sometimes played by adults, which imagines a contest that must be won if success with some unrelated though more important problem is to be assured. The sweet burn of the bourbon spilled down my throat as I created such a preliminary, putting upon Iseult Morraugh's unsuspecting, narrow shoulders the responsibility for what might happen by the way she would answer.

"Mary is hoping to do some research on St. Maureen," I say.

"Oh, really," Iseult answers, still fussing with her face in the mirror. I have almost won, almost across the pavement and no crack stepped on yet, but I push my luck further.

"Yes; of course, it's difficult for her, not knowing the Old Tongue and all." She continues to daub and trace, saying nothing. My lungs are about to burst. "I don't suppose there's a translation of her story anywhere?"

"Who would want to read that anyway?" Iseult says, now turning. "It's all full of the most awful nahsties one could imagine."

"Then you can read it?" Mary Abbey perks up. My elation is stopped dead by the unexpected turn.

"Ah, no. No more. Oh, I suppose I could make out a word here and there, but I've forgot most of it now. D'you know what it's about?" she asks Mary Abbey.

"Well, only generally," the poet answers. "She was murdered by Norsemen when she tried to save manuscripts and other treasures in a monastery."

"Hah," Iseult snorts and sits on the floor before the fire. The white skirt rises mid-thigh. "Rape's the word for it."

"That was almost a standard requisite for female saints, wasn't it?" Mary Abbey says, smiling.

"Ah, but with a difference for her," Iseult answers. "It's like the bloody English and this country, she was. I don't suppose there isn't a part of this country they didn't ravage. Not a part," she repeats, looking at me.

"Then you'll be able to come to our Thanksgiving?" I say to Mary Abbey. Her look lingers upon Iseult, her attention gradually leaving St. Maureen's ravishment, then turns to me.

"Yes, I suppose so."

"This is some harvest feast?" Iseult asks.

"It's an old American custom," I say, happy to plunge into the details. "Probably our only national custom distinct from others. The turkey naturally comes from the fact that there were wild turkeys around the place. Corn the Indians brought. The cranberries also grow wild in that part of the country, pumpkins, etc. By the way, Maxine Waters is bringing the cranberry sauce. Oh, yes," I say as she nods, "you knew that. She's quite a character, isn't she? You knew her husband?"

"Briefly," Mary Abbey says, lighting another cigarette. "He was very sick when I knew him, the last year or two of his life. He had retired from teaching. Maxine was my English instructor at the university. I handed in some poems as part of classwork and she let him read them. And he did write Aiken, as she told you. He was some years older than she, a very gentle, Victorian sort of man. Very frail and with white, white hair and dark eyes. He looked part Indian, you've seen his pictures, I guess. And it's terrible to say, but I never cared for his poetry. Can't read it."

"But what was the attraction between them?" I ask.

"Oh, I don't know," Mary Abbey answers carefully. "Maxine is such an outgoing person and he was so withdrawn, she's always so up and he seemed to be rather dry, ascetic. Maybe that was it. Who knows?"

"Children?"

"No, they had no children." Iseult has listened to us, legs curled beneath her, one hand on a slim ankle. Patricia, changed back to the habitual tweed skirt and heavy sweater, has been busy in the dining room, directing Emtie with the table setting, the sound of her singing trailing after her as she returns to the kitchen. Dressed for her walk home, Emtie takes a final squint at the table and bids us good night.

"God bless," she cries from the door.

"God bless," Iseult answers.

"We're ready," announces Pat and we all sit down. She has prepared mushrooms in heavy cream with dill, a salad of lettuce and avocado, hot bread and some fruit and cheese for dessert. It is all very delicious and I look around the table, once again relishing, along with the flavors of the food, my unique maleness in this female company. A beardless Brigham Young, home from the trials of sketching the development of capitalism to near-penniless youth, I relax in the comfort of their talk. Even Mary Abbey, her shyness overcome, joins in the talk of clothes and cooking, but it is Patricia and Iseult who carry the conversation. I recognize a peculiar bond has formed between them.

We finish the bourbon after dinner and there is more talk and much gaiety, Iseult and Mary leaving together to catch the last bus. I set the fire in the bedroom grate and Patricia stands before it in her long, voluminous flannel nightgown, warming her backside and making self-satisfied clucks in the back of her mouth.

"That was a good time," she finally says. "I like both of them."

"That's good," I say. "I'm glad you do. And by the way, that was a great meal."

"Not great, but better. Better, hmm?" she asks, referring to recent performances. I agree. She skips to the bed and burrows beneath the comforter and blankets. "Grrr. It if just weren't so damp all the time. And if only I could . . ."

"Don't worry about it," I say, slipping in beside her. The pregnancy now prohibits any sexual play, and her last attempt to gratify me had left us both cold and wary.

"I know," she says beside me, "but I feel so useless to you now." She moves her legs restlessly beneath the cover, eventually pressing against mine. And I realize I had expected an answer, expected her to say something more. We are silent, watching the wavering glow of the fire on the ceiling. "Hamilton." Her voice is soft, leavened with fatigue. "Could you make it with Iseult?"

"Is that an offer or an inquiry?"

"Now, be serious. You've thought about it, haven't you?"

"Well, I wouldn't say that . . ."

"She's thought about it. That's why she's here tonight. All those clothes aren't so much for me, you know. She has the hots for you."

"She's not my type," I say.

"What is your type?" Now more awake, Pat turns on her side, supports an inquisitive face upon one hand. "You know you've never really told me much about your other girls."

"I thought I put all of that down on the questionnaire I filled out for Edna Gates."

"Now stop that." She digs at a rib. "For example, have you ever paid for it? Stop giggling, I'm serious."

"Well," I control my laughter, "I suppose I have once or twice, but that was in Japan."

"Really? No kidding. You mean you've had Japanese girls?"

"You make it sound more exotic than it was. It was nothing more than the usual cosmopolitan orientation of the young American male."

"But you actually gave some girl money and then did it? Weren't you embarrassed?"

"Not a bit, because I knew that were it not for the language barrier between us, the Tom Sawyer in me would have been enough to bring her across. The money was just a convenient shorthand, a means of communication."

"Was she any good?" Her other hand tests my heart-beat.

"Adequate is more like it."

"Have I been good?" she asks evenly.

"You're the best."

"Really?" And I'm amazed by the uncertainty in her voice.

"Yes, really. What's the matter? Why all these questions?"

"Oh, I don't know." She falls beside me, her face under my ear. "I'm such a mess these days, unable to do anything for you, and then along comes Iseult and she's so obviously available. I've never seen a whore, I don't think, but she looks kind of whorish."

"Do you really think she's after me?"

"Yes. Why, are you interested?"

"Of course not."

"You're a liar," she answers. "I know you. You're interested in anything that can walk."

"Come off it. But you just said you liked her."

"I do in a way. I suppose it's because we share a common like—you. You know, I was thinking tonight—that things being the way they are and you being a man and all—that I really wouldn't mind. That's what I told myself. I kept saying, after all, the Arabs do it all the time—have several wives and when one is knocked up, the others are there . . ."

"You're nuts . . ."

". . . and then I watched her look at you at the table, and I saw that look in her eye and I said to myself, I would mind. I'd mind a good deal."

"You have nothing to worry about," I tell her, though

I wonder at how easily the words come out. Her hand has slipped under my pajamas and my belly tingles as it slips down to my groin. "Don't start anything you can't finish."

"I'm not starting anything," she replies drowsily. "I'm just being friendly. But I tell you one thing," she murmurs, "if that bitch makes the slightest move toward you, I'll slit her zilch up to her neck." The hand between my legs takes hold of me with a grip which, in truth, can only be described as friendly. In this way, Patricia falls asleep.

I suppose the reason Patricia picked Cape Cod out of the air, during that luncheon with Edna Gates, is because I had talked to her about it and especially Wellfleet. We had not actually decided where we were to be married until that moment. On the other hand, we really had no other place to go.

As a boy, I had spent several happy summers there with my parents and there were souvenirs of those summers that led me back there on my own afterward. For example, I can still smell my father's sweat as he bent over a fouled mainsheet. Or, visually, there is the two of them walking on a beach in the late afternoon, my mother stooping to pick up a shell, inspect it, discard it while my father continues ahead, winding up his lanky frame from time to time to skip a stone across the slack water.

There were also Arthur and Judy Levy. I had known Arthur in college, but only vaguely, and was aware of his presence on campus as most others, through his several enterprises such as Cram Caterers, Inc., Dance Co-op, Inc., and Research, Ltd. Besides making sizable profits, these endeavors also incurred for him some disdain, perhaps even some hatred. It was generally known that he did not need the money, in fact his father was very well-to-do, so the bankruptcy of the poorer undergraduates driven out of their sandwich business by Arthur's excellent service was generally decried over the hot barbecues and clam chowder wheeled into the dormitories on his army surplus, portable steam tables.

But it was not greed that drove him, and this I only discovered much later in Wellfleet, but the inherent need to solve a problem, to do something better. Even I believed, along with the others, that he had been motivated by revenge when he promoted the Dance Co-op, but this was not so. It was only that he carried the justification for revenge a step further, recognizing the feeling signified something was not operating properly, that a better alternative was possible. For all freshmen and most upperclassmen were either excluded from the weekend fraternity dances or were charged outrageous ticket prices to support the cost of brotherhood. Arthur was one of those upperclassmen so excluded, and the discrimination led him to create the Dance Co-op.

He rented a large hay barn near campus, contracted with a Meyer Davis Orchestra, offered the best cold cuts, set up several kegs of beer, arranged hay wagons with horse teams and, for good measure and with the thoroughness with which he does everything, threw in a couple of off-duty cops with crew cuts and bow ties to keep order. He sold tickets for a flat three bucks per couple, three bucks for stags also, and it was an instant, howling success.

"You know," he said to me, "the down payment on this house came from the profits on those dances." We were sitting on the porch of the big frame house in Wellfleet, occasionally hearing, for the lip of the bluff kept us from seeing, Judy and the boys in the salt marshes of Black Fish Creek below. On the far horizon, the thin spike of the Pilgrims' Monument in Provincetown was being brazed in the western sun. "I'll never forget"—his belly jiggled with laughter—"I'll never forget all those boys stopping me on campus—even Dean What's-his-name once —telling me what a wonderful thing I was doing for them. And there I was cleaning up." And he continued to giggle, the only flaw in him I could spot, for it identified him with the trite image of all other fat men. "Here, you need another." He took my empty glass inside. "So you've been busted," he shouted through the open door.

"Yes, busted," I said, looking out over the purpling bay.

"Well, maybe it's for the best. Even though you are about to get married. By the way, when is your bride arriving?"

"Next Friday," I told him, taking the new gin and tonic. He held a bottle of grape soda, his third one.

"Really, Hamilton, I don't think it's as bad as you think it is. Number one," he began to list the advantages of my position, his way of breaking problems down into separate departments, each successive idea thought of as the previous one was outlined. "Number one, you have a little money and from what you tell me, so has she. Number two, you've always wanted to write that book on the Dark Ages . . ."

"Medieval guilds," I reminded him.

"Well, whatever . . . and number three, maybe you just aren't cut out for academia. If you were, why would you be down there at that twat junior college? Right? I mean, you would already be at Brown or Harvard or wherever.

Right? Now, I'm just talking as an outsider, someone who doesn't know an aw-ful lot about the teaching business, but putting your qualifications, your background and your credits together with where you've been working just doesn't make sense." A pudgy hand wiped the sweat from his large, rubbery face. "As an outsider, I can't believe you were serious. It's like Mickey Mantle, let's say, suddenly turning down the Yankees to play for McKeesport, Pennsylvania."

"Well, it was a challenge," I finally said.

"Yeah, I bet," and he went into that giggle again which made me get up, angry with him and then with myself. Then it passed. "What's the cause this summer?" I asked.

"Vietnam, what else?" he answered, swigging the grape soda.

"All good demonstrators come to Cape Cod in summer," I said.

"Something like that. I met Judy in a Ban the Bomb demo in Provincetown, remember?"

"When was that?"

"The summer before we graduated. She was still in Bennington and was waiting on tables somewhere. Then came Korea—remember those times?"

"Yes, I arrived the day Harry Truman called up the troops."

"And all those meetings, the talks about West Korea invading East Korea and all that nonsense." The words came quickly, as if to jump over the subject and be on to another.

"It's a mess, isn't it?" I said.

"What?"

"Vietnam."

"Yeah," he answered after a moment. "Well, you're the

historian, what do you think? I don't know too much about these things, but what's the difference between this and say the Mexican War or the Spanish-American?"

"Well, there were territorial considerations in those two."

"And not here?"

"No, of course not."

"Well then?" And he shrugged and looked at me. "But maybe there were claims being staked out of a different kind, philosophical for lack of a better word. You know," he finished the soda, "I'm going to tell you something that may shock you, but a few years back—during the McCarthy bit—I could almost smell the ovens heating up, and one night I took down a road atlas and I studied, yes memorized, the quickest, most direct route to Canada."

"That does shock me. You didn't?"

"Yes, I did. So," he rolled his shoulders, "so I was wrong. And I may be wrong now in this. Maybe it's because I'm Jewish, but I smell an old, Presbyterian puritanism in this Vietnam business. Neo-Cromwellianism," and he laughed as I did. "Well, what you will. You remember John Foster Dulles during the Aswan Dam business, saying he was sure Nasser would see the morality of the conflict? Dulles's from Princeton or Nasser's from Mecca? I confess, it's the only time I sided with Nasser."

"Well, there's always the Kennedys—they're not Presbyterians . . ."

He shrugged and looked out at the water, which had now become almost black, though the sky was still a thin blue. "That's another thing," he continued. "I wonder if there's really any difference. I mean in terms of basic philosophy, in terms of the boys downstairs who bring up the ideas. Everybody belongs to the same club," and he giggled again.

It had grown almost dark and the distant lights of Provincetown glimmered on the horizon; those of Wellfleet were closer, unattractive. Traffic buzzed on the four-lane highway beyond the dunes. The voices of Judy and the boys came nearer as they climbed up the steep bank. They appeared at the top. Arthur's sons, around eight and ten years, each carried a bulrush spear as if they were guards for their mother, who held a dark, dripping mass in the front of her skirt.

"What are you two arguing about, Arthur?" she said in her light voice, looking at us.

"That *schlong* Johnson," he said, his belly quivering. "What do you have there?"

"We've found the most marvelous mussels," she said, coming up on the porch. "I'll fix them for supper."

Gnats and a swarm of mosquitoes drove us inside and we sat around the kitchen table while Judy prepared our supper, giving the boys eggs and cereal. She was barefoot, and her sturdy legs were marked with the black silt from the musseling. The short-cropped hair, chopped is more the word, though not unfeminine, accentuated a strong-featured face. As Arthur went to the refrigerator for ice, standing beside her and their backs turned to me, a passing envy swept me. It was his shorts which did it, a disreputable pair of Bermudas that hung below the knees yet was in no danger of slipping off his generous behind—the image of the two of them, of a contented and happy sensualism that adhered to no pattern, considered no influence save what they had discovered between them.

"Hamilton lost his job at Brown because of his marriage," he said.

"Yes, he told me," Judy answered. She chopped parsley and sprinkled it over the casserole.

"You know, if you want to keep on this teaching kick,

I maybe can help you." He brought me a fresh drink and stood stroking his belly.

"How is that?"

"Well, with the Foundation, you know. But it would mean going to Europe as an exchange."

"Foundation?" And then he told me of the Foundation and his position, and if he had told me this before I must have forgotten it as I always forgot what Arthur was "doing," for there had been a series of similar executive positions, always left by choice for some new one which had more interesting problems to solve and usually at greater compensation.

"Yes, it's kind of late, of course," he was telling me, "but I think there may be one or two spots still open. Let's put it this way; they might not be the best spots at this date, but they will be legitimate and, besides," he shrugged, "how about a wedding trip to Europe? I tell you what. I have to fly back tomorrow for a board meeting. I'll check around and just to make sure—just to get the machine turned on—you give me a résumé before you leave tonight. Use that typewriter over there. Then, your bid will be in; I'll find out what's available; I'll be back tomorrow night; I'll tell you what's up; you pick your spot and meanwhile the presses are turning and all I'll have to do is call in the name of the place and they'll fill in the blank space."

I've always been dubious of those moments when somebody was supposed to have picked up the phone and told Harry Truman he was going to be Vice President or when some German bureaucrat allowed that sealed train and its passenger to pull out for the Finland station. All too simple, things do not happen that way; yet here it was happening to me and I began to wonder if all history and all events were made or made possible not by the great names listed in encyclopedias but by a host of anonymous somebodies who knew somebody else. Stupidly, instead of asking the how, of exploring the mechanism, I asked, "Why are you doing this?"

"Well, I don't know," and his big, good-natured face attempted to leer and failed, "Maybe it's because you puzzle me."

"Arthur?" Judy said from the stove. "Stop that."

"Well, okay," he said, wiping his face, "maybe it's because I like you. Is that a better reason?" And I said it was.

I freely admit to the compounding of my error with the information that Alclair University was one of several choices given me. But the next evening, though, it seemed like the only one I had.

"Well, besides this one," Arthur told me, "there's a spot open at Leeds, one at the University of Madrid and the other is an American-type of college in Greece, set up for oil-company kids." He still wore an executive suit and tie. I had arrived at their house before his taxi from the airport. Were it not for the heavy patches of perspiration staining the silk jacket, there was nothing to relate him to the sloppy summer resident of the night before.

"It's really better than I had hoped," he told me with some excitement. "How about Leeds? Is there anything to drink, Judy? I'm dying of thirst."

"I've made some lemonade." She brought a pitcher and glass to him and he drank one right off, chug-a-lug.

"I don't know," I said. "England just wouldn't seem like Europe to me for some reason. No, I don't think Leeds is the place."

"Well, Greece, then." He poured more lemonade.

"American kids? I don't think so."

"Okay," he reflected, "I'll buy that. That leaves Madrid and the first one."

"Well, I don't speak Spanish, neither does Pat, and for some reason, right now, I'm wondering if I wouldn't get tired of Spanish food. Too much oil. I admit, it's ridiculous," I told his look, "but you know the first one sounds rather good. They speak English, and it's close to everything. We could fly easily, or take a boat, almost everywhere from there."

"You're sure that's the one you want," he said, looking at me intently.

"They've got a great library," I said, scrounging my memory for other things I had heard about the university. "Their history department is pretty good. They're an old school."

"Okay," he said, getting up. "That's the one."

Later that evening he made a phone call ("just to make sure we fill in the blanks first thing in the morning") and through the boys' rough-and-tumble I overheard him say, "That's right—that's the one he wants. Well, I don't know what his reasons are—that's the one he's picked." And so it was Alclair.

The many mirrors in the Red Dog people it with three times the number that are actually standing or sitting in it. Behind the bar are large cut-glass mirrors and on the walls are others, some with the gold-stenciled trademarks of whiskies and beer, and they reproduce and multiply the drinkers and talkers and the white globes of the lights into an endless, warm fellowship. For it is raining outside, a steady dark rain that has made the early afternoon old before its time, an unusually heavy downpour that sweeps refuse down the gutters and all pedestrians from the streets of Alclair except for the ever-present beggars who stamp morosely in doorways, impatiently waiting for the next sodden straggler.

"It is curious to me," Jack Crawford says, easing himself onto the barstool after his third trip to the toilet, "curious that they allow these poor blighters to clutter up the streets."

"It's for the tourists," I say. "Where else can you see genuine gypsy beggars?"

"Unlike any gypsies I've ever seen." He burps softly and sips first at his whiskey and then at a beer. "I really must go after this," he says, blotting his moustache. "There are forty papers that I must read tonight."

"Oh, it's early," I say, signaling the barman for another round.

"My dear fellow," Crawford says, in protest though he does nothing to stop the man.

"Of course, it does make one feel a part of history or tradition. As I was saying about Pat and me, there's Abelard and Héloïse and Dante and Beatrice. Yet to have an affair with a student and then to marry her, as I did, or to have a child by her—well, it's not the ordinary way of doing things and must affect one's life. Change it. I suppose you found this so?" He only looks into his whiskey. "But perhaps it was different with you."

"I cannot say," he says softly. There is a swirl of noise as a group enters through the alley door. It is not her hair that catches my eye but the black, glistening raincoat she wears, the gloss of rain upon the patent leather dazzling in the mirrors. I cannot tell whether she sees me before she sits in a back booth, the three young men accompanying her boisterously taking their places and calling for drinks. "I really do not know," Crawford says.

"You know it is strange," I continue, "but my wife is the result of such an affair. Yes, didn't I tell you that before?" He has looked at me, his glazed eyes startled into focus. "Her father was supposedly an English professor—this is what she was told anyway—and her mother one of his students. Except they never married. The mother's family wouldn't allow it, but she had the baby, Patricia. Twenty years ago it was, just about. That's all she knows about it."

"I'm sorry," Crawford says and then downs all the whiskey and chases it with a beer.

"I'm not," I say. "After all, I wouldn't have her today if it hadn't happened."

"She's a lovely girl," he nods.

"But it is strange, isn't it? I mean her being the result of such a union, our following the same pattern with one difference. Also your experience."

"My experience?" he asks incredulously. "My experience? What do you know of my experience?" The ruddy complexion has bleached around the eyes and corners of the mouth.

"Well, the other day in the office you mentioned something about . . ."

"I said nothing to lead you to believe I participated in such an affair."

"Now wait a minute, Crawford," I laugh and almost put a hand on his shoulder.

"You're dreadfully mistaken," and he almost adds, "sir." There is a vibrancy in his bony frame when he draws up on the stool.

"Oh, let's have another round and . . ." but his hand waves me off. He seems to gulp the air as if to oxidize the fumes in his head.

"Well," he says to himself. "Well, well, well." Then he laughs and clutches me around the shoulders in a surprisingly strong embrace and I am chagrined by its generosity, its forgiveness. "So that's what you thought," he says, having some trouble with the vowels.

"It was not that way at all," he speaks softly, head down over the beer as if in prayer. I can just make out the blurry outline of her head through the frosted-glass partition that separates the rear. The Red Dog is only two blocks from the University and caters mainly to the Alclair intelligentsia and students. So it is probably no more than coincidental that Iseult should be here. I also remember Patricia's suspicions, and I begin to wonder if she may have seen us come here, perhaps watching from her father's window as Crawford and I walked out the front gate.

The sorry plot of Crawford's downfall is dim in my ears. I hear him say, "He was a brilliant boy," but only vaguely, for there is a heavy throb in my head.

"Scholarship?" I repeat halfheartedly, trying to rejoin his conversation.

"Yes. His parents were rather poor folk. His father was a shoemaker. Italian, they were. And out of this came this brilliant young chap with a marvelous gift. He touched me as no other student ever did and I lavished upon him all of my learning. His was a unique and beautiful mind."

"Beautiful mind," I repeat, though at the moment I was far from the cerebral domain. Taking Patricia's observations about Iseult—and how quickly I did take them made me wonder—the possibility that I was perhaps being hunted creeps like a cool hand down my body to grab me, and I actually start with surprise.

"It was that and that only," Crawford tells me earnestly, apparently interpreting my jerk as a shrug of disbelief.

"You must believe that. It was his mind that I was . . . his translations were impeccable, a burning intensity. I spent more time with him than with any other student. I had contracted Harvard. I had planned his graduate work there. Possibly, he was to go on to the great collections at Munich or Vienna," Crawford continues morosely. I recall reading of men about to be executed who are seized by an unaccountable passion, who go to their deaths wearing the stiff baton of life, and I try to make a parallel rationale for myself. Here I am sitting listening to Crawford tell of a dead love and one who translated a dead culture at that, and for a second I put down the bulge in my pants to one more proof of the classic affirmation of life over death. Then I happen to catch my eye in the large mirror over the bar, and I have to smile.

"You see the irony of it, of course," Crawford says, also smiling. "The poems were merely dedicated to me as one scholar to another." His posture is different, ramrod-correct. He even adjusts, tightens the knot of his tie. "The relationship was completely misinterpreted."

"Dedicated to you, were they?" I say, picking my way back to his talk.

"They were marvelous," he says with remembered appreciation. "No one thinks of the Egyptians writing love lyrics, but of course they did. And the poor boy was unable to defend himself, or defend me either, for that matter."

"Why was that?"

"Because he was dead." He looks at me, obviously repeating this salient information. "With polio."

"Oh, yes," I say, as if remembering a minor point. "Well, that's really too bad. A damn shame."

"A genuine loss," Crawford mumbles. "The most brilliant student I've ever had. He would have become a great figure. A beautiful mind. Taste and elegance. And strength, all together."

He says no more, but his lips continue to move and his head shakes back and forth, back and forth. Then he downs the last of the beer and slips off the stool.

"Have another," I offer, but he lifts a hand and turns for the men's room once again. Like living through a dream, I know that Iseult is going to get up from the booth as Crawford passes by her, know that she's going to walk over to me.

"Well, Mr. Hamilton Phillips," she says. "Keeping the chill out?"

"Yes. Will you join us?"

"Thank you, I'll have a whiskey, please." The black raincoat is open and she even seems to thrust what she has of a bosom, two slight swellings beneath the pink wool of her sweater. "How's Patricia?"

"She's fine," I answer.

"I'm very fond of her," she says.

"And she's fond of you," I tell her, biting back more information.

"Look here," Crawford says returning, then noticing Iseult beside me. They exchange brief nods, then he turns back to me, choosing his words. "Getting soft in my senility," he says. "Too much booze, too much rain—whatever."

"Not at all," I answer. "Here, have another."

"Ah, no, those forty papers won't wait," he waves aside my offer. "But it is my responsibility and I have no right to share it with you—make you share it, and . . . and I apologize."

"Don't mention it," I tell him. "I won't." And he gives

me a soft look, a bony hand squeezes my shoulder. Then he's off, leaving the Red Dog with that peculiar sidewise gait, head high.

"What was that all about?" Iseult says, sipping whiskey. "What were you two talking about?"

"About love in Egypt," I say, noting that above the fluorescent pink mouth her eyes are made up in a facsimile of Nefertiti.

"It was all rather two-dimensional, wasn't it? . . . I mean those chaps with the square shoulders and feet all set down like this," and she mimics a tomb pictogram. "But we were talking about Patricia." She slips up and onto the stool beside me. "I didn't think I would like your American women."

"Why not?"

"I suppose it's the movies we see." She dips a finger into the whiskey, swirls it about and then sucks on it. "They always show your women striding about in whip-cords and boots, managing lumber camps or banana planta-tions. Or they are supposedly pretty, brainless creatures who somehow outsmart their men. But your Patricia is not anything like that."

"Well, she's not typical."

"I wonder about that. You get on well together, I imagine. You seem to."

"As well as any married couple gets," I answer.

"I'm quite envious, you know," she throws me a side glance from the Fourth Kingdom.

"Oh?"

"But of you both," she adds quickly. "The whole master-slave relationship," she says soberly and I must laugh. "Typical or not, I sense in your Patricia something very much like me, a way of looking at things, especially men. Some of us long to be enslaved." Her smile could mean anything. "But voluntarily," she adds.

"I thought slaves of passion went out with such notions as 'for God and country.' "

"Oh, it's not that simple. Say, the rain's stopped. Shall we have a walk?" She pulls the glossy collar of the raincoat up around her face. "Will you let me show you the footpaths and byways of my native city?"

Outside, we walk down the alley and onto Fleebus Street. Iseult moves smoothly beside me, hands deep in the coat's pockets. If I am, as already noted, a modest authority on Asian women and able to report that the mysteries of the Orient are no more nor less than what the serious student can discover in Cedar Rapids, Iowa, why then am I exposing myself to the risk of redundant observations with the European variety? There is no end to scholarship, as the never-ending flood of doctorate theses attests, but there comes a point where the gathering of information becomes the cataloguing of repetitious data.

From the doorway of an antique jewelry store, two barely feminine shapes in shawls and rags dart out to interrupt our walk and my reflections. They walk along with us, hands out and muttering.

"FerthlouvtheBlessedHol'MathuruvewrSavor." I find some coins. "Thenkyewsor-enHasialuvbayonya."

"You shouldn't have done that," Iseult says. "We'll have the whole pack of them down on us now." And it is true, for just as we turn the corner, we are set upon by several more smudgy shapes, pinks hands demanding.

"BlessinsbayonyasorferthluvthuHollyMather." I wave them away, indicating I have no coins left. The curse follows us down the street. "You shitty Yankee bastard. May you rot in hell!"

"There, you see," Iseult laughs. "You see where your famed American generosity gets you."

"But how would they know I'm an American?" She stops to give me the once-over.

"The way you look?" she asks incredulously. "Also, they know you must be an American because you're the only ones who ever give them anything."

"Why doesn't the government do something for them?"

"Ah, we do. We have places for them, but they'd rather be beggars. They don't want to be useful or work. That's just the way they are."

"It sounds like home," I tell her, though she's dismissed the subject.

The flower carts are being uncovered when we reach the edge of the Livia, and as if to compete with the russet and golden hues of the blossoms, Iseult shakes out her yellow hair with both hands, pulling the length of it from the collar, and spreads it like butterfly wings in the sun. It's a performance meant for me. I watch.

We continue to walk along the river, passing several gray fronts of government buildings, the pillars veneered with posters and official proclamations. A district of warehouses comes next, great blank buildings overcoming narrow, dirty streets where the round, red and white traffic signs appear like poppies growing from an ash heap.

I admit to a slight yen for this nubile stick of a girl, but it has less to do with desire for her than it has to with how Sandy Koufax or maybe Perseus might have felt showing up on old-timers' day and wondering if they could zing it across just one more time. And as she leads me into parts of Alclair that are new to me, I tell myself— in all honesty—that it really has nothing to do with Patricia, that she is back at the house, happy and content with the new lover I have given her. On the other hand, if my blond guide should suddenly leave me in this unknown neighborhood, how long would it take to find my way back to that house where Patricia is waiting?

"Where are we going?" I ask. "We're going rather far afield, aren't we?"

"Ah, no, you mustn't worry," she wrinkles her nose, smiling, "I know the way."

I am certain of that. It would be no contest for I'm sure Iseult would stand still and let me fire as many strikes as I wished. Then again, the whole logistics of adultery are new to me—where to go. Knowing the way, as she does, I have no doubt that this route among the warehouses is one she knows quite well, probably from past episodes with stevedores. I almost expect her to swing into a deserted, unpadlocked storehouse of mattresses. And, in fact, we do pause before a large sliding door, slightly open, but only to hear a fine tenor singing inside of doomed kings.

As an American who has read the required amount of European literature, I wonder where all of those private dining rooms are, those overcushioned nooks with unseeing waiters and well-set fires that could engorge an adolescent's imagination and completely unprepare him for the simplistic maneuvers in the back seat of a Ford. Is there an ironic fact in that the American high-rise, these glass-walled, see-all constructions that offer their scrupulous presence even in the Alclair skyline, has replaced all those hidden rooms, and the velvet drapery that once suffused the light now warms the shoulders of gypsy beggars?

"That's another thing I envy you Americans for," Iseult says. We stand on the high arch of an iron bridge that crosses the Livia. "You were able to name your rivers.

Here's this river that was named for us, thousands of years ago. And it's true of the rest."

"It's just a matter of time," I say.

"I don't think so. I sometimes think all of Europe came into being all mapped out and everything with names attached. We're so old, and you're so young." A wind from the sea pulls back the corners of her eyes. Like the spreading of the hair, here is another pose, something cribbed from an old movie.

"What are you looking for?" I ask. "A boatload of Vikings?"

"What a nasty thing to say." She turns on me, flustered and angry. "Besides, you blaspheme."

"I really don't think there's much left to blaspheme in the story of Maureen. It's like a manual written by some harem eunuch on holiday."

"How do you know, have you read it?" She tosses her hair angrily and moves off.

"Sure. Your father's translation, as a matter of fact."

"Oh, yes. Well, it may be just a dirty book to you, but it's something special to us. It's our story."

"Well, there's one thing certain. If that's required reading, the youngsters over here must have an extensive repertory—academically, anyway."

"Ah, well." Her good humor is back now. The pink lips curve up. "There's nothing new to any of it, is there? There's only so much one can do, isn't there?" Her head cocks to one side, her eyes slide over me. "You know, you've put me in a dilemma. Do you know that?"

"No," I say in all honesty, though thinking it would take little to resolve her dilemma.

"Well, there's your Patricia on one hand—whom I like,

absolutely adore—and then here you are—a pleasing figure
of a man, though a bit on the square side, but that's
amusing. Yes, that's amusing," she repeats, "almost endearing. Bookish. And what's more, you're a tease."

"Tease? I'm a tease?"

"All you American men are teasers. You walk about
as if you never heard about it and all the while you're
waving it before us like one of King's Henry's roses."

"That's a very pretty image, but I hardly think that I
waved . . ."

"Ah, no. Don't put me on," she says mockingly. "Do
you think I don't have eyes in my head? When I came
over to you I could see the steam rising from your crotch
like a bowl of porridge." The sudden transformation from
a rose to a bowl of porridge is too much, and I begin to
laugh. "You think it's funny, do you? Here I am, doing
my best to keep my Christian morality,"—the lightness in
her voice betrays her and she smiles broadly—"but you
don't help me at all and now you spurn, make fun of my
good intentions."

"Now, don't make it my fault." We come to a bus stop,
one she evidently takes, for she stops. "You're a very
pretty girl and . . ."

"Ah, the beast," she purses the small mouth. "Bit of a
sadist too, he is. But it is your fault. Just like it's not your
fault you're an American, but you are. It's the same thing.
Just standing there like you are is your fault."

"Well, I'll go away," I say, suddenly finding the scene
very tiresome.

"Here's my bus," she says quickly, though it's two
blocks down, so I shift my feet and wait with her. I should
be flattered, for how many times can an ordinary man

with softening midriff and no certificate to fame count on a young, juicy morsel like this throwing herself at him? And, in fact, have I not already possessed Iseult, taking her by the very act of will which makes me spurn her, as she calls it? Man's life, as finite and mundane as it may be, can still be illuminated as are the briefest of essays by footnotes which, though they only casually relate to the central theme, may also open up whole new worlds of knowledge and introspection.

And where does my student, my mistress, my wife, the mother of my child come into all of this? For though I have been playing the game played by every man—i.e., a quick, hot jolt with Iseult would not mean anything and therefore would be okay—there would still be a choice involved. And it's not morality I'm talking about, for I'm too much of a pragmatist to hide behind that punctured screen.

Let me put it this way. When I return home that evening, I find Patricia singing in the vast wilderness of this crumbling house. There are several enormous prints, reproductions of Miró, taped on the pressed-tin surface of the hallway. The curtains she made for the kitchen window do not entirely hide the grime-engrained casement molding but are still bright and fresh. With the two or three utensils provided by our highly selective landlord, she is serving a chicken paprika complete with *spätzle*. A quart mason jar holds martinis. The kitchen counter is dressed with a bright red cloth and there are two candles burning, one in the single candlestick granted us and the other in a wine bottle.

All very *suburbia faunae*, one might say, but the point is this; she never gives up. There may be setbacks, and the curtains may not hide all of the defects of the window-sill or the prints completely overcome the Icelandic waste of the hallway, but she keeps trying. I suppose it comes down to courage, that of the round chin in my office the day she said, "He might be my father," something of that order. Her uniqueness hits me as never before, and I realize, knowing her appetite for the sport and pregnant or not, Patricia would never have lost herself, become identified with a boatload of Vikings.

So I decide to say nothing about Iseult. To merely say I had seen her and nothing more would arouse Pat's already engaged suspicion. And to speak honestly and frankly, like, "I saw Iseult today and got a terrific hard on," would serve no positive purpose either. Instead I say, "I had an interesting conversation with Crawford," talking easily, able to tell Patricia all the details of this encounter. "It seems he had some sort of a relationship twenty years ago with some student—a boy," I add quickly, "who died leaving behind compositions that implied his interest went beyond the tutor-student phase."

"Poor Crawford. But it wasn't true?"

"So he says. And I believe him. I mean, he may have yearned to play Socrates but there's too much New England in him."

"And so he drinks."

"Each to his own. We're a crazy bunch, aren't we?"

"Here," she says, "come eat." She puts a spicy tossed salad beside my plate of chicken. For her, the usual bowl of oatmeal.

"You make me feel . . ."

"Don't be silly," she says, smiling, pushing up the glasses with a finger. "This is all I can eat and I enjoy fixing these things for you. It's the least I can do." She lifts herself slowly upon a stool. "But I can drink. Pour the wine."

"Well, what's new with you?" I ask, cutting into the chicken. It is delicious and I am hungry.

"Oh, Emtie and I had a merry day of housekeeping. Do you think the landlord would mind if I painted the john?"

"Why?"

"Well, I'm in there so much these days, I thought it would be nice to paint it a bright yellow or something. And I have one bit of news for you. Are you ready?"

"Sure."

"Well, you know how Mary Abbey has been so damn curious about who my doctor is and all?"

"Yes."

"Well, she came by this morning on her way to see him. And she told me the reason, just suddenly blurted it out like—well, she almost seemed giggly about it."

"You're not going to tell me she's pregnant too?"

"I'll ignore that inflection." She pours more cream over her oatmeal, and is silent as if to punish me.

"Well, what?"

"She hasn't been feeling well lately, there have been some symptoms so she thought she should have a," and her laughter hurts her, she grips the counter and gasps for breath, and after a long, agonized breath, ". . . she went for a Wassermann."

"A what?"

"A Wassermann. She's afraid she picked up syphilis in Venice from some Italian she had a thing with."

"That's too much!"

"It's the truth. Don't let on."

"That's too much," I say again, putting down my fork. Patricia continues to snort and hoot but my expression sobers her up.

"What's the matter with you? I find the image of Mary Abbey being poled by a gondolier rather endearing. Anyway, a shot of penicillin will fix her up."

"We mustn't let her come to Thanksgiving," I say. "I mean with you in your condition and her eating, using our silverware and glasses."

"You're crazy. Of course she's going to come. I have a notion to make her the guest of honor." And she busts out laughing again.

There are moments which seem to have an existence of their own, perpetual and independent occurrences suspended and preserved as if they were meant to be experienced again and again, always the same though set in slightly different surroundings, circumstances. We come upon them unexpectedly yet also familiarly, and they can be taken out, these ambered bits of memory, inspected and pondered, but they remain unreal and unrelated though perhaps the whole adventure would be meaningless without them.

I recall such a reference point in my childhood's terrain. Returning from play late one afternoon, I crossed the fields behind our house and saw my parents from a distance, though simultaneously I saw the boy in the meadow. My father, in shirt sleeves, had just repaired the rose trellis on the back porch, hammer still in one hand and a coffee can of nails in the other. My mother, coming through the kitchen door, about to call my name but then seeing me, seeing the boy in the field, raises her arm and waves. I can run over the incident again and again, as a film played forward and backward. The figure of the woman on the porch, the only one of the three figures that moves, appears, raises one arm and then backs through the door and, arm dropped, disappears. Much like the toy crossing watchman of an electric train set I once had, sliding back and forth through the door of his little house, lantern stiffly held aloft.

So I awoke one morning last summer, listening to the quiet wash of the sea below the small cottage I had managed to rent on the ocean side. It was an exhausted sound, the waves regathering their strength after the tumult of the night's storm, and Patricia's breathing beside me was almost apace with the tide even down to a long, deeper sigh as the seventh wave broke and sizzled. There were smells of wintergreen and sage and damp wood heating up; all seasoned by the sea air and the aroma of our skin.

At the window, I could look down on the shore a hundred feet or more below the sand cliff and assuredly I waited for them to appear and they did appear; two boys coming around the far edge of the cliff, two small figures walking on the beach. They carried buckets and would stop to pick up something, shells probably, then walk on. I was not surprised to see them even though it was very early. The vast plain of the ocean was still dark and the long red rays of the new sun struck the face of the cliff head on. They were there and I was above them watching, and I am convinced those two small shapes will always be on that deserted, unmarked beach, pausing to gather shells, leaving the small hyphens of their footprints, or perhaps a series of equal signs whose endless repetition tries to make up for the missing half of an equation, the lack of an answer.

There was a heavy sigh, a shift of body behind me, and

I knew Patricia was awake, that the moment was over. And I held my breath, unwilling to let it go, hoping that something would yet happen down there, some climax or point of reference—for the greater part of the beach still lay trackless and smooth—but it was no good. It was gone.

"Good morning," I said, still looking out the window. There were the wet sounds of lips and tongue being worked, a groan and the scratch of fingernails against flesh and hair.

"Morning," she said, her voice thick. "You know, you've got funny little pimples on your bottom. I've never noticed them before."

"Is that so?" I said, turning sideways, looking for something to put on. Clothing was strewn over the small bedroom, the wreckage of our giddy entrance the night before. Her suitcases were still in the car. "It's just the strain of getting married," I told her. "I always break out when I'm nervous."

"No, don't put anything on," she said. "Just stand there a minute." I stood by the window while she fetched her glasses from the side table. She was sitting up in the bed now, the sheet across her middle. Her breasts were lovely, haltered by a band of sunlight. Sitting tailor-fashion, an elbow on one knee, chin in hand, she pushes the harlequin frames against the bridge of her nose. "You know, I never really ever looked at you before."

"How's this?" I said, striking a health-and-culture pose, biceps straining.

"Be serious," she said. "Just stand normally." And I did, feeling a little foolish. "You know, you've really got a very nice build. You really have," she analyzed.

"Does that surprise you?"

"No, I guess I always thought so, or maybe hoped so. After all, it was your mind that attracted me first."

"Sure it was," I said, rotating my hips.

"Stop that," she exclaimed. She was very serious after all. "You look a little soft around the middle, though. You better watch that."

"The flesh may go, but the mind stays," I told her.

"Just enough hair, too," she continued, ignoring me. "And I'm so glad your minnies aren't big and pappy like some men's. I remember noticing that about you before."

"Minnies?"

"Yes, these," she said, lightly touching her own nipples.

"Minnies," I could only repeat, regarding my chest.

Her eyes were now upon my groin and they studied me calmly and with great deliberation, her mouth twisting to one side as if making some judgment. "And another thing," she said finally, "I'm really glad you were circumcised. Aren't you?"

"Well, I guess so. That's one of those things one has very little to say about. Actually, you might say it's the first of many decisions that are made for us."

"Don't be pompous." She pouted.

"Well, you must leave me some defense."

"Why do you need a defense? Men study women like this all the time. I see you looking at me all the time."

"Well, that's different."

"Why is it different?" She was quiet for a moment, then laughed. "And you don't know how relieved I was when I saw you didn't wear jockey shorts." Her arms stretched apart, breasts rising and vulnerable, the belly taut around the dimpled navel. "It wouldn't have made any difference, of course, but God, how I hate jockey shorts on a man. They . . ." and she stopped suddenly, blushing. "How did you get that scar on your knee?" she said quickly.

"I was kicked in a soccer game," I answered.

"How terribly in of you." She pulled her knees up beneath her chin, arms clasped around the sheet-shrouded legs. By accident or design, the sheet had raised and I could see a hard, smooth thigh rounding into the parenthetical curve of haunches, and the cloven print softly stamped within. "Oh, look. It moved. Look." I did not have to look, but I did. "I think it's cute," she said, definitely making up her mind now.

"Cute?" I exclaimed.

"Yes." She shivered more than necessary and, with a coyness obviously fabricated but with telling effect, she added, "And it's so terribly big." Her eyes widened with dramatic alarm as I approached. She even held the sheet over her breasts. "What of Edna? Her train arrives in Hyannis this morning."

"That's not until eleven o'clock and it's just past six," I said, pulling the sheet away without a struggle.

"That's five hours," she said almost to herself, calculating, just before I kissed her. Her hands joined over my neck and her thighs pushed against me, parted and then came together again.

"Take off your glasses," I told her. The thickly lashed eyes becoming mischievous slits. "Come on," and I started to remove them.

"No," she said, pushing me away and rolling over. "It's my turn and I want to see what I'm doing."

There were already a few people on the beach when we got up for breakfast, their voices rising distantly, yet loud enough to pull us from a sweaty slumber. The sun fell full upon the flat tin roof of the cottage and the bedroom was like an oven.

Patricia slipped on my shirt and went to the kitchen and by the time I had shaved and put on some fresh chinos, the coffee was going and bacon fried on the two-burner kerosene stove. The kitchen table, a fresh swatch of white oilcloth tacked to its top, served also as a divider between the kitchen area and the small sitting room. There was a rattan sofa and two wide-armed chairs of maple.

She was nowhere around, the bacon cooking itself and the percolator gurgling, and then with a slap of the back screen door, she entered holding some heather.

"They gave us a vase," she said simply, reaching down a glass receptacle from the open shelves over the sink. And the purple blossoms were put on the white table.

"There are also some *National Geographics* in the bookcase," I told her.

"This place has everything," she said. "How did you find it?"

"Just lucky. I really was lucky. It was so late, there wasn't much of a choice. I'm sorry about the stove."

"It works," she said. And she drained the bacon and broke eggs into the pan. Her black hair had been loosely wound up into a bun. The long thighs and legs moved beneath the shirttail with a mystery of their own. My body still hummed like a beehive, and her straining effort to reach a jar of jelly on the top shelf, a little exaggerated it seemed, was like a stick poked into the swarm.

But we were very hungry and so we ate. Over the second cup of coffee I told her about the change in plans, though with some change in facts, saying that I had turned down Brown for the better offer of Alclair.

"So we'll be spending a year in Europe," I said.

"That's super," she answered in a matter-of-fact voice which astonished me not by its lack of enthusiasm, for I could see she was pleased with the idea, but by what the tone indicated. If I had said, "We'll be spending a year in Peoria or at the library or in Central Park," she would have answered the same way. The point being that she did not really care where we spent the year as long as we were together and I had made the decision, that she was mine to do with as I chose, and whatever I chose to do satisfied her. She would participate with no hesitation. Putting this attitude on top of the way I felt and mixed with how she looked standing at the tiny sink preparing to do the dishes, all had its effect.

"Leave the dishes for a while," I said, leaning over her shoulder to turn off the water. She pushed against me.

"Good grief, again?" But she turned to kiss with grape-jellied lips. "What time is it?" she asked in my ear.

"Only about nine-thirty. Should we christen the kitchen?" I had been thinking about using the table with its fresh white oilcloth, but it meant removing the jar of Welch's Grape Jelly, clearing the rest of the dishes and wiping off the crumbs before making her play the patient. Patricia evidently thought of the same problem, for she walked into the front of the room, the shirt slipping down the long spine and off.

"Let's do one of the chairs," she said, whirling about, the motion loosening her hair so it swirled on her bare shoulders.

I have no idea how Edna Gates got from Hyannis to the inn in Wellfleet, but she did not seem too upset that we were not at the train to meet her. In fact, I imagine that she would have been disconcerted if we had met her, for it would have destroyed the opinion she already held.

Having dinner with her that evening made me realize that nothing ever disturbed her very much, for, like some decent Christians, she gratefully embraced the worst in everything, people and events. And I was reminded how much I underestimated her in another matter by the way she dressed here on Cape Cod. Seeing her in the neat canvas shoes, the denim suit with a lavender print blouse—all very right—I realized that I had expected her to be gloved, hatted and very much the clubwoman.

"Now, Patricia," she said after the coffee and after a rather enjoyable meal, "you must excuse Hamilton and me for a few minutes."

"Oh, come on, Edna," Pat said, scorn on her face.

"Now, dear," Edna said firmly. "Please."

"Oh, all right. You can find me in the bar," Pat said and left.

"Now, Hamilton, we can have our little talk," she said pleasantly. "Perhaps we should have had it sooner, but better late than never. I will confess that I was terribly worried about Patricia and you when she first wrote me, but now—I want you to know—I'm very satisfied."

"I'm glad."

"Yes, there was the age difference, of course, but thinking it over, I'm convinced it's good. She needs an older person. She's very headstrong and a willful girl. Though not intentionally rude, she sometimes does things which hurt others and herself. I think your age will make a difference. You seem to be a balanced personality."

"Mrs. Gates, Patricia needs no defense for what she is or how she acts."

"I'm glad you say that, Hamilton. It makes me feel more satisfied, though I don't entirely agree. Now as you know, the Colonel and I had no children . . ."

"Pat has told me all about this," I said, but she cheerfully waved me down.

"And it was my choice to adopt a girl," she continued. "Everyone makes mistakes, of course, and I cannot claim that I was the perfect mother—we both tried very hard with Patricia. And I think that the Colonel would have given your marriage his blessing."

"That's good."

"He was a very complicated man." She began to unravel his complexity and then stopped. "Now then." She opened the large purse she had held in her lap. "I've had our attorneys prepare these papers for you. The Colonel's estate and mine too, naturally, when the time comes—everything will all go to Patricia. She has, as you may know, already a small income from certain stocks and bonds we put in her name when we adopted her . . ."

"Mrs. Gates . . ."

"And in several years—when she is thirty, to be exact—there will be a small trust fund due. Not much, but comfortable . . ."

"Mrs. Gates . . ."

"Please, Hamilton, this is very important. Now there is a copy of the trust agreement. Here are the schedules for the stocks and bonds. And here's a copy of my will. You'll notice that the estate has been arranged to get the maximum benefit of tax deductions. There now," she beamed and snapped her purse shut. I realized that she had been very calm, very civil, and that everything had been done and said with the best intentions. Her good mood, the genuine glow that suffused her, derived not from the occasion, nor from my being or even Pat's, but from the knowledge that she and her attorneys had figured out a way to sign Patricia over with the maximum tax benefits.

"It all looks in order," I said, wondering if that were the proper phrase, and apparently it was, for she smiled winningly and patted my hand. She even put her arm around me when we walked into the bar, no doubt some tribal instinct of prospective mothers-in-law overcoming the Swiss banker in her heart. And there was Patricia, in hip huggers, loose blouse and sandals, frugging all by herself before the jukebox.

"Isn't she marvelous?" Edna Gates said.

Probably because the concept of formalizing our affair into an actual marriage still did not seem necessary, I had not acquired some of those items demanded by organized society. Fortunately, Art Levy came to the rescue and after half listening to the list of things I had not done he said his characteristic "no problem," and there was none. Somehow, his mysterious efficiency arranged for the blood tests, the affidavits and the other forms that would make us legitimate.

Whether as a last concession to Edna or not, I do not know, but Patricia insisted on having a church ceremony and two days after the dowry dinner I found myself standing beside Arthur Levy and before a very young, nervous minister. It was a colonial meeting house, the interior simple though elegantly restored, gleaming white walls and dark, polished woodwork. Patricia, with Judy Levy as matron of honor, walked down the center aisle past the rows of empty pews, followed by Edna Gates. Both wore yellow linen dresses, very formal, and Pat's glossy hair was crowned with a circle of yellow nasturtiums, a bouquet of the same in her hands.

The organ music swelled and she looked at me, as if on signal, with a wide grin, and I could almost hear the feathery flutter within her. For she was nervous, which surprised me, and took my hand immediately as we stood before the preacher. The ring, the worn narrow gold band with three small diamonds my mother had sent me, slipped on her finger effortlessly, the words were spoken over us with practiced ease and the music came up on cue. Edna Gates wept just enough and, afterward, I remembered her answering the question of who was giving Patricia away with a modest but no less forceful "*We* do."

It was late morning when we emerged as man and wife. The bay sparkled below Wellfleet, and groups of tourists strolled along the street and picked through postcards at the newsstand across from the church.

"Well, what do we do now?" Pat asked gaily. "Let's go to the beach. I've been here a week and I haven't been to the beach yet," she said, looking defiantly at Edna Gates, who only smiled.

"Well, you could drive me to the station," Edna said, batting her eyes. "My train leaves at two. We could have luncheon on the way somewhere."

"Oh, wait. Something else." Patricia stopped us from descending down the steps. "Hey!" she cried. Some tourists turned their heads. "Hey!" she yelled again. Several children walked past carrying fishing rods, three boys and a little girl trailing behind. "Wait a minute." Pat stopped them. "Here." And she threw the nasturtiums to the little girl, who, I'm happy to say, caught the bouquet against her chest—in both arms.

There was only enough time when we returned from Hyannis to change clothes before going to the Levys'. They had planned a party for us and though we knew no one, it was fun. The food was great and the drinks bountiful. Occasionally, I would catch a glimpse of Patricia talking earnestly with a group across the room, and the re-

freshed image of her bowled me over. And once I overheard her say, "My husband's field is the medieval, which
is why we chose to go there." After the party, the four
of us drove to Provincetown for some lobster and champagne, Arthur insisting on treating us, and then to a
discothèque afterward.

I had maybe thought of dancing at our wedding, but
this was the wrong place and the wrong music for me. I
might only embarrass Pat, so the four of us sat and
watched. The Levys seemed more comfortable than I;
however, it was obviously Patricia's crowd, her peers, and
she sat beside me with feverish eye and a tense quivering
of the spine. She was so keyed up that when a young man
leaned over and, shouting, asked her to dance, she bounced
up as if on springs and just as quickly sat down again,
giving me a startled, almost frightened look. Naturally I
nodded, a strange mixture of emotion filling me as I
watched her body jerk and contort in the same configura-
tions and frenzy that I had only—and I was conscious of
the adverb—only seen in bed.

The music cannonaded, a seemingly endless barrage
which overpowered and submerged us at the table, and the
Levys and I conversed in grins and smiles and shakes of
the head. They did not seem to think anything was unusual and Arthur even leaned over and shouted, "She's
terrific." And she was. Hair flying, breasts punctuating the
beat and hips rocking with a perpetual motion all their
own: Patricia was obviously the best on the floor and I was
suddenly alarmed by her excellence.

An interval, brief enough for more drinks to be ordered,
and the crash and slam commenced again. Patricia had not
returned to the table and I spotted her finally with a new

partner, the other one obviously used up. From then on, I could only get glimpses of her miniskirted butt, a spray of black hair above heads and arms, a flash of sandaled foot. Another pause, and then another number and then another and I was beginning to feel foolish. After all, this was our wedding night, I told myself, and whether it was there or not, I thought I saw a bemused, questioning look in Arthur's eyes.

It wasn't easy moving among the dancers, especially feeling so awkward and out of place, and when I saw she was not on the floor, I felt even more dispossessed. The music blared around me. Dodging elbows, battered by buttocks, I was the main course of starving cannibals. She was sitting down, her back was to me, head bending over the flame one of them held for her cigarette. They were all her age, girls and boys, laughing and screaming in each other's ears. She sat straight, almost primly, except for the incessant weaving of her neck with the beat. And for several terrible moments, I looked at the group, thinking it was not my right to interrupt. But I made my way to them, taking the long way around the small dance floor, and they took no notice of me when I got there. Patricia seemed to sense I was behind her and with a last, inexpert puff on the cigarette, she handed it to one of them, got up and came with me. There were no goodbyes, nothing.

We dropped Arthur and Judy off, Patricia unusually subdued during the ride back to Wellfleet. And I turned the car toward our section on the ocean side.

"Let's not go back yet," she murmured. "Let's just drive."

"Okay. I was afraid I had lost you back there," I said.

"Lost me."

"Yes, at the dance."

"That was a ball," she said, thoughtfully. Then she was beside me on the seat, arms leaning on my shoulders.

"Hoo-hoo," she breathed in my ear. "I'm glad you didn't try to dance—I was wondering if you would."

"What's all this testing business you're doing?" I said "If I don't have the qualifications—it's kind of late to discover if I've passed the grade."

"Hush," she said wetly in my ear.

"And we're going to be killed if you keep that up. You're too much sometimes."

"What a square. Who'd ever think my old man would be a square?"

"I don't smoke pot either," I said softly. "And for the same reasons."

"What do you mean?" she asked.

"Well, that cigarette at the place. I could smell it." She said nothing and we drove in silence. A finger traced the shape of my ear.

"It was just one last one," she said finally. "Just think, I'm yours now." And I had been thinking that very thought. "I feel like a snowflake in a box of cotton. Oh, my God," she said with a fierce tenderness. "Just think of it—you and me." Her nails pricked my shoulders. "I'm afraid to think about it sometimes, how much I love you."

"And I love you, too," I said, unable to lie about it. I slowed down, about to turn in a side road.

"No, don't. Keep going."

"It's hardly fair," I answered. Her fingers had moved from my neck, one hand stroked my belly.

"Love is never fair. I'm going to be the best wife to you, Hamlet. You'll see."

"I believe you," I said, keeping my eyes on the road.

"The first time I saw you in class I got all pimply and chills. One part of me said you were kind of goofy and the rest of me, most of me, said—screamed, 'That's him!' It was just like that. I had the hardest time thinking of some way of getting to you."

"You did."

"And I was on pins. What if you reacted the wrong way, what if you turned out icky—I had to find out."

"Wait a minute. You mean that story about thinking you were pregnant was all made up?" She said nothing but nuzzled my neck, her hands on my thigh. "Patricia? Answer me."

"I don't want to talk about it anymore," she said finally. "I don't want to talk about any of it anymore. My goodness, there it is again." She gripped me through my pants. Instinctively, I put on the brakes. "Keep driving," she commanded softly.

"Let's go home. I'm taking you home right now." And while I made a U-turn in the highway, she had adroitly unzipped my pants and took my erection in her hand. "We're going to become a statistic at any moment."

"What a way to go," she said. "I love you, Hamlet."

"I love you, Patricia," I answered, an insane desire to let go the steering wheel and take her in my arms nearly overcoming the sense of preservation.

"Oh, God," she said, thunderstruck, "isn't it wonderful." She meant us and not what she held, but then again I wasn't sure because, ducking her head, her lips caressed me—and it was all mixed up. It was a brief, tender gesture. "Now you can take me home," she said, nuzzling my neck.

"Like hell I will," I said. Within half a mile there was a side road, and we turned in, not knowing or even caring especially what lay at the end. The moon silver-plated the sand dunes on either side of us, the hollows in shadow. We walked down into one of these soft pits, still warm from the absent sun, and her hands went to the fastenings at the side of the skirt, then paused, and she spread her arms apart for me. Kissing, we slowly undressed each other, garment by garment, and were both happily amazed to find ourselves naked when we were finally naked.

"There's one more thing," she said, keeping me from pulling her down. I removed her glasses. "And one more," she said.

"What?" Her hand went to her breasts. The squarish gold key glinted in the moonlight. She turned her back to me, holding up the fall of hair. I unfastened the slender chain.

We awoke cold. There were signs of dawn above the edge of the crater we lay in and sand flies had begun to bite. We dressed and walked to the car and drove back to our cottage—all without speaking, but touching and looking. In the cottage, we fell on the bed and asleep almost at once. We rose late in the afternoon, just in time for a swim before nightfall.

Our days settled into a happy routine. The mornings were spent on the beach, back to the cottage for lunch and siesta, rising for a dip before supper and then long walks around Provincetown or over the dunes and home to bed again. Sometimes we visited with Arthur and Judy, and Patricia would invariably grow bored with the conversation and go poking about the salt marshes with the boys or read them stories if it were bedtime. On rainy days, I would read to her from my thesis and she would dutifully listen while doing her nails or perched on her head, feet on the wall above the sofa.

The olive-toned skin became honeyed in the sun and I

rediscovered her all over again. Long and lithe, she would walk to the water in her bikini and I could only stare in slack-jawed wonder. She was a dish, no doubt about it; a living, walking, breathing bird of paradise, and the stares and muffled exclamations of the neophyte Rotarians who generally surrounded our blanket were a gratuitous reminder of that beauty. They also reminded me that she was mine.

"But I just got wet," she protested one morning. Relentlessly, I gathered our things together and pulled her back to the car. "Gee whiz," she said, sulkily, slumped against the door. "I might as well just not bother ever to get out of bed." But I drove on, a steely master, impervious to any plea.

But they were not really a bad bunch, our beach companions, and after they realized that I didn't dip snuff or have other senile habits, we got along pretty well. On the ocean beaches they taught us to surf, their hands more solicitous upon that golden torso than I liked, but I ignored them, having momentary troubles of my own upon the treacherous board, and I knew in a few hours my lips would erase their fingerprints. Volleyball firmly established my domain.

"Sir." He stood over me, a squarely built Jack Armstrong, idly tossing a ball from one hand to the other. "We need a couple of players and we wondered if you and Patty would join us."

"Sure," I said, noting the hesitancy in my wife's eyes, which angered me more. "Come on, Patty," I ordered.

Back and forth over the net, the ball bounced and we moved around the positions. The girls squealed and the boys hooted and I was not unmindful of the jouncing breasts and tensing buttocks that were an important part of the game. I put my mind over matter, calling up all my playing-field valor and Marine Corps training, and the excessive cheers and compliments when I scored a point only made me work harder. They seemed amazed that I could run and jump, and the sea and the sand assumed a reddish tint in my eyes. Then I was at the net, Jack Armstrong facing me, and suddenly the ball was high between us. It was a setup. He had jumped too soon, coming down on his heels just as I went up. I felt like a gull, as if I could hang up there all day and the ball too, and I saw his face beneath the ball, the eyes wide and smiling. It was a most satisfying smash, catching him squarely on the nose.

"I'm terribly sorry," I said. "I hope it's not broken."

"No, it's okay," he answered, gingerly feeling it.

"You're a brute," Patricia said as we returned to our blanket. The game was over. "You take everything so seriously."

"I only play the game—some can play it better than others."

"Humph," she snorted and flopped on her belly. "You really surprise me sometimes," she said into her arm.

"That's part of it, isn't it?" And she began to giggle.

Patricia made of our tumbledown shack a nest of gingham with marvelous smells. From a collapsible oven, purchased at the hardware store, she pulled out a splendid duck *l'orange* one night when Judy and Arthur came for dinner. She demonstrated a skill with needle and thread that I had not known about, and insisted on making curtains for the windows.

"They'll be here for the next couple," she told me when I questioned the long-term value of her effort. And bending over to peer through her glasses at the minute hand-stitching, she was another person, another kind of beauty.

We also played the games all lovers play, I suppose, inventing little dramas on rainy afternoons as the sea pounded the shore beneath us and the tin roof drummed over our heads.

"Oh, Doctor, I have the most agonizing pain."

"Hmmm. There's obviously a pressure there that must be relieved. I'm afraid we must operate," I'd say, putting the patient in position.

Or sometimes the roles would be reversed. "How long have you noticed this growth?" she'd say.

"It comes and goes. But I'd rather wait and see the doctor about it."

"He's very busy and anyway, you wouldn't like him. He has a long, scratchy beard. I specialized in such therapy in nurse's school and this looks to me as if it requires immediate attention."

"Oh, very well," I'd answer.

One afternoon I came back from the grocery store to find her slouched in the doorway of the bedroom like Sadie from Tahiti. Where she had got the beads, the black mesh hose and the other paraphernalia I never knew. She rolled her hips. "Okay, honey," she said throatily, her heavily enameled lips twisted aside, "how do you like to have it?" But that was too funny and we could only laugh.

"But I practiced in front of the mirror all the time you were gone," she said ruefully, then merrily collapsed to rock in the obscene finery.

I can remember nothing of our evening strolls through Provincetown or Wellfleet, perhaps because the shapes and sounds of both were so familiar, but more likely because she was walking beside me. We'd walk past the blaring doors of the discothèques, nary a pause in her smooth,

sandaled gait, nor did she seem interested when I suggested
we go back. And I taught her to sail, new for her, renting
catboats in Wellfleet harbor and reaching far out to deserted sand sprits to swim naked, picnic, and later to be
awakened by the cool coverlet of the rising tide slipping
beneath our warm bodies.

Nothing except an occasional newspaper headline disturbed our play in this sunny arena. Characteristically, it
was Arthur Levy who brought us back to the practical
world and on the night of Patricia's triumph with the Long
Island duck. There were reports of very heavy bombing of
North Vietnam in that day's papers.

"There's going to be a demonstration," he told us. "Tomorrow night."

"Let's go," Patricia said defiantly, but we ignored her.

"I'm worried," Arthur said.

"So am I," I answered.

"Why don't we go?" Patricia asked again.

"What would it accomplish?" I turned to her. "What
good would it do?" She became red in the face, bit her
lips.

"What Ham is saying," Arthur explained to her, "is
that the debate is being reduced to a for or against proposi-
tion and at street level. We went through this once before
with Joe McCarthy—either you're for me or against me
and with no in-between. It is entirely possible that such
demonstrations have the opposite effect; actually harden
the government's position."

"What's in between?" Pat snorted.

"Well, there's negotiation, for one thing," I said.

"So we keep up the bombing," Judy said.

"It's not that simple," Arthur said. "It's become more
than just a civil war now. Well, Christ, I don't know," he
added.

"It's wrong, wrong, wrong," Pat said. "I think we should show ourselves. I'm going to demonstrate."

"No you're not," I told her, and we were suddenly, unaccountably at sword's point, which momentarily took me back. "You're not going," I repeated.

She said nothing more for the rest of the evening, except for some talk with Judy about the clothes she was taking to Europe. When they left, I started to help her with the dishes only to be told curtly she needed no help. The last plate set to dry in its rack, she stomped through the room, banging the screen door, and sat outside and smoked. After two or three cigarettes, she returned, going immediately to the bedroom, and when she closed the door, I threw down the *National Geographic* and came after her.

"Now don't be childish," I said.

"I am a child," she replied coolly. "And there are children being killed by us, probably at this very moment."

"And by them too."

"Does that make it all right?" She had straightened up the room ferociously, retracing the same path again and again, obviously unwilling to undress while I was present. "We have a chance to stand up for something and you chicken out. Chicken out!" she shouted, hurt and on the verge of tears.

"All right, you want to march? Will that stop the bombing? Will it?"

"We marched once before," she said.

"Yes, and what did it accomplish?"

"It did something for me and for you, too. You said so. You said it did."

"So, it was a personal thing, that's all. Look, Patricia." I took a breath. "Let's be honest. You're a girl from an upper middle-class background and you're . . ."

"Don't talk to me about my background," she screamed.

Her eyes were pinpoints behind the glasses. "Who are you to talk about my background—you—you phony, liberal pervert!"

"Pervert?" I gasped.

"Yes, pervert. Some of the things you've made me do . . ."

"I made *you* do?"

"I could send you to prison for twenty years! Twenty years!" she shouted in my face and then flounced on the bed, drumming her feet against the linoleum floor. "When I think of what I could be . . . where I could be . . ." and she began to blubber, "not tied up with a sniveling square and running off to some foreign country like rats from a sinking ship . . ."

"I'd hardly call America a sinking ship," I said.

"Oh, go away. Go away," she whined, falling over on the bed, sobbing. I was stunned, flabbergasted and it seemed best to obey her. The lights were out when I returned from a walk along the cliff, my mind no more able to sort out the maze of charges or the reason behind them. She was asleep, curled in a tight ball on the far side of the bed.

I awoke knowing it was very early, pulled from a restless, exhausting sleep by the sounds of vomiting. She leaned against me now, I held her over the commode while she heaved and gagged. Some strands of her hair had become fouled and I washed them off.

"That duck was awfully rich," I said gently.

"It's not the duck," she said wearily, her face wan and, minus the glasses, strangely defenseless. "But it rhymes with duck."

"But you can't be," I said, after a moment.

"Why not?" She staggered to the sink for a glass of water and gargled.

"Well, the pills."

"No pills would do any good the way we've been doing it," she said after a moment. "They're not completely certain, and God knows we never gave them a chance."

"Pregnant . . . my God, pregnant." All the complications fitted together in my mind like a terrible puzzle.

"How do you think I feel?" she said soberly. "I Was A Teen-age Mother. I can write stories for the *Ladies' Home* . . ." and she started to weep.

"Oh, come on," I said, putting my arm around her. The idea suddenly did not seem so bad. Slowly, her arm went around me and we stood by the front windows together. On the far horizon, a gray pennant of smoke floated above the flat, gun-metal sea. "There's a boat," I said, as if it were a cure.

"Where's it going?" she asked as a child for a story, sniffling.

"It's going to Europe," I said.

Turkey in the oven and pies cooling on the windowsill, our house is drenched with the aromas of sage, nutmeg and molasses, a heavy scent of cooking fowl vying with the pungency of yeast. Patricia, still wearing a nightgown with robe and slippers, moves in the small kitchen happily. She checks off the long list taped to the kitchen wall; "Turkey in"—scratch—"Rolls made out"—scratch—"Potatoes peeled" —scratch—"Greens washed—ah, greens washed," and she turns on the helpless romaine to pull it apart.

Emtie attacks the housework with identical, ecstatic frenzy, and whether in honor of the occasion or not, I do not know, but she has put aside her music-hall favorites and sings nothing but hymns. There's a hurried though no less meaningful moment of harmony in the kitchen when she goes for a dustcloth; shoulder to shoulder, heads nearly together, the two of them join in a phrase, Patricia taking the alto, "Lead kindly light . . ." The duet is abruptly dissolved by their separate duties.

I help with the moving of furniture, haul out the old ashes and run last-minute store errands. Dean Morraugh was more than happy to let me dismiss my classes for this purpose.

"Why, of course, my dear fellow," he said, his eyes glowing with a vicarious, nationalistic pride.

"I'm sorry the guest list got so long . . . we had wanted to have you and Mrs. Morraugh," I said.

"Tut-tut," he waved the three-fingered hand. "Not a jot to worry about. After all, the Morraugh clan will be well represented. Iseult is looking forward to it with great anticipation—great anticipation. She really admires the both of you tremendously," he said warmly. "I can't tell you how grateful I am for what you are doing with her."

"It's nothing," I said in all honesty.

"Ah, but you don't see the change in her as the missus and I do. Yes, all for the good." And he nodded and took a deep breath.

With Emtie's hymning assistance, I mount the hardware beside the front door for the small flagpole and insert the staff bearing the Stars and Stripes which Arthur Levy had given us at the airport, half in jest, and now I think more in earnest.

"Oh, long may she wave, sirrah," Emtie says, stepping back on the stoop, hands reverently clasped before her. I fully expect her to launch into "The Star-Spangled Banner," but she returns inside to her work.

The flag hangs and stirs in the slight breeze, unnaturally bright, almost garish in the gray neighborhood with its winter foliage, the dark brick fronts of the houses still wet from the morning drizzle. And I confess to an exultation upon seeing it, a lift which surprises me.

"Here we are," Maxine Waters' strident voice calls from the curb, and though there is no one else inside the taxi, she carefully lifts out a large plastic container and I assume the cranberries are included in the pronoun. "Isn't it beautiful," she says coming up the steps, eyes upon the flag. "As I told Dean Morraugh the other day, there's just no flag like it in the world." Down the hall and into the kitchen where she awards Pat the container, the large face gleaming with anticipated compliments. "Oh, my dear, it smells marvelous. Oh, look at the pumpkin pies. Ah, the turkey, how lovely. Oh, what a feast, what a feast! And rolls, too."

And all the while she is turning this way and that, stooping to sniff, arms flailing about with gastric ecstasy. A flash of instant hysteria crosses Patricia's eyes. The kitchen is small to begin with and there are stacked pots waiting their turn on the three burners, pies and pans of rolls balanced precariously upon narrow window ledges and sink. Maxine Waters is a massive dervish whirling within.

"I came early to help," she is saying, bending over to inspect the crackling bird in the oven while her rear end bumps a stool and sets it rocking. "Oops."

"The table . . . the table," Patricia splutters. "You can help Marie Therese set the table."

"Good. Fine," Maxine Waters says, taking a last deep breath with her into exile. I grin at Pat and she at me.

"How are you doing?" I ask.

"Super," she says, and she looks it.

"Anything I can do?"

"Yes, just stand there while I go over the list with you." She enumerates everything done so far. "Now the turkey will be done in about an hour, and then I'll put the rolls in. Oh, use that soup bowl there for the cranberries. Everything's going great. As soon as I get these potatoes ready, I'll go dress."

"You're terrific," I tell her. "You really are."

"Did you remember candles?" she asks. "There's the door. Everyone's so early."

"Come in, Jack," I greet Crawford. He holds a brown sack that clinks.

"Some reasonably good claret," he says, handing me the bag of bottles. "Ah there, Maxine. Happy Thanksgiving," he says in the dining room.

"And to you, Jack," she says, laying out the silverware. At the sideboard, I put down the wine.

"How about a drink?"

"It's a little early yet, isn't it?" he says.

"Oh, come on, Thanksgiving only comes once a year," I insist.

"Well, if you are." I pour two scotches for us. "Maxine? Sherry?"

"That would be lovely."

"Is this the Yankee Embassy?" Iseult Morraugh shouts in the hall before bounding into the living room. "To you," she cries to us, then reaches back toward the door and pulls in a youth behind her. "I've brought a friend, I hope you won't mind."

"No, we assumed you'd have an escort," I said.

"Did you now? Here's Judson Doyle." She introduces the round-faced, jug-eared character who stands behind, looking down at her with the sleepy, fatuous expression of a dog still hung up on a bitch.

"We were just having a drink," I say. "What will you have?"

"Gin and lime, if you have it, but nothing for him," Iseult says. "He's in training. He's a boxer." He nods his head energetically though no one has challenged the identification.

"Yes," his voice is a high tenor, "I've just finished doing my daily five miles."

"You must be starved, poor boy," Maxine Waters says, arranging the carving knife and fork.

"Where's Pat?" Iseult asks and then looks for her, drink in hand. Their salutations are very loud and cheerful.

"Well, how about some plain soda, then?" I ask.

"Nothing, thank you ever so," he says, contentedly smoothing his flat belly.

We move into the living room, leaving the last of the chores to Emtie, and I start fires in both fireplaces, for it is very chilly and damp. Maxine Waters stands before the mantel, her shelf of bosom poised as if ready to launch a lengthy opinion of Robert Frost. Crawford, drink in hand, pokes about the books on the table, carefully reading the titles along the spines and putting them down. Doyle takes the center of the floor, arms swinging as if to commence calisthenics.

"Well, how long have you and Iseult known each other?" I ask.

"Long enough, if you know what I mean," and he grins and winks in an obvious attempt at drollery. "A fine strip of a girl," he adds seriously to Maxine.

When I go to the kitchen for some ice, the girls are recovering from a fit of laughter. Pat is hanging onto the sink with one hand, supporting her belly with the other and her face contorted almost in pain. Iseult's long fingers cover her screams, but when I appear, they are suddenly composed.

"What's so funny?" I ask.

"Oh, nothing," Patricia says, then hoots again, looking at Iseult. "Well, I'm going to dress now."

"Need some help?" Iseult offers.

"If you like," and they leave me alone with the ice tray.

"Well, I'm off," Emtie says in the doorway. She wears her raincoat, galoshes and carries the black umbrella.

"You're not staying?"

"No, Missus says I can go. I have to take me father to the hospital to be purged. His bowels have been plugged up for a week."

"Well, I guess it's best to get him out of the house," I tell her. As I pass fresh drinks around in the living room, Doyle is showing Crawford and Maxine his ring stance.

"You see," he demonstrates, "it's nearly impossible to get to me this way. It's my reach that does it to them."

"Mr. Doyle is leaving for America next week," Maxine tells me.

"Yes, I've a tour of six months with two fights booked already," he says proudly.

Mary Abbey is among us, still wearing her white trench coat as if undecided whether she will stay. She stands in the corner glumly looking on. Underneath the coat is a drab outfit, and she appears to be an awkward freshman, still wearing the small-town Sunday-school best at her first fraternity brawl.

As I hang her coat in the hall, there are steps above me on the staircase, the two of them moving together down to the landing.

"And it's because of the way I'm carrying this baby," Patricia is saying, "that does it. Hewson says it's unusual but nothing to worry about, but it makes me sicker than I should be—all the time—and as for sex, well, forget it," she says just as they turn on the landing and see me. "There's the handsome brute that did it to me," she says. Pat is wearing the little-girl shift with the lace inserts, and, for the first time, I note that Iseult is wearing one almost the same, except in peach.

"Did what to you?" I ask, as they walk down to me.

"But not a single regret," Pat says, reaching an arm around me for a squeeze and a kiss on the cheek. Almost automatically, I put my arm around her and around Iseult as well, and we stand at the foot of the stairs for a moment, a blond and a raven head leaning against me.

"Homey, isn't it," Iseult says contentedly.

"Listen, we could make a small fortune as an act," I say. "Two girls and a man, and one of them pregnant besides."

"Pooh," Iseult says. "Always doing the dirty tease, isn't he?"

"Oh, you don't know," Pat rolls her eyes.

"It's the length of muscle in me forearm that does it," Judson Doyle is telling the group in the living room. "It's not knotted up as is the custom in other chaps, but long and supple. A spring of steel."

At the sideboard, I make more drinks, carefully noting that Mary Abbey's glass is decorated with diamonds, one of a set our bridge-playing landlord has left us. I remind myself to keep track of that glass.

"Isn't he marvelous?" Izzy refers to the prizefighter. "And what's more, he's a musician as well."

"Don't tell me he plays the violin?" I say.

"Ah, no. What is it you play, Judson?" she asks him. "What instrument?"

"The trombone," he answers. "It's good for me wind."

I look at Iseult, and particularly her make-up, which I have begun to anticipate each time we meet. There is little of it today, rather one even sheen of pink pearl covers her whole face.

"Well, I propose a toast," Crawford is saying, glass high. "To the Republic." It all comes back to us and we raise our glasses as one and drink to the picture of Jack Kennedy over the sideboard.

"And now to our host and hostess," Iseult says.

"Lovely, lovely," says Maxine Waters.

"Feel this arm," Judson Doyle says to Mary Abbey. She colors and looks apprehensively at the rest of us. "Feel it there, woman." One small, nail-bitten hand goes out tentatively and rests upon the fighter's bicep. "Ah, where's the old grip? There you are." The hand jumped as if she had touched flame. "What did I tell you?"

"It's very . . . very hard," she says in a small voice. She looks for a cigarette in her shoulder bag.

"Miss Abbey is a poet," Maxine Waters tells Doyle, as if to explain something.

"Give us a line," he asks.

"Ah, well . . . I . . ." Mary gurgles, clears her throat and then takes a large swig of whiskey.

"Here, do you know this one?" And he takes a pose in the middle of the rug, fists up and shoulders hunched over.

"Out of the night that covers me,
　　Black as the pit from pole to pole."
A left hook whips out.
"I thank whatever gods may be
　　For my unconquerable soul."
A vicious uppercut ends the quatrain.

Then suddenly Mary Abbey takes up the next stanza, Maxine Waters joining her at "My head is bloody, but

unbowed," for which Doyle staggers under an imaginary
punch but comes back more determined than ever. We all
supply bits and parts of the poem from memory, Mary
sustaining us through the entire length, finally all together
tumultuously as a flurry of dazzling punches pummels
the senseless air, "I am the captain of my soul!"

"The winna!" Pat holds his arm aloft and we all cheer.

"Splendid, splendid," Crawford says.

"Let's do more," Pat says. She pauses, thinks, puts down
her glass and strikes a declamatory pose, belly thrust out
beneath the silk shift.

> "By the rude bridge that arched the flood,
> Their flag to April's breeze unfurled,
> Here once the embattled farmers stood,
> And fired the shot heard round the world!"

"Marvelous," Crawford cheers.

"Hurrah," Mary Abbey shouts and just as quickly picks
up her glass and drinks.

"What is that about, a rent war?" Iseult asks me.

"No," I answer. "Well, in a way, yes. Concord," but
I see no recognition in her gray eyes and stop.

"Now you," she says.

"I can't remember anything. How about you, Crawford? Come on, Jack, give us one."

"Oh, do," Maxine Waters says.

"Well, hmm, it's not my field, you know," he says.
"Well, let's see." He takes a breath, and,

> "Wealth without moral splendor,
> Makes for a poor neighbor . . ."

And we wait for him to continue, but he looks at us
and then drains his glass.

"Now who was that?" Maxine Waters asks, thinking
hard.

"Well, it's a bit far afield, actually," Crawford says. "Sappho."

"Sappho," Iseult explodes. "You mean that old les with the Greeks?"

"Only a fragment, actually," Crawford is telling Mary Abbey. "The rest is lost."

"Say, I just thought of one," I say, bringing fresh drinks from the dining room, and I start to sing,

> "Over the river and through the wood,
> To grandmother's house we go . . ."

"Oh, honestly," Patricia says, but joins in as do the others.

"Dum dee-dum, dum-dee-dee-dum—here's the part," I lead them,

> "Hear the bells ring,
> Ting-a-ling-ding!
> Hurrah for Thanksgiving Day!"

Iseult's eyes are gray balls of yarn. She sits down by Judson Doyle on the sofa, the two of them forming a natural audience.

"Now, Mary," Maxine croons, "give us something of yours."

"Yes," Pat urges the poet.

"Oh, I don't feel like anything of my own," Mary Abbey answers in a flustery way. "But here's one:

> My country need not change her gown,
> Her triple suit as sweet
> As when 'twas cut at Lexington,
> And first pronounced a fit.
>
> Great Britain disapproves *the stars;*
> Disparagement discreet—

There's something in their attitude
That taunts the bayonet."

"That taunts *her* bayonet," Maxine Waters corrects her. "*Her* bayonet. That's Dickinson," she tells the rest of us with a possessive sigh. There's a momentary silence, the sound of ice tinkling, and then, clearing her throat, Maxine inquires, "It's my turn, isn't it? Well, now, let's see.

The plain, autumnal table Pilgrims set,
Serves notice, claims precedent
O'er meager feasts that subsequent
The harvest currency they spent
To wear faith's simple wilderness."

She seems too overcome to continue and merely looks into the depths of her sherry. Finally, Mary Abbey smiles and says, "That's one of Mr. Waters', isn't it?"

"Yes," Maxine Waters answers, happy and relieved. "That's a lovely line, isn't it—the plain, autumnal table Pilgrims set?"

"Yes, lovely," Mary says.

"I better put some food on the table before we all get smashed," Patricia starts to go.

"We haven't decanted the wine Crawford brought," I tell her. "We must wait for that a bit." And while I turn the corkscrew into the cork, Pat and Iseult, followed by Maxine Waters, tiptoeing with anticipation, start transferring platters and dishes from the kitchen.

"Go ahead, with all your might," I hear Doyle say in the living room. He's standing before Mary Abbey, jacket pulled back, exposing his shirtfront to her disconcerted gaze. "Come now, give me a good stiff one."

"Oh, I really don't want to," she says, suddenly laughing and looking around for rescue.

"Go ahead," Iseult shouts from the doorway, a dish of potatoes in her hand, "hit the bloody bugger!"

"Oh, very well," Mary says absentmindedly, "but I must have a drink first. Where's my drink?" She looks around.

"Just behind you there on the table," Crawford says.

"No, that isn't mine. Mine had diamonds on it," she says. A cold wave flows down my back. There are three glasses on the side table: clubs, spades and diamonds, three glasses put there by Iseult, Patricia and me, but I could not remember which of us had been drinking from the diamonds.

"Well, it's all the same," Pat says, laughing, looking at me and then deliberately giving me a wet kiss full on the mouth. "All one big, happy family," she says, giggling.

Mary Abbey shrugs and drinks from the glass behind her, stands before Doyle, takes a few practice swings and then bangs him square in the midriff. He merely smiles down upon her, as she shakes the pain from her fingers. Her squinty eyes boggle.

"Come now, everyone to the table," Pat says.

The candles have been lit. There is a sparkle of silver and plate and a glow of red wine. The turkey glistens before my place, a hulking drum major to the parade of dishes that are stationed the length of the table: mashed potatoes, scalloped oysters, boats of gravy, asparagus, salad, hot rolls, and the red of the cranberries in the center.

"Oh, just smell it," Maxine Waters says, her nostrils dilating, bosom shivering.

"There's only one thing missing," Mary Abbey says. "There should be a couple of great hounds in the corner to fight over the bones."

And down we sit, all except for me, as I start carving. It's a beautiful bird and cuts easily. Maxine helps each to potatoes and the cranberries as the plates come by her; the others sort out the remaining dishes themselves. All served and we are about to dig in.

"Somebody ought to say something," Patricia says. "Maybe I could pretend to be Pat Nixon and say a few words." She is very pretty in the candlelight at the far end of the table. Maxine Waters is quickly on her feet—her wine glass held high.

"Oh, say can you see . . ." she begins the anthem rather high and we rise to it, joining in. Our guests look on in wonderment, Judson Doyle standing like a rod of iron, Iseult holding her napkin and with a bemused look on her face. But we have become very serious. Patricia's school-girl face is set, determined as Mary Abbey's. Crawford sings looking straight ahead at the fire in the grate. Maxine pitched it so high, we all have to drop an octave to make the bridge of the song, then return where we started for the release. The final notes seem to echo through the house.

"Well done," says Crawford as we sit down.

"Well, here goes me training," Doyle says, pouring on the gravy, napkin tucked in his collar.

"You must get used to it, bucko," Iseult tells him. "In America, they eat like this every day. Isn't that so?"

"Lovely, lovely food," Maxine says, shoveling it in.

"The turkey is great, Pat," I tell her. "And the dressing is marvelous." There are more compliments from around the table.

She bows to accept them, picking at the food on her plate, one slice of white meat and a dab of potato. Craw-ford is also eating, and Mary Abbey resembles an orphan still damp from the storm. There is little conversation as the turkey is rapidly stripped down to the bone under repeated servings, none of us very far behind Maxine's three platefuls.

"Have you tried the cranberries?" she keeps asking. "Here, you must have some of these."

"I have, I have," Crawford defends himself. "They are very good, most unusual."

"This was a recipe of my husband's mother," she says.

"It's a treat for us to be sitting here at this typical American meal," Iseult says, the corner of her eye on me, "with such a distinguished group of Americans. A poet, two eminent scholars and the wife of a distinguished poet."

"Give us a line," Doyle says, one asparagus bud hanging from his mouth.

"We've done that," I say.

"Ah, yes, fame," Maxine says. "It can do terrible things to people." She pauses to get her footing on the trail of a monologue.

"Who's for more turkey?" I ask, but there are no takers. "Well, I guess we're ready for the pie." Maxine Waters glances sharply toward me but patiently waits while Patricia, assisted by Iseult and Mary, clears the plates and brings in the pie.

"What's this?" Doyle looks at his plate.

"Pumpkin pie."

"Pumpkin—what's a pumpkin?"

"Squash. It's like a squash, you lugger," Iseult tells him.

Everything served, we take on the pie and I wait for Maxine to continue, curious as to what method she will use to swing the talk back her way. Jack Crawford obliges her.

"One of the virtues of my field is that one does not have

to worry about fame. The interest is so limited," he says humorously, sipping wine.

"And you're so lucky—so lucky," intones Maxine Waters. "It can be so debilitating—"

"What can be, what are we talking about?" Iseult asks.

"Fame," I tell her, and her mouth shapes a perfect O.

"You just don't know, you just don't know," Maxine says with a pained, mournful expression. "You must guard against it, Mary dear. You are about to achieve it, and be wary of it. It's tragic to see a great talent waste its energies on all the minutiae that come with fame. And the hangers-on—oh, if you only knew."

"Tell us about it, Mrs. Waters," Patricia says, and I look at her quickly but her face is blank. It is an unnecessary request in any event.

"My husband wasted himself, a tragic, tragic waste," she says, after taking a sip of water. "Poets, you know, have this reputation," and she winks broadly and laughs, "and everywhere they go they are set upon by hoards of— well, my husband in his last years used to call them *anonhorai*, which is the Greek for . . ."

"*Anonkorai*," Crawford corrects her. "Camp follower," he adds the translation.

"Are you sure about that?" Maxine leans across the table, one hand at her throat. Her expertise in the use of the future perfect or the construction of compound sentences gives her an unshakable assurance in all other matters.

"Yes, quite."

"I'm almost sure that—for you see, my husband was a very fine scholar in addition—a junior Phi Beta Kappa as an undergraduate and all on scholarship, for his people were just good, ordinary farming folk. Well, no matter, those people. Oh, those people! And what a tragic waste of energies."

"Well, certainly, you must have been a stabilizing force," I say. Her wan smile fends off the compliment not too successfully.

"A woman can do only so much," she says. "In any event, the real damage was done by the time we met. He had already reached the peak of his career, of his development. And the women, my dear . . ."

"That's something I won't have to worry about," Mary Abbey says on her second cigarette.

"Yes, well, wait and see," Maxine warns, apparently hearing nothing but her own voice. "He used to say that he felt like a steward or ship's doctor on one of those cruise boats—hired by these colleges only to attract women students and not for his talent and what he could give. And he could have given so much," she says, with a pained face and hands outstretched.

"Sounds like a jolly good berth to me," Doyle says, burping. He looks suddenly at Iseult, apparently receiving a sharp toe in the shin beneath the table.

"Yes, you're a man and you would say that," Maxine says with great understanding. "He even said it himself—sometimes. But it's different with the creative mind, you see." She explains it patiently. "All the time his great work was to be—a poet's great work should come just when he is about fifty, it's then or never, I'm afraid," she laughs knowledgeably, "and all of his energies were being drained away, debilitated by these wasteful people, instead of being put into his work.

"If I could only have met him ten years sooner," she says, taking another sip of water. "Well, who knows. One can imagine what may have happened all day. No," she sighs, "I'm afraid the damage had already been done." A deep breath raises the tablecloth over her bosom. "He was fallible—no more or less than any other man, but fallible and the temptation was great."

"How about some more coffee? Pat, more coffee?" I break her concentration; she has been staring at Maxine with a glazed fascination.

"Just as I first met him," Maxine continues hurriedly, "he was recovering from a disastrous affair with one of his students at one of these dinky little schools. One of those little—well, there are names for them—who hope for some mention in a biography as a footnote."

"Where was that?" Pat asks.

"Oh, I don't remember—it doesn't matter." Maxine dismisses the tiresome question with a hand. "But it took years for him to recover—years, my dear," she tells Mary Abbey, "and even then it sometimes preyed on his mind and what a loss. What a loss, for all the time he should have been totally involved in his major work." She angrily strikes the table with a spoon. "Ah, it was tragic," she says, rolling her eyes to the ceiling.

"I'll get more coffee," says Patricia, rising with the pot in her hands. I try to catch her eye as she leaves but she does not look up.

"You must have been a great comfort to him," Crawford says. "A rehabilitative force almost." The hard look in his eye surprises me.

"Ah, but it was too late, too late," Maxine says, full of the tragedy.

"It's like that with me, you know," Doyle says. "They're always after me, the women, to break my training."

"Really?" Maxine says, her best smile put forward.

"Ah, sure," the fighter says. "They smell the virtue of my rigorous conditioning and they want to despoil it. It's like a lure to them. Many a night on the circuit, I've come in to find one of them in the sheets waiting for me."

"A tragic waste," Iseult says, biting a piece of celery in two.

"I suppose this explains his output at the end," Mary Abbey says casually, lighting another cigarette. "I mean, why his poetry dropped off." There's a tense moment, Maxine looking upon her former student with the bristling recognition of betrayal.

"It was very fruitful, considering," she says finally in a meaningful voice. "He published four books . . ."

"One of them a collection, another a translation," Mary says softly.

"And with many new poems," Maxine says defiantly. "No, his work continued, but think what it might have been. I often said that if I had had his talent put together with *my* determination that it . . ."

The sound that interrupts her is strange and chilling, only in that it is not immediately recognizable, like the unidentifiable creak in an old house that turns out to be a shutter. Eyes flick around in the candlelight, questioning, startled, and then Iseult starts to rise.

"I'll go," she says.

"No, I will," I stop her.

Patricia is hanging over the small sink in the corner of the bedroom, gagging and spitting. The spasms are so violent, so wrack her body that for a moment I think she may bring up the embryo as well. I hold her tight, pull back the long hair from around the red, gasping face.

"Yaaghk," she grimaces between heaves. Then, still looking down the drain of the sink, she adds, "It's gone."

"What's gone?"

"The key. The Phi Bete key is gone."

For the first time, I notice her jewelry box open on the foot of the bed. "Are you sure?"

"I'm sure. I came up to get it, and looked through. Everything else is there, but it's gone."

"But how—who?"

"Emtie, probably," she says with surprising serenity. She straightens up, gargles and washes her face. And as if to change the subject, "Those were the worst mashed potatoes I've ever made. They were lumpy."

"They were not. Now wait a minute. When was the last time you saw it?"

"I can't remember. It doesn't matter. I just came up here to look at it when Mrs. Waters was talking about her husband, thinking maybe he might have been . . ." and she slips into an embarrassed silence, glancing furtively at me from beneath a damp lock of hair.

"You didn't. Ah, Patricia." I try to admonish her but nothing comes of it.

"Hamlet." She leans against me, a slight acid smell still on her. "I'm homesick. I don't want my baby born over here among all of these foreigners."

"They're not foreigners. We are."

"It's the same." Then, fixing her hair, regrooming her hostess self, "Go on downstairs. I'm all right. I'll be down in a minute."

Downstairs, Iseult has taken command, clearing plates, serving more coffee, with Mary Abbey helping until Judson Doyle begins to lecture her on smoking. The poet sits by him and smiles benignly. We move to the living room, I poke up the fire and take orders for more drinks, almost forcing a round upon everyone, for our guests now seem no longer comfortable. Doyle tries to liven things up by balancing a sherry glass on the back of his head while walking on his hands, but it does not help. Mary softly pats his shoulder and he desists.

Our Thanksgiving feast has come apart; the mood is gone and each of us seems eager to return to his separate routine. Our guests wait only in order to say goodbye to Patricia, who gives them this opportunity for grace by wandering in looking very pale and shaky, a pregnant Ophelia who suddenly gives meaning to much of the plot.

"Lovely party, old chap," Crawford tells me, and we shake hands and then, before he sidles out of the door, he holds Pat at arm's length for a moment, caresses her cheek.

Mary Abbey, looking both embarrassed and apologetic, lets the prizefighter escort her, shaking hands with both of us and glancing up with a sort of amused terror at him when he shouts at us, "See ya in the States!"

We find Maxine in the kitchen ostensibly helping Iseult, who had already announced she was staying on to clean up, though with each plate she passes onto the sink, the poet's widow rips off a piece of turkey from the carcass. "This has been a grand occasion," she says brightly. "How do you feel, my dear?"

"So-so," Pat shrugs. She goes to the sink, but is waved away by Iseult and comes back to rest on a stool.

"I see that Mary Abbey has taken Judson Doyle along with her," I say to Iseult's back.

"And good riddance," she answers.

"I must say," Maxine Waters says with a disapproving

shake of the head, "that Mary has changed a good deal. She's not the sweet person my husband and I once knew."

"May I call you a cab, Maxine?" I ask.

"But I hate to leave you with all this mess," she answers, her glance lingering over the remains of the turkey.

"We'll manage," Pat tells her.

But she decides to walk and we send her on her way, half of a pumpkin pie and some leftover cranberry sauce hugged in her arms. When I return to the kitchen, Pat has poured herself a glass of wine; Iseult continues sudsing and rinsing.

"Well, it seems we have had a theft," I say.

"Oh, don't," Pat starts up.

"A theft of what?" Iseult turns about quickly.

"A piece of Pat's jewelry is missing . . ."

"It's worth nothing," Pat says quickly. "Really, I don't want to talk about it."

"You don't suppose that your girl . . ." Iseult says. Then, very angry, "Ay, the thieving bitch. She did it! As sure as I'm standing here, she took it."

"Oh, please," Pat says wearily, sips her wine. "Let's forget it."

"Forget it?" Iseult explodes. "It's a disgrace to us and you ask me to forget it."

"Well, it was probably my fault," Pat begins.

"Not at all. That traitorous bitch." She gnashes her teeth, and I fear for Emtie, guilty as she might be. "Burning oil is too good for her." She looks about the kitchen as if for a weapon. "Oh, if I could get my hands on her."

"Cool it, Izzy," Pat says, a hint of impatience in the tone.

"Well, you'll never see it again. She's pawned it by

now. Oh, I know the type. It's the shame of the nation. I hope it wasn't very valuable," she says with some interest.

"It wasn't worth anything," Pat answers, though she is looking at me. Then she gets up like an eighty-year-old woman. "I have to go to bed. It's been a big day for me. I betcha that first barbecue wasn't as exciting as this one."

"The patio in Plymouth," I answer, "really started something."

"Secrets of the Pilgrim grill," my wife adds. Iseult regards us raptly. "Good night, all," my wife says, and, passing me, puts three fingers in my belly. "Keep it down, lover."

The warning does not go unnoticed by Iseult, who snorts and turns back to the dishes. There are still a few ashtrays to be dumped, and isolated cups and glasses to be collected in order to restore the front room to its Union Station waiting-room atmosphere. And one of the glasses I bring to the kitchen is the one with red diamonds.

"It's sort of funny about Mary Abbey going off with Judson Doyle," I say to Izzy. "You don't suppose he'll break training, do you?"

"Hah!" The blond head goes back and a dish is slapped into the rack. "Him and his training rules. That's the only soft thing about him, is his training rules."

"I'm sorry to hear it," I say evenly.

"Why? What's it your business? It means nothing to me, I can assure you."

"Well, he seems like a strong, healthy young man and since there's the possibility that Mary Abbey may have a venereal disease—only temporarily, of course—it just seems a shame, that's all." Iseult presses against the sink and closes her eyes, perhaps in mourning for the fate of a national champion.

"That's shameful." She swings around. "You're putting me on?"

"No, I'm afraid not. But on the other hand, it may be nothing—perhaps nothing more than a bad cold. The results of her Wassermann are not known."

"You're a pig, do you know that?" she says. "And talking about such dirty things on one of your holy days at that."

"Thanksgiving is not a holy day," I answer. "In any event, it's somehow appropriate. Kind of keeps the tradition going, if you go for keeping tradition going. Supposedly, Columbus brought the first dose back from the New World. No, I think it's altogether fitting—holy day and all."

The dish towels are folded, plates and silverware put away and the garbage neatly packaged, all done with precise haste, indicating an eagerness to quit this place.

"How about a drink?" I say.

"No, no, thank you. I must be on my way."

"You mustn't be disturbed about this theft, if it is a theft."

"I'm not disturbed," she answers quickly. "Well, of course I'm disturbed," she decides.

"We're used to being stolen from, you know. In my country there's a whole tradition surrounding servants stealing from their masters. Whole refrigerators of food are emptied out at the end of the week and smuggled out the back door."

"What do you do about it?"

"When they are caught—and they are nearly all Negroes —we lynch them on the nearest tree." Her gray eyes are like coins, her mouth ajar.

"You're a terrible man," she finally says.

"Come on, have a drink. One for the road."

"There you're teasing me again, and with the poor creature sick upstairs."

"Well, then do a favor for me. Will you return the book your father loaned me, the story of Maureen?"

"I'll do that," she says, grateful for the alternative.

While she puts on her coat, I look for the translation of Maureen's martyrdom. It's not among the books on the mantel, nor is it with those on the floor. "I can't seem to find it right at the moment."

"Well, no matter. I must be off," she says, not looking me in the face, a flurry of superfluous attention to her hair, the coat collar, the rest of her. We stand at the door.

"What will you do tonight?" I ask.

"What will I do tonight?" she repeats resentfully. Then, thinking it over, "I may get bonkers, stony blind."

"You know we . . . I really like you."

"Don't do me any favors."

"We can be friends, can't we?" I say, which brings a snort, and I lean forward to give her a kiss, purely a gesture of friendship.

"What are you about?" She spits out. Hands come up like claws and I back away. She grabs at the knob, swings open the door and takes the steps down at breakneck speed.

Another inspection of the books confirms the suspicion I had when I first looked; the translation of St. Maureen's delaying action with the Norsemen has disappeared, has been taken. "I think we've had another theft," I tell Patricia in the darkened bedroom. She lies on top of the bed, knees up around the great beach ball of her belly.

"What?"

"I think Mary Abbey has taken that book Dean Morraugh loaned me."

"Oh, yeah." She's not at all interested. "Why does she want it?"

"It remains to be seen. How do you feel?"

"Oh, all right." Her voice is small. She rolls over on her back, pulls up to a half-sitting position against the pillows. "How did you and Izzy make out?"

"Terrific. She's a regular mink. You want to hear about it?"

"You're not going to be one of those dirty old men Edna was always warning me about, are you?" She takes my hand and plunks it down on the high mound that holds our child.

"I don't even seem to get the chance to be a dirty young man. Look, Patricia, I promise you I'll get the key back."

"Don't promise that," she says. "Anyway, I don't even care about it anymore. It doesn't mean anything anymore. You're so romantic, so gullible."

"What do you mean?"

"How do you know I didn't pick it up in a hock shop somewhere . . ."

"You don't mean that."

"Well, I could have," she says soberly. "I could have just as easily, because that's all it means now. I mean, everything that happened before is . . . all gone. It's finished." A soft ripple, like a rolling bubble of gas, has just passed under my hand.

"That's him," Pat says, a silly grin on her.

"Really?" I press my cheek against her to listen for something.

"You know I was lying here," she continues, "thinking of how you used to tell me about things. Just before we would fall asleep. Remember? And I had it all figured out to ask you something silly, like why did the Kerensky government fail, and then the small descendant flicked me in the ribs and I said to myself, it's time to kick all that."

"He's not making any movement," I say.

"He's all right," she assures me. "Did you hear what I was saying?"

"Well, what do you want me to tell you now?"

"About the future," she answers, but this I cannot do.

5

"Now, Marie Therese," I say to the wide snow field of her face, "let's go through this again." In the front hall by the staircase we stand. "You say the beggars came to the door."

"Right, sir. You and the missus had gone down the street and I was just fixing your tea when the doorbell rang."

"So you came from the kitchen to the front door, like this." I walk the route. "Then what?"

"I open the door and there's this beggar woman and her little boy. They ask for a few coppers, so I go back to the closet to me purse to get some."

"Not closing the door?"

"Well, save me, I didn't think at the time," she says. Roses bloom in the snow.

"So then you come back to the door and you find the woman alone." She nods quickly, blue eyes bright. "And then you hear something upstairs . . ."

"Ah, the dirty little beast. I rush up the stairs to find him in your bedroom, his fists full of the missus's things, and a great blanket of a bag on the floor. Oh, how we wrestled, sir! I shake it out of him, drag him down the stairs and send them on their way with a curse, God forgive me. Ah, if I'd only known, if I'd only known, sir. I thought I'd taken everything from him. That's why I never mentioned it to you or the missus before—it seemed all right."

"Okay, now, Marie Therese," I say. "I'm going to stand here at the door—outside and ring the bell, and you answer it just as you did before." The eyes haze over, but she retreats to the kitchen. I stand outside, check my watch and ring the bell. She comes to the door, self-consciously, unsure of her lines in this comedy. "Right. Now, I've asked for money and you go to get it, come back to the door and then rush up to the bedroom." She turns on her heel and is off at a trot to the closet near the kitchen. I run up the stairs to the bedroom and start gathering jewelry and clothing together. I can hear her running back to the door, panting and puffing up the stairs, two at a time. She barrels into the bedroom, frightened, nearly skids to a stop and waits uncertainly, flicking at some dust on the windowsill with her apron.

"That took approximately forty seconds from the time you left the front door to go to your purse," I tell her. "Now I can't see how the boy had the time to gather all the things together you say he did in forty seconds."

"Ah, he was a very devil, sir. You should have seen him, you should have heard him curse me when I took the things away . . ."

"Marie Therese," I interrupt, "let me say it would have been impossible for him to do all those things." She stares back at me, eyes clear as mountain water. "Impossible, do you understand?"

"They train them, you know. It's terrible things they do with their children. You don't know, sir. They train them to be thieves."

"It would have been impossible," I repeat, looking straight at her, but her eyes freeze over, deflect my stare.

"For you see, there's more than just the medal missing."

"Saints preserve us," she says.

"There are three of my wife's sweaters and a bottle of perfume . . ."

"Ah, but the missus gave me a bottle of . . ."

"I know about that. This is another bottle of perfume I'm talking about. Three sweaters and a bottle of perfume." She sucks her lower lip and looks at the floor.

"Ah, he was cunning," she finally says. "He must have stuffed them up his jacket and I didn't see them. Ah, forgive me, sir, and I thought I had protected your personals and I failed."

"Are you sure this is the way it happened?" The red patches on her cheeks enlarge, the color spilling down her neck. "Are you sure about this, Marie Therese?"

"Preserve me, it is, sir. Ah, Mr. Phillips, you can take the stolen articles out of me pay. I'll work it off, for whatever the sweaters were worth."

"That won't be necessary. I don't want that. We just want the things back, especially the medal. It means a great deal to my wife—it has no real value."

"Ah, I know, I know," she says with a maddening certainty. "It's a holy medal for sure. Its value is for the soul."

"Marie Therese," I begin and then turn away to put down the noise rising in my throat; an incredible, frustrating laugh of defeat. "I want to believe what you say but the facts are just against it. The time is just against it."

"He was terrible fast," she offers in a soft voice.

"It could not have happened the way you say it did. Not in forty seconds. Are you sure, are you sure this is how you want to explain it?" She rocks a bit on her feet, her face has become expressionless, numb.

"You don't mean, sir, that you—that you think I may have taken—ah, God save me," she nearly screams, and it looks as if she might swoon. "Oh, sir, I swear on my mother's poor heart, on the Holy Writ itself—oh, never, sir." Her look is reproachful. "Do you think that of me?"

And, for some reason, I shake my head.

"Don't you think you're being icky?" Pat asks, pulling a long strand of wool yarn from the bag at her feet, the knitting needles clacking. "I mean, that Phi Bete key seems to mean more to you than to me."

"But what about the sweaters and the perfume?"

"Well," she shrugs, "I never noticed them gone, I hadn't worn them for a while. Maybe I don't need them."

"But is that an excuse for someone to steal them?" I ask. We speak softly in the living room, doors closed, since Emtie is preparing the tea tray in the kitchen.

"You surprise me," she says, pausing to undo a stitch and then continuing, "I never thought you'd be so hung-up on possessions."

"It's not the possessions, it's the whole idea. Maybe I'm fed up with the holier-than-thou attitude around here. I get it in the classroom, from everybody. We're always the baddies, we're always the immoral ones."

"But why should they be any different?" she asks.

"Should I serve tea, missus?" Emtie says from around the door. I wonder how long she's been standing there.

"Ah, Mr. Phillips, you don't know how I feel about this. The shame of it and to think that I recommended the girl in the first place. Iseult tells me your wife is upset— Mrs. Morraugh sends her deepest sympathy."

His office is gloomy and the windows are dark with clouds, but a beam of sunlight, almost a trick of stage lighting, strikes his head, dazzling the fringe of hair and the bald pate. It's an apocalyptic effect that I am sure Dean Morraugh has somehow arranged.

"Well, it has been very distressing," I say, sitting across the desk from him.

"Distressing? Distressing? My dear fellow, you're very mild in your language. To think that she has lain in your bosom like a serpent all this time, and all the while has been pilfering your belongings and you've been so good to her. Oh, I know, I know. Iseult has told me of the things your wife has given her, and then, of course, there's the privilege of being in your home. She's a perfidious, lying creature, make no mistake. Well, we shall deal with her, have no fear about it, we shall deal with her." His voice is coolly ominous and I can almost hear the rack and wheel being greased up in some subterranean chamber. The sunbeam has been shut off momentarily and his head disappears with it. But my eyes slowly accommodate the shadows. The colorless stones of his eyes are fixed with a murderous glaze.

"Well, it may not have been Marie Therese, but if it was, I'm sure she's been punished enough by herself with the guilt," I say, for I begin to fear for her.

"Ah, you don't know these people the way I do," he says swiftly. That light is turned on again and I must look away momentarily from its brilliant intensity. "Being an American, you always think the best of people. You don't know these people the way I do, you don't know the struggle we've had to give them self-respect, to break down their old lazy, thieving habits." He gets up from his chair, leaving the spotlight, and goes to the window. "You don't know how this depresses me, Mr. Phillips. All the blood, all the blood and the planning and the dreams go for naught when something like this comes up. And to think I recommended her. It's a blot upon my name." He speaks looking down at the street below.

"Oh, I wouldn't say you're responsible, Dean Morraugh . . ."

"But, I am—I am. She *is* my responsibility," and the fact of it makes him clench his jaw and smash the three-fingered fist into the undamaged hand. "And by God, I'll take care of her. I'll teach her a lesson she'll never forget." The abbreviated fist smacks again. "She'll wish she was never born." It cracks again.

"I think we should be fair," I say, sorry that I told Iseult about it. "After all, we really are not certain that she did do this . . ."

"She did, she did," he waves me down. "Make no mistake about it. I know the way these people work, behave. I know them, you don't. What approximately is the worth of the lot?"

"Well, the key has no value except as a memento," to which he nods and grievously sighs, "but I totaled the rest up for the police and it comes to . . ."

"You've been to the police?" he asks quietly.

"Why, yes."

"You've been to the police? You've told them about her?"

"No, of course not. I just reported the theft, gave them the list of articles. I thought that maybe the medal might turn up in a pawnshop or—"

"Good Christ on the cross, man, do you know what you've done?" He springs back to the desk, back into the spotlight, the roly-poly softness of him gone. "What police did you go to?"

"Well, the local precinct or district or whatever . . ."

Morraugh picks up the phone on his desk and shouts, "Get me . . . no, never mind." He slams it down, then starts to pick it up but pulls his hand back as if the instrument were hot. "Blue balls of fire," he says and turns away, hands clasped behind his back. The shoulders are squared, tense. "Do you know what you've done? You've ripped it good and proper, that's what you've done."

"Well, it seemed like the usual thing to do."

"You know what they'll do, don't you? She's the logical suspect. They'll get a search warrant, and they may find your precious things and they may not—but they certainly won't find her. She'll be off to England or to Holland before them and with a warrant out for her. That's what you've done, Mr. Phillips." His voice is that of a firing squad commander.

"Well, what are the police for?"

"What do you know about police? We have our own ways of handling these things." He still is not looking at me.

"It sounds as if your ways of handling things would be more extreme than what the police will do."

"What do you know about it?"

"Dean Morraugh, you apparently are very upset about Marie Thesese's actions reflecting upon you, but we don't think about it that way at all." I speak to the dark shadow of his back. "We consider her an individual, responsible for her own actions, so it is just between her and us and the police. This is the way we would like to handle it. It has nothing to do with you."

"Responsible for her own actions?" he says wonderingly, as if I have introduced a new thought into Western civilization. "Responsible for her . . . why, man, how can she be responsible for anything, least of all her own actions? We've been slaves in our own country for centuries, without a pot to piss in, and suddenly a girl like that is responsible for her own actions? Have you no sense?"

"Well, let's say it's a lesson to be learned. It's hard, I know, but it's one way to learn respon—"

"What are you talking about?" He wheels around, the face white and mouth wet with spit. "Who are you coming over here, leaving your valuables about, tempting a poor creature that's never had a penny for her . . ."

"We didn't leave them lying about," I try to explain, to describe our bedroom with its lack of bureaus, lack of drawers. "Anyway, I fail to see why we are responsible for tempting her, as you call it. . . . Look, we're not the ones that have broken the law."

"The law, the law," he cries, wringing his hands. "Ah, the poor creature, the poor creature. What will happen to her? She'll go to the streets of London." The thought of Emtie singing music-hall favorites under the streetlamps of Piccadilly while drumming up trade seems farfetched.

"Oh, come on now, Dean Morraugh." The ball bearings roll over me and he swings around to the window, arms against the casement, supporting a deep concentration. "You know," I continue, smothering a desperate laugh, "ever since we arrived here, we've been cross-examined by all of you about our problems in America. And here we are with the same kind of situation, the same kind of thing we used to call the white man's burden. The same thinking. It's all right to take the law into your own hands to punish someone, but don't give that person the chance to behave responsibly to stand up with the law. Treat them like children, take care of them but don't give them the chance to be responsible—because that means freedom, too.

And when they do wrong, punish them like naughty children, outside the law. It's the same kind of thinking to be found in Mississippi, the same kind of thing your friend Smith-Royce likes to throw his barbs into, but here it is right here. It's the same morality."

"What do you know of morality?" he says quietly, face leaning against arms. "If it works then it becomes moral, that's your brand. It it's practical then it's moral. Dump your liquid fire on those innocent people in Vietnam and if you burn enough of them, blast enough of them—if it works out then it has been moral. . . . You've kept your moral commitment."

"Now wait a minute . . ."

"Don't give me a lecture on morality, Mr. Phillips. I know about your brand of morality. My daughter put me on to you from the beginning." I can only look at his back and he turns around at my silence. "Yes, that's stopped you, hasn't it? You didn't think I suspected anything about you, did you—giving me all that kalabash about this university being like the Industrial Revolution? Do you think I believe that sort of nonsense? Who do you take me for? Didn't anyone tell you of what I did in our revolution? That was my field—intelligence." I am trying to shift thoughts and subjects to catch up with him. "A man like you who could have a teaching post nearly anywhere he wants . . ."

"Not really . . ."

"Don't tease me, Mr. Phillips, I was once a man of violence." He means it, no question about it, and takes one, two steps toward me.

"But I couldn't uncover it, and it was there all along," he laughs lightly at his own blindness, "and then Iseult showed me the piece in the magazine. And it was one of your own magazines at that." That's even funnier to him. "Tell me, Mr. Phillips, why did they send you here? Is it because of the scholarships we're giving to the African students? What was it?"

"Why did who send me here?" I ask.

"Your CIA. Come on, let's have it," he urges chummily, one secret agent to another. "What was the reason? It's all up now, you might as well come clean."

"Dean Morraugh, I don't know what you're talking about."

"It's all in print, it's all been exposed. Your foundation has been supported for years by your CIA."

"Look Dean Morraugh. This is a dreadful mistake you're making. These were peculiar circumstances . . ."

"Indeed, indeed," he says wisely.

"But I needed a job and I had a friend"—and as I talk I wonder about Art Levy as a friend—"and he has something to do with the Foundation and . . ."

"Yes, yes. Of course, you needed a job." His voice is thick with sarcasm. "And of course, you have a friend who just happened to send you here. Come now, Mr. Phillips, do you take me for a fool? Don't you think I know how these matters are handled?" There's the barest smile on his face, the genial face of an inquisitor being lenient before the screw is turned. I can only return the stare and shake my head dumbly. Exasperation with me and then sorrow compete for his expression, the former winning out. "Ah, well, there are more important wheels to fix," he says and becomes frantic once more, some inner conflict pushing him to the phone yet pulling him back until he finally stands transfixed in the middle, hands clasped before his face. "Ah, that poor creature you've done in. You're a heartless people, Mr. Phillips—heartless. I must go to her," he says quickly, compassion rising in his face to spill from the gray eyes. "Yes, yes," he says to himself, for I obviously no longer exist. "Yes, I must go to her." He pulls on a heavy trench coat, scarf, and dusty bowler. "Go to her," he whispers to himself and leaves me sitting in his office with the busts and stuffed bird.

Patricia pauses in her sweeping of the rug in the hall when I come in, pauses to straighten herself up, a hand pressed into the middle of her back to brace a burdened spine. "Well, they found the perfume," she says, motioning to the hall table. There's a bottle of Chanel near a stack of bills that have been the day's mail.

"I'm sorry," I say, suddenly very tired. "Was anything else found?"

"No, just the perfume," she says, continuing her sweeping. "I made some cinnamon toast for tea," she says, not looking at me. "I didn't feel like going out in the rain to get anything else. Oh, and there's a number you're supposed to call." She leans the broom against the wall and walks to the kitchen. "It's the detective at the police station."

"Ah, yes, Mr. Phillips." A clean, careful voice comes over the receiver. "We searched the girl's premises and found only the one article which your wife had identified."

"There was nothing else?"

"No, I'm afraid not. Either she has given it away or sold the other things. We gave it a thorough job, you can be sure."

"Was she there?"

"No, she wasn't, but we have a warrant out for her,

and we'll find her, never fear." His voice is quietly assured, with an amused inflection, as if anyone like Marie
Therese could ever escape them.

"Well, what do we do now?" I ask.

"There's nothing more for you to do, Mr. Phillips. It
will all proceed now on its own, as it were."

"Look here, can we just forget it?" I ask.

"Ah, no, Mr. Phillips, we can't do that." He's patient, a
little disappointed. "Since we found the one article, the
charge is automatically made by us. It's out of your hands
entirely now. You have nothing more to do with it any
longer. I'm sorry it's happened to you. You're from the
States? I have a brother over there living in the city of
Pittsburgh, Pennsylvania. I don't suppose you might know
him?"

"Well, then she'll have a trial?"

"Oh, yes, all fair and proper."

"Well, will she have an attorney—we want to make
sure she is represented in court."

"Ah, that's very good of you, Mr. Phillips. Very good,
indeed. But it's all been taken care of and she'll have a
good barrister standing with her, you can be sure of it.
It's a shame it's happened to you. Of course, we see it all
the time, and if more of our people did what you've done,
we'd all be better for it, that's for sure." The cool, detec-
tive-policeman's voice talks on. I can almost visualize him
getting comfortable in his chair, eyes roaming importantly
around the station house, while he talks to the American.

"Yes, well, thank you. You'll keep us posted."

"That I will," he says, obviously sorry the conversation
is over.

In the kitchen, Patricia sets out the tea things, a stack

of cinnamon toast, dry from storage in the warm oven, the cups and pot. I sit on the stool and look at her, thinking of all those times last spring and during the summer— all of those happy, crazy moments that have become dim in my memory, lozenges dissolving upon the tongue. She looks at me curiously now and then, and her hands move nervously to her hair, pull it back and refasten the large silver clip gleaming in the black fold.

"What are we going to do?" she asks finally.

"There seems to be nothing we can do," and I look at her.

The large brown eyes are like a child's, ready to cry with resentment from some undeserved punishment.

"I feel we've done something very wrong," she says. "It's like . . . like putting dresses on Fiji Islanders or something."

"Well, it's become even more complicated," I say and tell her about my supposed status as a secret agent. "So it seems Iseult's interest was not in my body but only some sort of counterespionage."

"You have a nice body," Pat says soothingly, though that makes me feel worse. "But I've had good news," she continues, sipping her tea. "I got a note from Mary Abbey. Her Wassermann was negative."

"That's good. Where is she?"

"She's flown back. She wrote from the airport. She also said thanks for the book." Her smile widens into a laugh but there is more desperation than amusement in it.

I sit beside her on the kitchen stool beneath the light hanging from the ceiling. The wind rattles the leaves in the garden and the long branch of a rose tree scrapes at the window.

"Maybe we should go home," I say after a moment.

"Where's home?" Pat asks.

"My usefulness is at an end here. I'm no longer a teacher. I'm a foreign agent, as far as they're concerned."

"Why don't we become tourists . . . American tourists," Pat says, licking cinnamon from a finger. "We're good at that."

"See America first," I suggest.

"You know," Pat says, "I said the other day that Phi Bete key meant more to you than it did to me, and I'm beginning to think I was right. I don't need, haven't needed anything like that to tell me who I am, not since I became your wife. You do remember that I am your wife?" she says, nudging me, then pulling one of my arms across her heavy belly.

And though I snort to underscore the question's absurdity, it strikes me that if I had not forgotten her, I had not accepted her. For several months I had been behaving like someone driving a car while looking out through the rearview mirror.

But the past is never dead, since it is part of the human predicament to be able to remember it. Pieces of the past rise through the memory like sparks from burning leaves or, as some science-fictionists tell us, like the sounds and noises of history that remain suspended in the echoless chamber of the ionosphere.

"You mean to tell me," Patricia said, "that up there somewhere is Marc Antony's speech over Caesar? In Latin? I don't believe it."

"I don't either, but it's a theory," I answered. We were leaning against the rail of the small Cunard liner that took

us from America. We searched the sky for famous say-
ings. Two days ago we had passed the silhouette of
Martha's Vineyard and, far beyond, that of Cape Cod
slipped by on the port side, the beach where we had
walked and sunned only a faint line on the horizon.

"How much longer will it be?" Pat asked, continuing
our morning stroll.

"Oh, about seven days," I said.

"Seven more days on this tub," she murmured grimly.
"He doesn't believe in flying. The ocean voyage will do
us good, he said. It will relax us. Hah!" And the black
hair swirled with derision.

"Well, we would not have gotten the sense of traveling,
the idea of going somewhere, if we had flown over," I
argued.

"Listen, if you had what I have, you would certainly
get the full flavor, the full sense of traveling, all right.
Yagh," she gasped and made an exaggerated lunge for a
stanchion, for there was only a gentle swell on the sea.
Actually, those first bouts of morning sickness were long
past and in her third month there was only a slight thick-
ening of the long cello of her torso.

"Oh, it's not that bad," I said. "I think it's a nice little
ship . . ."

"A nice little ship," she echoed me.

"And the food is pretty good," I continued, guiding her
around a lifeboat. "Come on, just two more turns around
the deck."

"You're the living end." She stalked the deck beside
me, hands deep in the pockets of a stadium coat. The hood
was thrown back, her face framed by an olive-green cowl.
"Say," she moved up to me, "wouldn't you like to drop

off in the stateroom for a few minutes?" Her tongue bathed the leer on her lips. Patricia trying to look lascivious sometimes resembles a drunken pumpkin.

"Keep moving," I told her. "It's almost time for bouillon."

"Bouillon! Crimininnies."

"And by the way, I don't think you showed the proper attitude during the lifeboat drill yesterday," I said.

"Oh yeah." Her face was dark.

"Well, it's one thing to complain about life preservers, but there was no need to keep talking about 'all that smoke in the cabin'!"

"Everybody's so serious in first class," she answered. "They seem to be having much more fun in the tourist section. Can't we go in now?" she begged just as we rounded the aft deck. "We haven't done the top bunk," she added as an additional motive.

"Just one more turn," I told her.

"A nice, quiet, relaxing sea voyage, he says. I might as well be back with Company C. Left-right, left-right," and she marched down the deck.

My reasons for going by ship did have something to do with the sense of travel, of going from one place to another, but there were other reasons. The pregnancy had created a new relationship between us and we needed time, perhaps, to adjust to it before settling down into the entirely strange atmosphere of Europe, time to fondle a few memories, good-luck mementos, before confronting the unknown.

When there were just the two of us, the idea of going to Europe did have a kind of exciting escapism about it, a running away from what someone once called "the great promiscuous grave" of America. I felt as much of an orphan as Patricia was, in fact, and there is a remedy for such conditions in becoming a foreigner in a strange land, a sort of double negative of identification which becomes a positive. So there had been the idea of the two of us doing the expatriate bit, return tickets tucked into our passports. But no definite schedule.

But there was a calendar, it turned out, a daily measurement of time ticking inside Patricia which established a schedule for us with every heartbeat. There were three of us now, and I admit an initial resentment to this intrusion, but after her first outburst that morning in Wellfleet, Patricia seemed very happy with the idea of motherhood and I caught the mood from her. But our plans had to be changed.

"You know, having this baby," she told me later in our stateroom, "is a little like putting everything back on the right track. It's not just me being illegitimate and this kid being legit, but it's like finding the piece of a puzzle."

As she changed for dinner, I sat in the chair glancing through Fielding's travel guide to Europe, trying not to look at her. She wore only a mini-length chemise, and her legs were brown and bare.

"According to Fielding," I said, "there's only one decent restaurant in Alclair."

"You're not listening to me," she said airily. "Anyway, why do you want to eat out when you've got me for a cook?"

"I'm listening," I said, turning with a heavy heart to the section listing the gastronomical treasures of Paris.

"It's almost like starting all over again for me," she said, her voice coming from the small bathroom. She stood before the mirror to shave her underarms, one foot resting on the other. It was a pretty sight made piquant by the studious, absorbed look in her face as she carefully pulled the razor up and over the soft nook. "It's not as if I ever thought I wouldn't have babies," she said as I sliced into the heavy cuisine of Germany, "but I never really associated the two things—you know, doing it and being pregnant. That's funny, isn't it?"

"Ignorant is more like it," I said. Water splashed in the sink.

"Oh, don't be square," she said. According to Fielding, the name of the best bartender in Munich is Erich, but Pat was half nude, the narrow straps of the chemise slipped down over her arms so it hung from her waist. She leaned over the sink washing under her arms and the marvelous breasts swung free. Set in the large aureoles, the dark, stubby nipples seemed larger than usual either because of the cold water or from some pregnancy change, but for whatever reason, they put a torch to Fielding's travel tips.

"No you don't," she said, quickly grabbing a towel when I came toward her. "Have a peach." She diverted my attention to the remains of Edna Gates's bon voyage basket. "You're such a stinker." Her eyes glinted within the harlequin frames. "You'll just have to wait." So I had a peach, and it was nearly time for dinner anyway.

The old habit of looking for an orderly sequence of events, of passing from one era to the next as in history, was probably the main reason for taking the boat. By plane we would have slipped from America to Europe in six hours, and it seemed to me we would lose something in gaining time. What measurement I hoped to find, I cannot say, but halfway between the new world and the old, the engines of the ship stopped and we floated silently in a calm, overcast sea.

"The steward said they're making some minor repairs on the generators or something," Pat told me. "Come out on deck. It's creepy."

And it was very peculiar to stand on the deck of a silent, motionless ocean liner with not a ripple on the becalmed water, everything colorless as it was soundless, save for an occasional scrap of conversation coming from some other deck, and to wait expectantly—for what? The sound of an oarlock somewhere out there, the past rowing into the present.

"It's strange," Patricia said, leaning out over the flat water, "but I just thought of that spot in Wellfleet where Teddy Roosevelt sent that message to George V."

"Marconi's radiotelegraph? What makes you think of that?"

"Well, first, it was such a dopey message—all that business about the people of the United States sending the people of Great Britain good wishes and all that—who needs that? He could have said that in a letter. He should have said something like, Me and Alice just wanted to say hello to you and Mary—Hoo-hoo! Something like that."

"Man's words are not always up to his great moments," I told her.

"But it's more than that." She lit a cigarette and dropped the match overboard. We could hear it hiss when it hit the flat sea.

"Do you really think it's possible the dit-dots of that silly message are still floating around up there?" We both looked up at the blank slate of the morning sky.

"Sure it's possible, but not probable. Why?"

"Well, it would be all too depressing," she said. "Here we are going nowhere in the middle of the ocean while overhead float the dull tootlings of Teddy Roosevelt. It's like being part of one of those goofy murals in a post office. It's all hung up." She took a final drag on the cigarette and tossed it over, and once again there was a hiss of fire and water, only louder. The cigarette floated in the sea beside the drifting hull. A short distance away, the match bobbed gently on the surface. "You know," she shook her hair back, "I could sure go for some of that bouillon."

"It's probably too early for bouillon," I said, meeting her side glance. "However . . ."

Several days later, when the green bulk of the first European landfall raised mysteriously on the horizon like a resurfacing Atlantis, I recognized the hiatus in mid-Atlantic had also marked a turning point for us. That interruption of our passage, brief as it was—for the engines began to throb just as we happily overcame the restrictions imposed by the upper bunk—was a vacuum into which all the scraps and souvenirs of the past had disappeared. We held each other and passed from one into the other as deftly as we passed from one hemisphere into another, the actual, instantaneous beat of our hearts sending the only viable message.

"What's the Morse code for 'Hoo-hoo'?" Pat asked, her fingertips delicately tapping my back. As a historian, my days were numbered.

December 10, 1966
San Terenzo, Italy

DEAR HAMILTON,

Your letter was forwarded to me and, as you can see, we also have forsaken the native shore for this pleasant hideout on the Mediterranean.

Yes, the balloon went up and I'm genuinely sorry that an innocent bystander like you got caught in the ropes. I'm also sorry you feel the way you do. I never told you about some of our operations (actually, our interests in information assessments represented a very small fraction of our total "good works")—well, there was simply no need for you to know about them. Anyway, it got you a free ride to Europe, and I thought I was doing you a favor.

Apparently, the coverage was not much where you are or you would have known about it sooner. The story broke here about a month after you left and we were front-page stuff for a couple of weeks. I had to resign, of course, and be properly shocked and astounded by the revelations. And it's just as well, for Judy has been after me to take a rest, and I was beginning to get bored with the operation.

How do I justify what I was doing with the way I talked, my own feelings? Well, what are my own feelings? I sometimes really don't know. But I don't suppose my little schizoid is unique. There must be millions who work one way at the office and talk another at home. Our little service, hopefully, was one way of keeping the argument in the classroom and out of the streets. We never tried or expected to win anyone over, but just keep them talking—to keep the drums going. We all know what happens when the drums stop.

If you think it will help, I'd be glad to write your dean a letter of clarification of your status. I brought some of the firm's stationery with me for a few last strings. Actually, one of my last acts was to veto a similar proposal to do same for the rest of our legits on the theory that the whole bunch would be given away, by process of elimination. But if your credibility gap is hurting you, I'd oblige you.

This is a very charming place we're in. The boys are in school in Switzerland and Judy and I are having a second honeymoon, like upper MC drop-outs. There's a grotto here where Byron is said to have taken his morning dips, and as I write you, I can look over the balcony to the bay below where Shelley set sail that last time. In the morning we stroll along the seawall built in the fourteenth century to keep out the Arabs and in the evenings we sit up here on the balcony and sip wine (yes, I'm actually developing a taste for the stuff) and watch the sun do a tightrope act on the sea. There's a bunch of South American exiles living below us—who managed to get over the wall also, but what their reasons were are unknown. Every night they get out guitars and sing very sad songs. Their bossa novas float up the air to us, Judy and I dance on our balcony. I imagine myself to be David Niven or someone as we do a stately pavane in the setting sun.

We're sorry Pat is having so much trouble with the baby. Judy had a similar thing with Joshua, he seemed to be growing in her throat rather than her womb, and she had to sleep sitting up for months.

Again, I'm sorry you got caught up in this, Hamilton, and if you cannot understand or forgive, I hope someday you'll be able to laugh at it. It's all terribly funny in an insane way. I still think I may have done you a favor and one with no strings. They're hard to come by these days.

Judy sends her love to you both as do I.

ARTHUR LEVY

Now that Emtie no longer comes to us, Patricia moves heavily about the house chores with a self-absorbed pleasure. Whether it is because of some "nesting" instinct or just to keep occupied, I cannot tell, but the effect upon her is for the good.

We take long walks together, on orders from her doctor, though we would probably do so anyway just to get out of the house. She steps beside me, self-contained and self-absorbed, feet marching straight before her with a slow, regular pace that sadly reminds me of her background with Company C. We return to a one-dish supper she has almost absentmindedly prepared, for she has served up, with a silent assurance, a series of excellent stews and cassolettes—sometimes shared with Jack Crawford.

Naturally Iseult never calls anymore, and we are not sure if she is even in the country. Maxine Waters sometimes joins us at a Chinese restaurant, and even with her, Patricia displays the same casual, friendly indifference with which she treats me, not even interested anymore in the details of Robert Lewis Waters' life and loves. Gratuitously, Maxine offers to testify on our behalf in the coming trial, which makes Patricia laugh so hard that she nearly turns blue. It is with Crawford that she seems to be most communicative, most at ease, and he calls several times a week to take her for long excursions to the zoo or along the docks or, if the weather is poor, among the cases of stuffed Arctic birds of the museum.

One afternoon, I return after a particularly trying session in American History. "What was the difference, Professor Phillips, sir, between President Lincoln's objection to England's interference in the *Savannah* matter and the American intervention in the Vietnam civil war?" I speak of commitments, of SEATO, noting the luminous eyes in the otherwise serious, sober face, and, throwing all caution to the winds, if only to bring the laughter from eyes to mouth, some response, throw in John Foster Dulles. So, feeling inept and unfit and up to here with undigested theories and platitudes, I arrive at our front gate just as the cab pulls up. She is laughing, the wonderful trill of old times that starts with the high, breathless surprise of a girl-child and descends into the hearty register of a field hockey goalie.

Crawford helps her out with courtly deference, says something to me and then goes off in the taxi. "What do you two talk about?" I ask.

"Oh, animals and birds," she says, withdrawn and foreign once again. "He knows an awful lot about animals, especially lions and tigers." And as I open the door, a marvelous aroma wafts out the front hall. "I made onion soup today," she says simply.

Patricia's self-absorption, the single-minded contentment which apparently has no room for me, is disturbing. I seek punishment for an unknown crime, redemption from guilt that lies upon my unconscious like ground mist, and perhaps for this reason my imagination tortures me with fear: her behavior is similar to that of someone on the edge of death, that exclusive, subjective preparation which shuts out all who stand around the bed. For I think of the long trip we have made together, of how we have changed each other and of how, on those nights when the moon breaks through the clouds, my eyes cannot face its brilliance. I remember her saying this once. What would I do without her?

Though the Clerk Street Courthouse was built in the early days of the eighteenth century, it was not until the present that it took on the Hogarthian rabble and atmosphere which the American tourist now sees with delighted surprise—"a find" happily captured by Kodaks. The slums that surround the hall of justice were once the dignified, correct chambers of British lawyers, where open, good-hearted debate decided the most efficacious method of prosecuting rebels brought to the dock across the street, or perhaps established the maximum possible fine that could be collected for nonpayment of rent. Baggy-socked strings of children, snot-nosed and grubby-handed, spew from the slack-jawed doorways and crash up and down the splintering, sagging steps inside. There is a continual bickering, a pepper pot stew of words inside these tenements, and though not as precise or authoritative as the walls once heard, the subjects are the same, unpaid rent and the penalty for being outside society.

The courthouse has fared better, its original purpose and continued use assuring a certain preservation. Lawyers no longer walk across the street, but ease their Mercedes and Austins through the narrow byways—tires crunching cartons and rubbish in the gutters while the drivers dreamily digest luncheons eaten across town, near Liberty Park, where opinions and a bit of steak are shared in clubs that glow and smell of lemon polish. The cars park, double-park, and generally block the small streets around the courthouse, and fines of a few pennies are paid to the ragamuffins on guard.

The courthouse is a small, handsome imitation of the Pantheon, its limestone exterior pitted and stained by time and urine, with birds' droppings, and everything plastered over with public notices, both in English and their own singular script. Inside, there is a long dark hall from which one emerges into the bright arena of the courtroom beneath a large dome, and it is just so; a large round chamber with curves of spectator benches circling three quarters of the way around the ring and nearly to the ceiling. Two narrow aisles, like Alpine paths, trisect these rows. In the pit, as it were, are several long tables and a few more pewlike seats and all facing the fourth quadrant and the high bench of the judge with a choir loft to one side and a smaller pen just opposite but only slightly elevated from the floor. It looks as if it has all been carved; the benches, jury box, judge's roost and witness cubby, all carved by some great artisan from a single enormous piece of oak, and polished and rubbed to a rich golden glow.

This is hallowed ground, as is almost every public building, for each one is marked by either blood or some memento of the long struggle for independence. Clerk Street Court had just been built in 1810 when it was the scene of the first of many trials which sent native heroes to the English gibbet. The young patriot, so unlucky to initiate the series, had not only been trapped in his fiancée's garden, but was also careless enough—the story goes—to have been trapped by the grenadiers between her thighs as well. This outrage, this successful attack upon her chastity, so angered the girl's father—a noted defender of revolutionaries and only a few years from the hemp himself—that he refused the young man's case. So the boy went to his doom undefended, though he would have been hanged in any event. But the fact that he went to his death with no one speaking for him is celebrated in legend and song, perhaps giving this people an existential insight the rest of us are only just discovering.

I take my seat in the first ring of the gallery. Candy wrappers crinkle and bones crack around me as other spectators leisurely have their lunch while waiting for the session. Some have brought thermoses of tea and a cup is passed down to me. The pit before us remains empty and the gallery waits for the afternoon's entertainment reading racing sheets and newspapers and munching chocolate creams. An official enters, strolls about the floor, leans up to check something behind the judge's bench, and papers are put down; his every move silently and gravely observed, then interpreted in hoarse whispers upon his exit.

One by one, the jurors enter through a small door high above and take their seats in the box with an uncertain, self-conscious manner like a choir that has forgotten its music. There is a wave or two to the spectators, to relatives who have come to watch them do their duty, and these sit forward now in their seats, attention gathering to a point on their foreheads and with murmurs of assurance that "he'll do the job, all right." Black-robed barristers, white wigs plopped on their heads like large fuzzy moths, file into the pit, taking up positions behind the long tables, upon which thick dossiers and folders of documents are plunked down with heavy authority. They talk among themselves self-consciously and in whispers that tease the spectators to the edge of their seats. Some stroke plump fronts beneath the black gowns, turn and survey the expectant gallery, as if to identify themselves to anyone seated there for some future reference or need.

There is a rustle of excitement around me and the name Gil Morraugh is whispered, for the Dean has just appeared at a side entrance and enters briskly into the pit with golden-haired Iseult behind. A flicker of the cold eyes behind the rimless glasses acknowledges my presence but no more, though Iseult passes, then turns back and comes to the railing. "Come to see justice done, have you?" she flings at my face before rejoining her father at one of the tables.

The people stir around me, almost moving away as if her words had splattered some offensive matter, and suspicions further hooked by the smirking glance one lawyer gives me after a whispered consultation with Dean Morraugh. Some guards have now appeared on the floor and a hush falls, an electric tension whirls in the circular chamber.

"All ye, all ye," a voice speaks from behind the desk and everyone is on his feet, some of the spectators nearly preempting the cry, jumping up with a practiced formality. The judge takes his seat, arranging his voluminous gown with near-matronly care. He is a short, plump man with a red face and a thick, fat nose. As if to show his rank, his wig seems more bleached than the others.

There are several matters, pending from previous trials, brought to the court's attention and which do not concern the jury. Nor does the judge seem particularly interested in the points made by several barristers, listening to their arguments with a distracted, almost bored gaze toward the ceiling made even more obvious by an impatient thrust of his hand that is meant to adjust his wig but actually sets it more aslant. Immediately upon the last words from the pit, he quickly passes down decisions, as if all were rehearsed, granting a retrial for two cases of burglary and denying a motion to set aside the fate of a convicted murderer. The barristers, successful and not alike, gather up their papers and pass through a side door, duties satisfied.

"Now then, can we get on with it?" the judge implores from the high bench. He takes out a heavy watch, looks at it and places it on the desk. There are assenting nods around the pit, a settling-down in the gallery and a leaning-forward of the jury, the top row threatening to topple over the one below and so on—an avalanche of peers.

A door opens and closes somewhere, and rising up from the depths of a lower region comes white-faced Marie Therese to stand in the prisoner's dock. She wears her usual blank look but I notice her neck, for the first time, exposed and plump and seemingly ready for the knife. She stands for a moment, hands clasped before her, casts a nervous smile of recognition toward the Morraughs and then stares reverently up at the judge. A clerk reads the charges.

"Accused did take from the residence of . . ." and the bare details of the charge strike my ears like sharp stones. I can feel eyes in the gallery fix upon me.

"Well, what's the plea?" the judge asks when the clerk finishes.

"Ah, your lordship!" Emtie cries out, to be struck silent by his pudgy hand and a fierce glance of his eye. He leans forward, his attention on a tall, gangly attorney with a wig too small for his large head, who has risen majestically in the pit.

"Sir. This is a most distressing and pathetic situation brought before this honored court, and I consider it not only an honor but my duty to represent this maligned and innocent personage." The judge has begun to fuss with his robes, fix his wig, fiddle with the watch. "Then, sir, the defendant is desirous of entering a plea of not guilty under provisions of Article 418 of the Penal Code which sets forth in no uncertain . . ."

"Yes. Yes. Yes. I am aware of the law, counselor," the judge interrupts. "Now then, you've entered your plea—

the jury will be made cognizant of the factor of your plea on their commission—and we may now proceed with the counselor for the State, that is, if you have no statements, counselor."

"Sir, I bend to the formality and rule of procedure," the Lincolnesque figure says, eyes twinkling, "with an alacrity that bespeaks my confidence in its ultimate justice." There is a droll look from the judge and a murmur of approval from the spectators.

"That told him," one says to another.

"Ay, he's the man for it," comes the hushed answer.

Another black-robed, wigged figure is now standing, addressing the judge, and I glance at Emtie, her head quickly turning away indicating she has seen me, has been looking at me. She stares down at her feet, passing the time of her trial as all those who stood in the same spot before her passed the time. What words of defiant patriotism rang in this chamber before the black cap of imperialism's verdict inevitably was set? Now all gone, replaced by the routine listing of stolen articles, barroom brawls and cracked skulls.

There is a police officer in the witness chair and from his voice I recognize him as the man with a brother in Pittsburgh, Pennsylvania.

"Would you tell the court what you found, Sergeant?" he's asked.

"Yes, sir. We found a bottle of Chanel perfume which was identified by the complainants as their property."

"Thereupon, you filed a warrant for the defendant's arrest, under Article 32."

"Yes, sir."

"Why was this necessary, Sergeant?"

"Well, sir, the defendant was absent from her premises."

"Absent from her premises?" The State's counselor repeats the phrase, looking up at the jury. "And you had to send out a search for her . . ."

"Sir." Young Abe is on the floor. "We ask if this is an entirely justified phrasing of the events?"

"Yes, yes," the judge nods. "There's probably a simpler way the State's counselor can put the questions, isn't there?"

"Quite right, sir. Where did you find her, Sergeant?"

"We found her walking down Mountflorry Street."

"Walking down Mountflorry Street?" the prosecutor asks, again eying the jury.

"We have ears, counselor." The judge leans forward. "There's no need to repeat the information." A snort of approval runs through the gallery. "Now, did you have anything else?"

"No, sir."

"Very well, then. Does the counselor for defense wish the witness?"

"No, sir."

"Very well," the judge says, obviously pleased with the speed of events. "We shall now hear from you."

"May it please the court," the tall barrister begins in a slow, dry voice, "we intend to show this preposterous charge has no foundation and despite what seems to be clearly damaging evidence, as just testified to by the estimable member of the constabulary, our facts will demonstrate that what may seem to be is not actually the case." The judge leans back in his chair with a sigh and stares at the ceiling, obviously preparing for an oratory.

"Here is a young woman of outstanding virtue and decorum," the barrister continues, "who is the sole support of an aged mother and father, accused of a crime that is not only beneath her in moral contemplation but is dead set—dead set, I remind the jury—against the righteous and fervent code she learned in a Christian home. And dare I say, sir, that we take pride in our nation because of the distinction we have in all the world for our Christian homes."

There is slight applause from the gallery, silenced by the sharp eye from the bench, and someone near me says, "He's right there enough." The judge continues to lean back, picking at his teeth with a fingernail.

"We do not judge the conduct of others," the barrister continues after acknowledging the gallery and a lingering look in my direction, "our laws are for that and administered by such esteemed courts as the one before which we have the honor to appear. But it is germane to our case to say, if only in passing, that there are other homes and other nations which may mock our determination within the Christian ethic—which may judge us by their own valueless agnosticism, arriving at empty and false evaluations simply because they do not possess the clear-eyed vision, framed with charity and love, given to those true children of God who follow the selfless concepts of His Son's works."

A rather burly fellow sitting next to me gets up with dramatic obviousness and moves down the bench. A woman also slides away from my right. The contaminated has been isolated.

"This then, gentlemen of the jury, is the conflict in this case—between this child of . . ."

"Counselor," the judge interrupts. "I think the interest in this case has been established. Now, are you to go on about it much more, because I would like to hear your witnesses before the jury has its tea. It's going on three o'clock now and I *could* ask the jury to forego its tea, but I would not wish to. I'm sure you agree."

"Quite so, sir," the barrister answers, glancing up at the troubled faces in the high box. "May it please the court, the defense will call but one witness, but one of such magnitude and standing in the hearts of his countrymen that he is all we need. For, in truth, sir, this trial is actually an assault upon a pure, Christian character and we fight fire with fire . . ."

"Ay, that's the stuff," someone says behind me.

"And so call upon one whose own character is of the highest order to speak for the character of my client."

"Call your witness, counselor," the judge says wearily.

"I call," and he pauses for the full effect, "Dean Gil Morraugh."

There are oohs and ahhs around me as Dean Morraugh strides to the witness box, takes the Bible in the three-fingered hand and swears the oath. His stance is militarily correct and he looks up at the jury with a commanding eye that snaps them to attention.

"Now, sir," the barrister says, "am I correct in assuming that you are the same Gil Morraugh who presided at the birth of this nation? Who, indeed, was one of the great assistants at the bed of liberty . . ."

"Counselor, I think the court is aware of Dean Morraugh's credentials and background," the judge says. A smile passes between Morraugh and the judge, an old buddy signal of recognition, and I can imagine the two of them planning an ambush behind a hedge. "In fact —and this is off the record," he tells the stenographer, "in fact, the last time I saw Dean Morraugh in this courtroom

was when he was a defendant, on trial for his life—and
we had a devil of a time springing him. Do you remember
that, Gil?"

"It was a great blast, Sergius." Morraugh rubs his hands
together, chuckling. "They never knew what hit 'em."
Titters and chuckles, thighs are slapped and sides nudged—
the courtroom bursts into applause.

"All right, now, let's get on with it," the judge says,
solemn once again, restoring decorum. "Back on the
record. Proceed, counselor."

"You've known the defendant long, Dean Morraugh?"

"I have."

"Would you tell us of her background and character?"

"Her father was a trusted and valuable member of the
Twelfth Brigade, distinguishing himself in several con-
frontations and notably at Croon's Look, where he received wounds that make his elder years painful and en-
feebling. Her mother was a Flunin, a credit to the piety
and devotion known to that family by her own good works
and deeds. This only child of their later years, willingly
sacrificing her own life for the comfort and welfare of
her aged and noble parents in the purest Christian devotion, has been known to me for . . ."

Dean Morraugh drones on, embellishing Emtie's character with a yoke of virtues that seem even too heavy for
her sturdy shoulders. She stands and listens, open-mouthed,
a look of distant recognition upon her face, which grows
pink and then scarlet with embarrassment as the rich
qualities of her character are uncovered for all to see.
When Morraugh finishes, he returns to the table and sits
beside Iseult amid muffled applause.

"He did the job," someone says.

"Sure, it's all over," another agrees.

Next comes Emtie's turn, and, led by the defense counselor, she repeats the story of the beggars ringing the bell—going for pennies from her own purse is asked for twice—and then the scramble upstairs and the courageous defense of her employer's property. Haltingly and shy of voice—the judge asking her to speak up—she tells the whole story and it obviously makes an impression on the jury.

"Think of it," a woman says behind me. "Just think of her doing that."

The State waives cross-examination, the defense has nothing further to say, and the judge, happily snapping the cover on his watch, turns to charge the jury. He speaks to them simply, unhurriedly, and looks at each one in sequence, as if they were members of his family.

". . . now with all that, you must also keep in mind, and it is my duty to remind you, of the evidence introduced by the State and which the defense has chosen to ignore. I refer to the bottle of perfume found in the defendant's home and identified as one of the missing articles. It is . . ."

"Your honor." My words stop him cold, though he continues to look up at the jury, and then, still uncertain that he has heard right, he turns a startled look toward the gallery. Chairs scrape below as those at the tables wheel around—all but Iseult, I note—and waves of whispers swirl around the chamber. "Your honor," I repeat, directing his attention.

"Just a minute." A gavel is used for the first time. "This court does not tolerate comments from the gallery."

"I know, sir," I say, "but perhaps what I have to say may help matters."

"Who is this man?" he asks the barristers in the pit. The spare defense counselor rises wearily to his feet.

"If it pleases the court, this is one of the complainants

in this case—if I am correct, sir?" he turns to ask me, though his back receives my nod.

"There's the bastard," a voice mutters behind me.

". . . and I plead presumption to make excuses for him, since as a foreigner, he is probably ignorant of our means and manners in law . . ."

"Yes, yes, yes," the judge waves down the man, then regards me across the space of the pit. He takes out his watch, looks at it, and winds the stem, the sound coming across the space like that of a cranking winch. "I assume that you wish to testify in this case? There's no need for you to do so."

"I know that, sir."

"Well, then, this is a shade irregular—how does the State feel?"

"No objections, sir."

"Defense?" There's a hurried conference between Morraugh and the barrister, who then rises.

"If it pleases the court, we would like to stay any objection we may have until after we hear what Mr. Phillips has to say . . ."

"Very well. Come down, Mr. Phillips. We will hear you."

I step over outstretched feet and obtrusive knees, and down the steps into the pit. I take the oath in the witness box, conscious of Emtie's heavy breathing nearby. She had given me one frightened look as I passed her and now stares at the floor.

"Very well, now, Mr. Phillips," the judge says, one hand supporting his head, further displacing the white wig. Up close the blue veins in his nose are discernible.

"Well, sir, its about this bottle of perfume," I say. My voice sounds distant, almost as if someone else were talking. "There's been a mistake about the bottle of perfume, for actually—as it turns out—this is a bottle of perfume which my wife had given to her some time before. It had been a gift."

"But it had been identified to the police as otherwise," the judge says, fixing me with teary blue eyes.

"That's true, sir, but my wife had mistakenly identified it." Then, taking a deep breath, "For you see, sir, my wife is with child, and though this state is a blessed one and is the holy, natural fulfillment of a woman's holy role as given by the Creator," which brings a hard side glance from him, "well, sir, there are also sometimes complications. Tension. Nerves. It is due to the nervous tension brought on by her—by her blessed condition, that led my wife to falsely mistake this bottle of perfume for the one that is actually missing."

"And you've only just discovered this?" he says dryly. "Well, then, I don't suppose there are any objections from defense counsel? No, I thought not. State? No. Well, it seems there's been a mistake, and one which has caused a number of people a good deal of effort, I might add." He looks at me sharply. His nose seems to swell with anger and it has become purple. "If there's no objection from counsel, I shall dismiss the jury and void this deliberation. The defendant is released and you, Mr. Phillips, may step down."

Cheers from the gallery answer the crack of the gavel, backs are slapped and the barristers form a black group around Iseult and Morraugh, her hair shining among the dull white wigs. Emtie and I stand alone, with no one to talk to but each other, she still regarding the floor—though now out of the paneled dock.

"I'm sorry, Marie Therese."

"Ah, well," she says. "It's over now." Then she looks me full in the face. "And you were a real gentleman to come here and speak for me. I had wanted to ask you, but still didn't want to get you involved in it—with the missus so close to her time and all. Ah, but you were a gentleman to do that for me, sir, to speak up for me defense, and I won't forget it. You have the prayers of my parents until they are taken, that's for sure." There's a thin gold chain around her neck, but whatever it holds is hidden in the deep canyon of her bosom.

"Emtie," I say, trying to phrase it right, and then choosing the simplest, "We need you."

"Ah, indeed," she says softly.

"Would you come back?"

"Well, I don't know. The Dean Morraugh has asked me to help his missus during the week."

"Perhaps for just certain days if not for the whole week."

"Ah, now," she says brightly, "as it happens, I've got Tuesdays and Thursdays open."

"Well, Mr. Hamilton Phillips, you think you've pulled it off, do you?" Iseult's thin face is set and her eyes are those of her father. "But you won't get away with it, Mr. Cloak and Dagger," and she almost shakes her finger in my face.

"Come on now, Izzy. There have been mistakes made all the way around. Can't we forget all this and . . ."

"Ah, no." She shakes her head, and turns to Marie Therese. "Can we take you home, dear?" she says softly, her narrow back blocking me off, an arm going around the plump shoulders and moving away like a grieving survivor.

The courtroom is nearly empty, and I wait until the

last of the spectators file out before leaving. Out in the street, the urchins run up to me like pigeons after peanuts but just as quickly disperse when they realize I am on foot and there's nothing to gain. But a beggar approaches as I round the corner, and I put a hand in my pocket but then leave it there and walk on. She merely shrugs and steps back to her post inside a doorway.

6

"$\mathbf{W}$E MUST LOOK LIKE HELL FROM SHORE," MY father once said to me. We had been sailing our small sloop in Wellfleet harbor with me at the tiller, and I had not changed our tack fast enough; so we sat, nearly stopped on nudging waves, sails luffing, sheets and blocks slapping and rattling above our heads. And my father, who never had the time or the inclination for racing but who nonetheless took great pride in executing all the points of the sport well, spat over the side disgustedly. "You have lost the advantage made on the last leg, Hamilton," he told me.

Patricia and I seem to "lie in chains," rocked about and at the mercy of a wind we no longer control. For some reason, we have lost our momentum, and the steely eyes of Dean Morraugh, or the scarcely disguised scorn I confront every day in the classroom, leave no doubt how we must look from the shore.

And behind us, the happy, gurgling curlicues of passage have disappeared, become undistinguishable from the open ocean. It is true of people, as history indicates it is of nations, that there comes a point when direction must be changed, and if done correctly, the advantages of the previous tack are preserved, even furthered. The new tack is shot across with a waxing of the original impetus. But to make this maneuver carelessly, to do it inexpertly or unmindful of course, is to slop around at the mercy of circumstances. The new course is unknown, a hazard by itself, and it is necessary to start all over again.

"Where's the guidebook, Ham?" Pat demands. We stand with Jack Crawford in the doorway of St. Michael's Cathedral. "I really think," she continues with an exaggerated upper-class drawl, "that we could afford two guidebooks so I could have one of my own."

"Here, take mine." Crawford holds one out.

"No, thank you," she replies sweetly. "I'm more than willing to make do with the little my husband provides." Flipping through the pages, she reads, "A splendid example of Romanesque and early Gothic architecture, begun in 1100 and boasting the fourth highest vaulting in Europe. Note the frescoes devoted to the childhood of Christ. Note them frescoes," she repeats and wanders away by herself.

Crawford and I slowly walk down the aisle toward the altar beneath tattered ensigns hanging from clustered columns, remnants of regiments organized in this colony to further the cause of imperialism in another. Before us, the altar lights burn, wavering in their red jars.

"Actually, what you have done," he continues, "is that you have insulted them on two counts." He looks up at Europe's fourth highest vault, the watery eyes straining, then takes in the flags. A finger goes to the moustache in contemplation. "And it's also a matter of honor, perhaps. Yes, honor."

"How so?"

"Well, first that cock-and-bull story about making a mistake about the two universities. Yes, yes, I know—it was true; but you see, they don't believe it and they certainly don't believe it now with this CIA business."

"But that's not . . ."

"Of course, of course," he shakes his head. "But it explains for them your actions, which before were inexplicable. You know, these Europeans expect us to behave in a certain way, and when we don't, they find it very disturbing. You didn't behave their way, but then this CIA thing came along and Morraugh could say to himself, 'So there's the reason.' I dare say, if it were not for the other matter, he might have been pleased to have a supposed American spy on his faculty."

"But the other matter did come up," I say. We pause before the altar, beneath a huge wooden crucifix, and Crawford makes a creaky genuflection, crosses himself, then turns with his back to it all and leans against the stone communion rail.

"And there you did it again," reflecting, a wry smile exposing the horse teeth. "You did two things, actually. First, you repeated the initial mistake—well, not mistake, but I'm talking objectively now—of not acting as they think an American should act. What you did in the courtroom was unnecessary to the outcome, for I'm certain the woman would have been acquitted. Am I right?"

"Yes, I suppose so." There are steps on stone as Patricia explores rooms to the right.

"And in standing up there like that, you went counter to their concept of you. You were expected to seek damages, to demand punishment of the wrongdoer . . ."

"I did think about it, especially because of the medal . . ."

"Tut-tut," he waves me off, "but you didn't. That's the important thing. By behaving differently than expected, you turned the tables on them. But the second matter is more important." He pauses, and moves to the front pew to lounge with sprawled limbs, idly turning the black fur cap in his hands. "To refer to the Greek," he continues, "you have exposed their *hubris* by committing an *aidos*. Rather complex concept really, *aidos*, for it means both honor and shame and there's also an additional meaning referring to the"—he looks down the length of the empty pew—"ah . . . to the genitals. It's as if you ripped off Hecuba's cloak and bared her teats."

"It's difficult to think of Marie Therese as Hecuba," I say, looking around for Patricia to hide my smile.

"Yes, quite." Crawford stands up quickly. "But I refer to the whole episode. Your act there in the courtroom was out of harmony with their concept of you, out of harmony with their order of things, the order they had planned. And being so, it revealed their own arrogance to them, their own failures. By exposing their arrogance you made them feel shame. It's as simple as that," he says, completely satisfied.

We find Patricia in a crypt behind the altar. There's a single sarcophagus of pitted stone and on top of it lies the effigy of a Norman warrior, the crucifix of a long broadsword clutched down his length.

"Who's this?" I ask Pat, and she gestures with the guidebook. It is a rather forlorn motion and I notice her eyes are luminous. There's a second effigy, much smaller, lying beside the other, and also wearing knight's armor; an Arthurian doll.

"He was sent over here by Henry II," she tells us, "and this was his son." She pauses and caresses the projectile-shaped helmet of the miniature. "But it seems the boy became frightened in some battle—though your lovely guidebook says his horse may have only shied—anyway, the great hero here," she points to the regular size, "turned around and killed him because he was a coward. A coward in battle at six years old. It's always been the same, hasn't it?" she says.

"Hmm, yes," Crawford says, "it has something to do with . . ."

"You know what they remind me of?" I say quickly, cutting off another lecture. "They remind me of a pen and pencil set." And then before anyone can say anything more, I add, "Let's go get a drink."

Though it is just after three in the afternoon, it is growing quite dark and the streets of Alclair, as usual, are glistening wet, and the multicolored images of signs and storefronts play upon them like the lights of exotic deep-sea creatures that have swum too close to the surface and are unable to return to their native depth.

Large yellow roses bloom on the leaded pane in front of the lounge, and the name of the place,

"THE NORMAN PRINCE",

is also set in the same hue so that we are ambered as we drink. It is especially unflattering to Pat, overlaying a jaundiced tint to the paleness that is often her complexion of late. The great brown eyes appear larger and darker and I notice that the fingers holding a cigarette to Crawford's match have bitten nails. She shifts uncomfortably in the worn, plus settle and then smiles at me, a hesitancy behind the glasses that I cannot be sure is not from the slant of light off the windowpane.

"Well, now, Hamilton," Crawford says, after sipping his whiskey. "How do you think this war will end?"

"Do you mean will it end, or how will it end?"

"Yes, that's another question too," he says. "But it seems so out of character for us. Perhaps you don't agree.

Perhaps it's being over here reading mostly European views of it. And all these frightful riots, burning the flag and all of that . . . civil war between whites and Negroes . . . universities seized!"

"Well, the demonstrations are new to us. No, that's not true either," I correct myself. "There were tremendous riots during the Civil War too, when Lincoln introduced the draft. And we have a long tradition of what Thoreau called civil disobedience. Somebody's always been marching up and down, protesting something or other . . ."

"You're getting away from the original question," Pat tells me. She takes one, two, three puffs of the cigarette and crushes it out in the ashtray.

"Well, I'm sorry to say, I'm only equipped to tell how things were, not how they are and certainly not how they are going to be," I answer.

"Don't be flip," and I'm surprised by the flash of anger in her eyes.

"No, he's quite right," Crawford assures her, a fellow academic closing ranks. "But what disturbs me is the mood, at least from the reports one reads, the tendency to utilize undemocratic—to use the new phrase, para-political—measures. This seems new to me. Thoreau, after all, went to jail, he did not try to burn the jailhouse down."

"The Nuremberg trials changed all that," Pat says, matter-of-factly, and looks to me. My mind goes back to a lecture last year at Scott Junior College. I hear myself saying the same thing, spouting the theory of moral resistance to one's government in a classroom of nurtured beauties, female descendants of an American Junkers class. I feel a retroactive chagrin.

"What she means," I say to Crawford, who is finishing his whiskey, "is that there's a new wrinkle in politics now . . ."

"Yes, yes," he snaps with an old maid's impatience. "I'm aware of all that. I simply just can't relate to America anymore." Palm against palm, his hands pressed together, squeezed between his knees. "I was raised in an era of orderly discussion, of rules of debate, of points made and points answered. All of this violence, this contempt for democratic procedures, is foreign to me . . ."

"Well, maybe democracy is no longer possible . . . maybe it's old-fashioned; it can't be programed. Maybe there isn't enough room on the computer card for all the holes necessary for a democracy. Then there's the new factor of time. Maybe the jet age is . . ."

"Don't talk like that." He takes my shoulder and his eyes are moist, searching. "You of all people mustn't talk like that."

"Well, in the disharmony—"

"Look," Pat interrupts me. "I have some groovy onion soup at home. Let's all go back and have something to eat." Her concern to keep Crawford well fed, to defend and bolster the condition of his liver, companions his interest in her; the trips to museums, the long walks along the quay.

"I don't think I shall ever return to America," Crawford says suddenly but softly. He looks away from us, wipes his nose with a handkerchief and then turns back, tipsy gaiety masking melancholia.

"Now, you stop talking like that," Pat says sternly.

"Ah, no, my dear, you misunderstand. No, I was down at the Embassy the other day. I'm applying for the Peace Corps. They seem to want people my age, which is very nice. Shall we have another?" he asks, now fully recovered.

"I've got this onion soup at home," Pat reminds us darkly.

"But where will you go? Where do you want to go?" I ask, signaling the waiter. Pat "humphs" against the cushion and looks sullenly at her bitten nails.

"I was thinking of Africa," Jack Crawford replies, smoothing the moustache. It strikes me, after all these months, how very much he resembles Dean Acheson from the nose down. "Yes, I think I could be very useful in Africa."

"How do you mean," Pat says, "like in somebody's cooking pot?" Crawford finds this very funny. The big yellow teeth are bared and there's a whinny to go with them.

Of course, we have more than just "one more" and when we finally taxi up to our house, Crawford is pressing upon us the significance of Horus' triumph over Set after the murder of good King Osiris. Patricia stands silent and grim at the front door while I manage the key into the lock, and then walks determinedly down the dark hallway to the kitchen. But the soup though very strong is still all right, at least to our numbed palates. We cloak her with compliments, but she shrugs us both away.

"Why are you so angry?" I dare to question just as she slams the bowls of soup down on the counter. She stops, her tongue goes out and licks a bit of perspiration that lies in the cleft above her lip, and I am almost foolish enough to try to kiss her. The need for her rises in my throat. "But aren't you eating?" I ask, seeing only two place settings.

"I have work to do," she says, the brown eyes narrowing. "Marie Therese didn't show up today, and the house is a mess. You and the sacred bull of Memphis get in here and eat this so it won't be a complete waste."

But we are too far gone for even the recuperative power of the concentrated stew, and an hour or two later, I sense

Crawford's description of the dual monarchy of the Upper and Lower Kingdoms has wandered off and disappeared into the rushes of his sluggish mind. How long I have been sitting across from him on the sofa, answering him, head thrown back and mouth agape on gurgling and snuffles, I do not know. But with a final "That's very interesting," I turn out the light and go upstairs.

Pat is already in bed, but not asleep, for as I stretch out beside her she turns on me quickly. "Where's Jack?"

"On the sofa. Why are you so angry?" I ask.

"Why?" she repeats, jumping out of bed. "You know what his problem is, and you sat there and deliberately fed him drinks."

"My dear," I begin, trying to put together a telling phrase about individual responsibility and about the unique fellowship among men which transcends the particular *Angst* of each.

"My dear, balls," she snaps back, and clutching a blanket moves through the gloom in her white flannel nightgown, resembling an enormous, angry jellyfish. And there is an element of fluidity about the bed, a swirling of waters through which I hear first one and then the other shoe drop on the living-room floor as Pat repeats the now familiar routine of tucking in Jack Crawford on the sofa. Just before I go down for the last time, I reach over and pat the empty, warm pillow beside mine. Her use of the word "balls," though said in pique, is somehow a good sign, a viable testament—in every sense of the word—to . . . and it is suddenly morning.

"Sir, Mr. Phillips." The syrupy voice comes from a high bench in the rear. "You have made quite clear the theory of Manifest Destiny as a possible cause of the United States' war with Spain. My question, sir: Is it not possible that this same or a renewed version of Manifest Destiny is at work in the Vietnam situation?"

"Parallels in history are not very useful," I answer. "For one thing, we have seen that there had been an interest in acquiring Cuba since the days of John Adams and for a number of reasons. Morrison gives economic and political reasons for the Spanish war. For example, the talk of a canal in the Panama area was very high at this time, and the need of protecting such a venture through control of islands such as Cuba was thought to be essential. No, I'm afraid, the circumstances, the actual facts, do not make for an easy parallel."

"But, sir, Mr. Phillips," comes another voice, this time from the front, "is it not peculiar that your Mr. McKinley and President Kennedy were both assassinated at times when the United States was embarking on imperialistic ventures?"

"I'm afraid the gratuitous acts of singular individuals cannot be placed in any rational order," I answer, already hearing the next question.

"But then you believe there was no plot to kill President Kennedy?" it comes from the front again, in an accent already practicing for Oxford study.

"There is no evidence to believe otherwise," I say just as the bell rings. But they are slow to move, lingering over the delights of unknown conspiracies.

"Ah, we were afraid it would happen. Mrs. Morraugh and I have been keeping a close look on Marie Therese these last few weeks, for the poor creature has not been herself, that's for sure." Dean Morraugh crosses one stubby leg over another and fools with a paperweight on his desk.

"But where is she?" I ask him. "What's happened to Marie Therese?"

"She's been in the Melrose Clinic for the past ten days," he says sorrowfully. "A piteous case, indeed. It's a complete breakdown. The poor creature has had so much on her mind, what with her parents' infirmities and the state of the world in general. And then, of course," and almost shyly his eyes turn on me, then roll to the corner of the room, "there was the strain of the business in court, don't you know."

"Well, I'm sorry," I tell him, in a tone which says that I'm not, that this is one responsibility we will not shoulder. "What of her parents? Who's caring for them?"

"Oh, the missus has them arranged for in an elderly home. They'll be well taken care of," he says dryly, his mind on something else. "It's too bad it's happened right now, just when Mrs. Phillips needs her the most." The moonface breaks into a grin. "Yes, it's too bad."

"We'll get along."

"Oh, I'm sure you will. I have no fears that you'll get along, Mr. Phillips. And how are the classes going? The reports are good." Who the secret agents are that file these good reports are a mystery to me.

"They seem to have difficulty believing the Kennedy assassination was not a plot. Even poor old McKinley— they're trying to tie the two together." The sparse eyebrows arch up.

"Ah, indeed. Well, it's only natural—I confess it's in me as well. But you must understand we have a history of conspiracies over here. You Americans are all so individual, you have a background of one man or another changing events." It is difficult to tell whether he's ironical or merely weary of me. "By the way, Iseult was asking for Mrs. Phillips. I'll be pleased to tell her she is well."

"How is Iseult?"

"Fine, thank you." He fusses more with the paperweight, a heavy piece of crystal. I'm standing and start to leave. "You know it's strange you mention your President Mc-Kinley," he says, going to the big bookcase, one finger searching the titles, then stopping at one. "I was doing a little reading of your history the other night and I came across a most interesting paragraph here. Do you know this book?" He holds up the volume as he turns through the pages.

"What is it?"

"*McKinley to Harding* by a . . ."—he looks at the spine "by Kohlstat."

"No, I'm afraid not."

"Ah, well, you can't read them all, can you? I bought this when I was in your country working on my degree at Columbia. There were grand bookstores down at the bottom of the city in those days."

"Yes, on Fourth Avenue. They're still there."

"That's splendid," he says, looking for the section. "Ah, here it is." He adjusts his glasses. "It has to do with your Mark Hanna—he was an important man to McKinley, was he not?"

"Somewhat," I answer, wondering if he wants a seminar on the subject.

"The author apparently rode with Mark Hanna on the train that took the assassinated President home for burial." There were more "s's" than necessary in his pronunciation.

"And he quotes him—that is, Hanna—as saying, 'I told William McKinley it was a mistake to nominate that wild man in Philadelphia'—he's referring to the first Roosevelt, of course, as Vice President . . ."

"Yes, of course . . ."

" 'I asked him if he realized what would happen if he should die.' " The three-fingered hand moves freely in the air for emphasis. " 'Now look, that damned cowboy is President of the United States,' " and the book snaps shut and he's looking at me, a glint in the steel eyes and a smile on his face as if he's just proved the existence of life on Mars.

The Melrose Clinic turns out to be one of a row of brick mansions near the zoo, all identical and in a neighborhood of large lawns, high hedges and graveled walks. There are heavy sprays of rhododendrons, some nearly as high as the half-timbered second floors of the establishments, and it is disquieting to come upon this ersatz Tudor architecture, accustomed to the genuine Georgian character of the rest of the city. It looks like a well-to-do suburb in Kansas City.

But the smells inside are those of sickness and medication and of the continual polishing and scrubbing that goes on in such places. A nurse at the door takes my name and asks me to wait in the small foyer beneath a massive staircase. There I'm joined after several minutes of absolute silence —perhaps I half expected to hear screams, muffled cries and gibberings—by a pale young man who introduces himself as the resident physician.

"You're the American, aren't you?" he inquires with a smile, anticipation sharpening an already very pointed face, and I wonder if I should say something amusing or do a few handstands. "Well, she's coming along. Yes, she's coming along. And you've brought sweets," he indicates the box of chocolates in my hand, "how very nice." Like a hostess leading me to the hors d'oeuvre, he backs away, turns and guides me toward the rear of the house.

There is a large shedlike annex which takes up the space of what had been a rear garden, a construction of corrugated steel with green plastic skylights and partitioned within by temporary walls of wallboard on metal stands. I have the feeling that if health and mental stability were ever restored, the entire area could be turned in minutes into a meeting hall for Girl Scouts.

"Here we are, Marie Therese, here's a nice American gentleman come to see you," the doctor says, and he nearly bows or curtsies—depending on one's point of view—and leaves us alone.

She is all in pink and her complexion is the color of a bowl of strawberries and cream, her face as inanimate as the bowl. She sits propped up against the white pillows in a corner bed, hair neatly combed, and I feel strangely embarrassed for her, since she is in her nightdress, just a pink wool shawl about fleshy shoulders. She would have been mortified by my seeing her in this intimate dishabille, these quaint open lacework trimmings of spinsterhood.

But of course she is not aware I am there at all, or if so, is not really sensitive to my seeing her, or perhaps she does not care. It is impossible to tell, for her eyes are wide and vacant, two lustrous mirrors set beneath the forehead, and without a shadow of cognition within them.

"Hello, Marie Therese. You look fine. I've brought you some sweets." The box of candy rests in her lap and she continues to stare at me, and for a moment I suffer that illusion one has when confronted with insanity, that the beholder is being put on in some way, that the illness is actually in the visitor's mind rather than in the patient's. There is the faintest suggestion of derision in those empty eyes, the hint of a smile, as if her dead pan were on the verge of cracking up, the secret of her actual sanity given away.

"We miss you very much and hope you are your old self again. Mrs. Phillips also sends her best. But the important thing is for you to get well." I continue to talk to the pink planes of face, my gaze shifting to the white planes of the pillow, the only difference between the two being the color. Tucked in beneath the pillows I see a doll. It has a cloth body and arms, rather like the old-fashioned Raggedy Ann, but the head is of celluloid, very worn and even cracked at the forehead. The eyes, which once were an unblinking blue, have been almost erased, giving them a weary expression, disquieting in the infant face.

"Is this your—is this your baby?" I say, reaching for the little head above the coverlet. She moves quickly, cunning rippling the blank eyes, and clutches the slack figure to her bosom to rock it back and forth. There are guttural snaps and hisses in her throat and moist cluckings. "It's a lovely baby, Marie Therese," but the eyes have gone dead again as she bends over the broken head pressed against the pink shawl. "Well, we want you to know that we hope you get well very soon. We like you very much, and everything that has happened is all forgotten." It is useless to continue, and I wonder for whose benefit do I talk?

I am sorry to open the little drawer of the bedside table. It is the habitual reflex of a visitor or relative paying a duty call, and, bored with the narrow interests of the sick, the conversation stilted by neighboring beds, one first leafs through magazines and newspapers. Then cards and letters received by the patient are read over and finally the meager collection of personal belongings are assayed. I am sorry to do this, for lying beside a well-thumbed missal is the Phi Bete key on its thin chain. I knew it would be there—this talisman of achievement lying beside the black prayer book, the only two personal belongings in the white metal drawer.

It is heavy in my hands and the chain winds around my fingers. I think of the history of this pitiful "holy medal," as Emtie used to call it. She is oblivious to everything but the doll she has in her arms. I think of this scholarly amulet and of all who have worn it, and I imagine the pride and pleasure it must have brought the first wearer and then the affection with which it was passed on to the second and the euphoric secrecy with which it was worn. I imagined the ultimate, poignant recognition that its charm was limited. Then comes the deliberate, meaningful surrender to the third owner, against whose soft breast it tap-tapped the gentle reminder of an unknown past, irritating inconsolable desire. I think of all these hands who have held it, of the heartbeats measured on its golden flank and of all its different values and I realize that things, people, perhaps if not historical events, have a way of coming full cycle. And if the relationship or repetition is only apparent, only an illusion, it is no less real to the one to whom it happens. The chain slips through my fingers, and the key drops into the metal drawer beside the prayer book where it belongs.

"Well now, Emtie. We will come back again. Now don't worry about anything. Do you understand, Emtie? Don't worry about anything." She pauses in her crooning and cradling, an arch of eyebrow and a piercing look gives me—for the second time—the idea the whole business is an act, and then she carefully arranges the doll beneath the covers and recomposes herself, hands primly interlaced at blanket's edge. I almost expect her to say, "Well, now, Mr. Phillips, me love to the missus," but she only stares.

"It's a rather common form of hysteria," the whippet-like doctor tells me in the foyer. "We see quite a bit of it here, don't you know. Ah, we're just having our morning tea. Won't you have a cup with us?"

In fact, it is also feeding time at the nearby zoo, for as I leave the place, the neighborhood trembles with the thunder of lions and the cries of lesser animals. Patricia's fruity alto greets me when I open our front door, filling the hall with "Strawberry Fields." I peer tentatively around the kitchen-door jamb, testing her mood before going all the way.

"Hi," she says, straightening up from the oven. She pushes the glasses back on her nose and with a foot neatly kicks shut the oven door. "I've just made some super cheeseburgers."

"You're in a good mood today," I say, taking one of the stools.

"You bet," she says cheerfully, licking some melted cheese from a finger. "I always feel good when I make decisions."

"Like what?"

"Well, like I don't need Marie Therese and I don't care if she ever comes back."

"That's a choice bit of de facto reasoning," I say.

She starts to take a swipe at me and then changes her mind, pulls up a sagging knee sock. "No, I really never needed Marie Therese. That was your idea, and I appreciate what you meant by it. But it's good for me to do all the housework. Keeps my mind off things."

"What things?"

"Oh, just things," she shrugs, the lower lip pushing out. "Ouch!"

"What?"

"He just kicked," she answers, a hand on her side. "Feel." She comes near, leans against me and places my hand on her belly. I sense a gentle undulation. There's a big grin on her face and her eyes squint happily.

"I know of a woman who had a baby just last week," I say.

"Yes, but it wasn't me," she answers. "And it wasn't you either." She puts her face against my neck and we stay like that for several minutes, the smell of cheeseburgers wafting around us as the whispers of Alclair's afternoon traffic come across the back gardens. Brown limbs and black foliage are brushed and teased by a sputtering sun. "It seems like such a long time ago," she says, finally.

"Yes."

"Are you sorry? I know it wouldn't do any good, but are you sorry? Who was it said that to forget past mistakes is to repeat them again?"

"No, I'm not sorry," I answer, "but I do think you're carrying this mother image business a little far. I mean with Jack Crawford." The echoes of his morning discipline, a roscid series of hacks and spittings, still seem to reverberate in the stairwell from the commode high above. "It's almost as if you were trying to . . ." and the phrase "adopt him" meets a silent death in my mouth. She's looking at me warily and her eyes tell me she knows what I was about to say. Her kiss says she's glad I didn't.

"He needs to eat," she says finally. "And I hate to think

of him going to that lonely room." She pulls away to
check the oven. "By the way, where have you been
today?"

"I've been to the zoo," I tell her.

During that long train trip out to Illinois with my
mother to claim my father's ashes, I remember sitting in
the observation car watching passengers disembark. It was
wartime, and the train made more stops than usual, almost
a local on a thousand-mile run. All day long I watched
strangers get off, to be met by others on the different station platforms along the route, and then as the train moved
on, the stationary figures, their journey over, would gradually grow smaller and smaller and finally disappear.

I think of this experience now, for it's difficult to remember Patricia, to remember what she was like when she
was not pregnant, though I try to go back over it again and
again. And all the other items and elements of our past,
actually the only past I care to remember, have become,
like those strangers on a train, even more strange, more difficult to see as they are left behind by present momentum.

This "long-legged bait" carrying the little fish our
mingled breaths and juices put there in the heat of Wellfleet rolls beside me on the street, bumps me out of bed,
and I'm nearly prepared to accept the permanency of this
great humpty-belly of a creature. She also seems to sense
the possibility, for neither her mind nor body rebels any
longer; there is no more sickness, no more depression and
a serene mantle has fallen over her with the same ease as
do the voluminous smocks that cloak her swollen body.

How much of this contentment is attributable to Jack
Crawford moving in with us, I do not know. Superficially,
he has replaced Marie Therese in the household, for he

helps with the housework, does the shopping and generally looks after Patricia. It takes me several days to get used to meeting the distinguished authority on ancient Egypt in our kitchen, an apron tied about his waist, and hands splashing in the soapsuds, red ring of Harvard and all. And as a bachelor chef, Jack also contributes some of his culinary specialties to our fare, and although they mostly alternate between baked macaroni and creamed chicken on toast—their soothing, protective effect on stomach linings well known—these dishes also afford Patricia a break now and then.

"Jack is cooking supper tonight," she says. Then, seeing the look on my face, "Now, come on, his macaroni is really getting pretty good."

But there is more to his presence than the mundane chores he performs. We spend most of our evenings together, usually sitting in the living room, a fire in the grate. We seldom watch television anymore, and especially not the pictures of the disturbances in America, but quietly talk. Jack and I go over lecture notes or read while Patricia sits knitting, on the sofa. Now and then I look over my book and watch her. There's an enigmatic flicker around her lips, a composure of eyes and face set within the long dark hair that would have stopped Leonardo in his tracks. Or put on a lower level, she calmly works over the flashing knitting needles with all the complacency and self-satisfaction of Wendy. I am not Peter Pan, nor ever hoped to be, but it is a startling resemblance.

"Well now," Crawford says rising, "I suppose it's just time for a nightcap," destroying whatever allusion might be made for his role in our little hutch.

"How many is this?" Patricia asks simply, not looking up from an intricate stitch.

"Why, just one before dinner . . ." Crawford pauses in the center of the room.

"Two," Pat reminds him.

"Well, yes, but I didn't finish it until after dinner." He holds up the glass, then puts it on the table, adjusts some pillows and gently sets her back against them.

"Oh, come on," I say, throwing down Schlesinger's *The Age of Jackson*, "let's all have a drink." Pat's eyes are sharp but she's obviously outvoted and we do. I am impatient with all of this sudden intimacy, this mutual care; perhaps jealous is the word, but it passes as quickly as it came, replaced with the idea that whatever this thing is between them, somehow or other it is returning more of her to me.

Then there is Christmas coming on, and it does seem right to have Jack Crawford with us. We even talk of having a large Christmas dinner, and on one morning, he and I meet Maxine Waters on our way to morning classes.

"I would love to come," she tells us, "and I have a wonderful recipe for baked oysters." The flicker in the big eyes indicates a flash of intuition; that if we were not aware of the recipe, we knew where she got it. "But you see, I'm going to England for the Christmas recess. There's not a single English edition of my husband's work, and I have some appointments with publishers."

The three of us pause across from the great iron gates of the University. The morning traffic slushes by, and there's a bit of gray snow on the cap and upon the gun, cradled in the arms of the national hero.

"But I will be back in time for the Beverley dinner," she adds, "and we can all have a Yuletime toast there. You are going, aren't you? I'm dying to meet them and I understand their dinners are right out of the eighteenth century. Sit down at eight and up at one in the morning."

"I don't know," I reply. Beverley Biscuits is the largest employer here and the family has been generous with the profits made from vanilla tea cookies. Liberty Park was their donation to Alclair as are the restorations of several monasteries and churches. Their will did not always win out, however, for they had wished to mount a fine Flemish statue of St. George on the pedestal which once supported King William and which now bears the wide stance of the stone gunman.

The Beverley generosity is also extended at the Yuletide to those foreign dignitaries in residence, and Maxine, by dint of her marriage, and Pat and I, probably because of my appearances on Smith-Royce's program, have been included. Not Jack Crawford, and this disturbs me. It puzzles me because I am disturbed; perhaps Patricia's affection for him has rubbed off. In any event, it seems that one more place could have been accommodated at the cookie king's castle.

There are the usual messages and mysterious packages arriving and especially many boxes from America with Edna Gates's return address on the shipping labels. There's a long note from Judy Levy.

"When we will return I do not know," a part of it reads. "Arthur has suddenly got all involved with some Italians here who want to make a big resort out of this place. Byron and Shelley and all that. They plan condominiums all along the beach and he's helping with all sorts of promotion ideas. He knows nothing about this business, of course, but that's SOP, because he's never known about any of the other projects he got into until he started. Please let us know as soon as the baby comes."

And the next afternoon, Pat greets me at the door with, "It looks like Mary Abbey has sent us a copy of her new book." On the hall table is a small package with American stamps and neat green handwriting. "Should we wait for Christmas to open it?"

We do not wait, opening it after our first drink in the kitchen, and it is the copy of Morraugh's translation of Maureen nu Nailly's martyrdom—the same one that disappeared from my mantel at Thanksgiving.

"I thought it over," Mary Abbey writes, "and decided that it was a bit like cheating. So I will forego the fame and fortune that might be mine by way of Grove Press, and send this back to you with all my affection and what's left of my discretion. Perhaps it should be wrapped more Christmasy; it is, in my meager way, a gift.

"I do not mean to be dreary at this time of year but only tell you a bit of news and do so to indicate one of the reasons for my change of heart (ha ha), and to put from your minds the idea that my behavior is guided by purely righteous motives. (Please do not tell Maxine Waters what I am about to say.) Now, how to say it? Well, it seems that I do have a pox of sorts, but not the Italian kind as I had—hoped (?). Call it the American Pox, if you will, and how it will turn out nobody knows. X-rays—then the knife if necessary, if practical. I am not at all depressed, strangely enough, but I do feel a great urge to concentrate on *my own work*—so you see . . .

"Oh, yes. About Judson Doyle. He's had a disastrous exposure here—and *exposure* is the word. He's been knocked out in almost every fight and his poor nose is . . . but in another way he's made it. I have seen him a few times, but mostly on late-night television, where he has become all the rage on interview shows. He calls me now

and then when he's in New York and we have long tele-
phone chats, but he's always being rushed off to some other
show and we never get together. I invited him to one of
my readings, but I don't think he came. Conflict of celebrity, I guess.

"Do you think you will come back soon? I am in the
phone book and . . ."

"Well, Merry Christmas," Pat says, her mouth turning
down. I leaf through the pages of the book, expectantly,
but the gymnastic convulsions of Maureen's sacrifice are
the same. "It's strange," she continues, supporting her
belly, "but that note we got from Judy Levy depresses me
more—that is, if I am to be depressed. You know what?"
she says, turning back to the stove.

"What?"

"I think I'll make biscuits tonight," she announces, rolling
up her sleeves.

Christmas morning is heralded by the bells of Alclair, a
cascade of peals and sonorous clangs that are surprisingly
robust and not at all worn out by the banging they received throughout Christmas Eve. Crawford's morning
gargle contributes a cacophony to the pealing which is dis-
tinctive if not seasonal, and Patricia's singing rises with the
heavy aromas of pancakes and sausages and coffee.

The small tree Jack Crawford brought home several
days before and which the three of us trimmed looks rather
pathetic before the huge front window of the high-ceilinged living room, rather like a display piece left behind
in a bankrupt department store window, not worth taking
with the rest of the inventory. But it is ours.

And it is surrounded if not bolstered by barricades of
colorfully wrapped packages; as always, one is surprised
by the number of things there are. Most of the boxes have

come from Edna Gates, who obviously fulfilled her Yuletide duty with courage and Christian determination.

"Edna has had a charge account at Macy's since the year one," Pat tells Crawford as the wrappings come off, revealing everything to be from the same store.

"A veritable cornucopia," Jack Crawford replies with an anxious sniff. Though he has only just put the ham in the oven, he's already worried. It's his first try with a new recipe.

Instead of one or two ties, selected with care, there are about a dozen, obviously grabbed by the handful. There are sets of lingerie for Patricia, all very plain and useful. And so on. Most of the large boxes contain items for the baby. Multiple combinations of gowns, layettes, blankets, caps and booties. A collapsible crib and a portable bath. In short, Edna has sent us everything for the nursery except the four walls, the paint to use on them (one can of pink and one of blue) and a window overlooking a sunny park.

We play in this pile of plenty, roll in the mass of paper and wrappings like children, while Jack makes several trips back and forth to the kitchen to check on the ham. But, again like children, we soon tire of commenting, tire of mouthing surprise and wonder, and silently rip open the last of the packages, which contains a gleaming set of electrical appliances that cannot be used here without a transformer.

"Where did we put that can of pineapple rings, Patricia?" Crawford asks from the door. He holds the recipe torn from the pages of a woman's magazine.

"It's early for that, isn't it?" she asks.

"Yes, but I just want to get everything ready." He fidgets with his moustache.

"Oh, come on. Let's open everything else," she answers, gathering up all the crumpled and torn paper.

We next turn to the packages from my mother. Instinctively, Patricia winds the yards of white lace around her shoulders and hair like a cowl. For me, there's a set of memoirs by one of Richard I's Crusaders in cracked leather bindings, which must have come from some Holy Land bazaar. My mother has sent nothing for the baby unless she intends the framed photograph of herself to serve as a gift.

"Isn't that peculiar?" I say, looking at the image. "Why would she send that?"

"I think it's nice she has. Where was it taken, do you suppose?" Pat leans over to look at the picture.

"It's in a small garden. Perhaps it's part of her house. She looks in good shape. And happy."

"That's why I think it's nice to send it," Pat says seriously, then plunges into the clutter around her. "Now here—these things are for both of you," and she hands Crawford and me our gifts. "Try it on, if it fits."

"It's great," I tell her, putting on the sweater. "So that's what you've been knitting all this time."

"All this time is right," she cracks. "I started that thing back at Scott," she says, and the brown eyes grow soft within the harlequin frames.

"Just what I needed," Crawford is saying. He smoothes the large, heavy scarf around his neck down over the thin chest. He receives the gloves I bought him at the last minute with the same genuine gratitude.

In return, Crawford presents me with two very fine bottles of French cognac, appropriate gifts and obviously meant to be shared in the spirit of the season. He then hands Patricia a very small package.

"Small but hopefully . . ." He stops, flushing.

"Good things come in small packages," she says, her face brimming with joy. On the thin gold chain is what appears to be a small, golden cross save for a circular finial at the top.

"It's called an *ankh*," Crawford says, unwrapping and then wrapping the scarf around his neck. Pat holds it above her face, eyes hazy and distant. "The Egyptians used it for the symbol for life, though actually," and he turns about, seems to be addressing himself in the mirror above the fireplace, "actually it represents Aton, who was . . ."

"It's beautiful," Pat says softly and it's enough to interrupt him. "It's just what," and she pauses with half a laugh, "it's just what I always wanted." She gets up and kisses his cheek and turns about, the cowl of white lace thrown back, for him to fasten the chain around her neck. As she holds up the long hair, her eyes meet mine and they are glistening.

The perfume I got her was meant to be a sham, a mundane, ordinary present designed to put her off guard so that the second gift, still in my pocket, would come as a surprise. I feel the small box, my fingers tracing the corners and teasing the thin ribbon around it, as Crawford finally makes the clasp work.

"There," Pat says. "Isn't that lovely?" she asks me. "I think that's the nicest thing anyone has ever given me," she says.

Part of me resents this intrusion, resents this small trinket which has usurped and made my second gift worthless. But it is only a very small part. In fact, gratitude to Crawford overcomes my bitterness, gratitude and thanks to whatever god's influence came with the *ankh* that had de-

termined the sequence. For if she had opened mine first
and found my old Phi Bete key, she probably would have
reacted with the same delight, the same tears, but it still
would not have been the same. Mine was a foolish gift, and
like most sentimental gestures not really truthful. The
civilization that created it might be dead, but the belief
the *ankh* stood for is still alive; by contrast my little device
is but a poor imitation of the past.

"Well, how did you like it?" Dean Morraugh asks,
taking the book from me.

"Very much," I answer. "It was not exactly what I expected."

"Was it not?" he says, carefully replacing St. Maureen's
story back in his bookshelf. "Ah, well, our saints are full-
blooded creatures, don't you know—none of these namby-
pamby types."

"Perhaps when the weather gets better, we can visit the
site. My wife and I would like to see it. Where is the
monastery located?"

"Oh, down on the south coast," he says, moving to the
large window. "But there's nothing to be seen there."

"No?"

"Ah, no. It was completely destroyed, don't you know.
After the Berserkers had done with her, they burned the
place to the ground."

"But I thought . . ."

"That she saved the place?" He turns an incredulous
look to me. "You see, you don't understand it at all. Ah,
no, it was all burned to the last parchment."

"But what about Friar What's-his-name? How did
he. . . ?"

"Ah, Friar Georgio apparently hied it to the bell tower

when he saw them coming toward the monastery. He locked himself in and fortunately they could not knock through the walls. No, fortunately for us all, he saved himself."

"And nothing else?"

"Ah, Mr. Phillips, you Americans ask for too much. It is enough that he saw what happened and lived to preserve her glory. This wasn't the Alamo, you know."

Though I agree, I'm about to say more but the bell rings, summoning me to my class in American Foreign Policy.

"Look," Pat says to me, several days later, "I think you should go to that do at the Beverleys' without me." We are taking the afternoon stroll through Liberty Park.

"Oh, come on, it will do you good."

"No, really." She sits on one of the benches that face the duck pond. Only sea gulls paddle on the water and the parade of folding chairs that usually dress ranks along the paths has been withdrawn for the winter.

"I just don't feel like going." Feet tucked beneath the bench seat, she stuffs her hands into the pockets of the camel's hair coat that can no longer be buttoned.

"You really don't have to stay home with him," I say. "Jack's feelings will not be hurt."

"Oh, it's not only that," she says.

"What's the matter? Don't you feel all right?" I sit beside her.

"Oh, sure," she shrugs. "I feel all right."

"Well, what then?" Two gulls march stiffly around the bench, heads cocked and yellow eyes fixed upon us.

"Oh, it sounds silly, I guess—but I must be homesick."

"Homesick? For where?"

"That's what makes it silly," she answers. "For where?" She sucks her lower lip.

"Look, as soon as you have the baby, I'll resign from this place and we'll take a long trip. Maybe we'll go to that place where Arthur and Judy . . ."

"No, that's not what I want. You don't either. Hamilton," she faces me, a hesitant smile on her face, "why don't we go down to the airline office right now and buy tickets? I could be packed in no time. Most of the stuff we could have sent. Why don't we go back right now?" She speaks all in a rush, a bubbling of words.

"Right now?"

"Oh, I know it might look bad for your career . . ."

"My career," I repeat, for it's a strange term.

"You could take a year off and work on your thesis," she continues, while I remember my unfinished study. "It's the war, I suppose, and all the mess going on. I just feel like we should be there, be home." And the long hair which has hidden her face as her head was bent falls back as she looks up. "Do you know what I mean?"

I look away from her, unable to face the seriousness in that student face and I suppose not really very happy with the maturity that has suddenly aged it. The relationship between knowledge and age should not be new to me, but, let me admit it, my own canister of years has become very heavy.

"I'll think about it," I say finally.

"No, it's no good to think about it," she says with half a voice. "The moment's over now, anyway. Actually," she gets up and holds out her hand, "I feel much better, now that I've had my say."

We walk through the park, toward home, hand in hand.

"Do you think your mother will ever go back?" she asks.

"To the States?"

"Yes."

"No, I don't think so. It doesn't sound as if Crawford will either, does it?"

"No. I guess some people never do," Pat says. A cat high-hips it along the path besides us, then slinks beneath the rhododendrons.

"We all have return tickets tucked away somewhere," I say. "But some people never use the second half. The stubs turn up in old trunks along with worthless stock certificates."

"You really don't want to go back, do you?" she asks, squeezing my hand at the corner. There's a timid stealth in the fingers.

"How many times have I told you never to ask direct questions?"

"Do you?" she repeats.

"I don't know. Maybe not." We cross the street and she leads me into a greengrocer. She picks over the lettuce, selects some romaine; checks out the beets, chooses carrots; then hefts a couple of Spanish melons. "Well, why should we?" I continue, taking the bag of groceries from her. "It's all so familiar . . ."

"I've never seen the Grand Canyon," she says moodily.

"That's not what I mean," I say, turning from the gulling look in her eyes. "Everything that's happening back home is familiar—you can find it all in any history book. All the antecedents of what is and what is going to happen can be found in any history book. Even an American history book. That's what I mean by familiar."

"Once again, dear doctor, you have opened the door to

understanding," she says, but before I can reply, crack her head open is more like it, we must separate around a hop-scotch game some kids have going on the sidewalk.

"You didn't need to say that," I say as we move together again. "I'm sorry if I sound . . ."

"No, what I mean is this—" She stops suddenly. The pouty mouth is firmed up and there's a quick, businesslike adjustment of the glasses. "When the Sunday papers come from now on, are we only to read the travel section and throw the rest out?" She thumps the melons against my chest and walks on, a wild swing of arm encircling the next question. "I just want to know what you're going to do. Because," she pauses at our front gate, "I'm with you, Hamlet. Whatever you want to do is okay by me. But I need to know."

We walk up the steps, Pat taking them slowly, a regular one, two, three pace with a breath-taking pause at the top. I'm unable to answer her yet, and in any event we are met in the hallway by Jack Crawford, just putting down the phone.

"You just missed Maxine Waters," he says.

"*Tant pis,*" says Patricia, taking the groceries and going to the kitchen.

"How did she make out in England?" I ask.

"Ostensibly she called to see if you were going to the Beverley party tonight," Crawford says, "but I also received a lengthy report on the state of letters in England. There's hope that matters will be improved with the publication of Robert Lewis Waters."

"Shakespeare, Coleridge, Tennyson and Waters. They wouldn't make a dime in Philadelphia."

"No, I dare say," Crawford muses, smoothing his

moustache. "However, it might be said that one more blank in the tradition has been filled in." And he falls into a hemming and hawing, a vocal shifting of feet.

"I think it's time for a drink," I say.

"Do you think so?" he asks. "Bit early, isn't it?"

"No, it's just that the days are getting longer," I tell him as we move to the bottles on the dining-room sideboard. We both choose some of the local whiskey and as I roll its smoky softness around my tongue, I meet Jack Kennedy's eyes above. For some reason, I'm curious to see what magazine or paper the picture was clipped from. I reach up and remove the picture from the wall.

The paper and its cardboard backing are a loose fit in the dime-stone frame, so it nearly falls apart in my hands. The paper is flimsy and fragile without the frame. On the opposite side is a brief report on the chances of a Common Market. There are several advertisements ("Speak Spanish in Two Weeks!") and one photograph, the picture of a bikini-clad girl being pulled by two leashed poodles ("Despite her busy schedule at the film festival, Silvia Romano finds time to exercise her poodles on the beach").

We become aware of Patricia standing in the doorway but I continue to wrestle with the parts of the picture, trying to fit everything back together again. Crawford's voice makes me look up.

"What is it, my dear?"

"I'm sorry," Patricia is saying. Her voice is curiously distant, her lips seem gray and there's a dull look in her eye. "I think we should get a taxi. Maybe I should go to the hospital."

7

I F IT IS OF ANY CONSOLATION, THE AMERICAN TRAVELER
in Europe will find the way has been prepared for him,
that he has been preceded by the image of another American. Sometimes accompanied by a picture of Pope John,
as on cottage walls in Ireland, or hanging by itself above
bars of London pubs or in French cafés, the rotogravured
image of John F. Kennedy is met almost everywhere. One
may come across the earnest schoolboy gaze amid the
clutter of plaster gods and armless nudes of a souvenir shop
by the Ponte Vecchio; and it is unsettling.

Sadness comes first, but then comes pride and, perhaps
because it's more agreeable, a sense of belonging. One is no
longer quite the stranger in Europe one might have been,
no longer a type with no other identification than a passport. The flat, two-dimensional face, and all of its many
mass-media variations, has somehow filled in a few of the
blanks, rounded out our character. From that image, often
still with ragged edges where it was torn from a magazine,
others have learned a little more about what we were and
what we might have been and, of course, what we are.

"That comes down first thing," Patricia said, motioning
to the framed photograph above the Chippendale side-

board. We had only just entered the house and our land-lord was yet showing us through.

"Well, let's wait until he leaves," I said. "It was meant to be a compliment, I suppose. What's the matter, afraid the ghost of Colonel Gates will break the china?"

"No," she shrugged and took off her coat. Even with swell of belly, she looked very trim in the tweed traveling suit. "It just makes me . . ." and she shrugged again.

"Here we are, Mrs. Phillips," our landlord said from the doorway, almost tugging at the cap he wore. "May I show you the kitchen?" And we followed him down the small flight of stairs into the back room. "All very modern and neat, wouldn't you say?" he said, presenting the place.

"Where's the refrigerator?" Pat said darkly.

"Why, right here," the man said proudly, bending over and opening the small door beneath the cabinet. There were two shelves inside with an ice compartment the size of a cheesebox. "Hmm, that light seems to be off; I'll tend to that."

"That's a refrigerator?" Pat asks, adjusting her glasses as if to see more.

"Yes, and very popular in the best of homes," he answered almost gaily. "My wife gave us an assist with the utensils—so you have everything you need, for sure. Now around here's the bath, newly tiled too." Around the corner and within a smaller room is a square tub. "And since you Americans like the shower," he continued, holding up a rubber tube with a spray head on one end, "we've got this for you. You just plug it in and slosh it down."

"Where's the rest of it?" Pat said suspiciously, for there were no other fixtures in the room and I could sense the horror growing in the dark eyes; the thought of trekking to a garden privy.

"The rest of what?" the landlord asked blankly.

"The other parts of the bathroom," I supplied.

"Ah, the water closet," he brightened. "Why, it's separated, of course."

"Of course," Pat said, shooting a glance at me. Her brow had become low and menacing.

"There, you see." The landlord led us to the foot of the stairs and pointed into the darkness at the top. "All the rest of it is up there—right where you need it, close to the bedroom, don't you know. Well, I'll be off. If you need anything, don't hesitate to give me a ring." And he was gone.

We wandered about the large rooms of the house, experienced by our brief tenancy in Wellfleet to the transient's inspection of belongings left behind by previous habitants. Instead of the *National Geographics* we found stacks of *London Illustrated News* in a corner of the dining room. In the hall closet there was a dress sword, its hilt encrusted with artificial gems and an elaborate crest of some religious order. The sideboard held a mixed batch of crystal and glass, three cordial glasses remaining from a set; someone had substituted a rolled up paper napkin for the carafe stopper.

"Wow," Pat said as she surveyed the bedroom. Even with our trunks and suitcases, there was still enough space left over for a square dance. The Queen Anne chair was in one corner, the large bed against the inside wall and beside it the huge, empty armoire with the door hanging open, as if our predecessors had made a hurried exit.

"This reminds me of one of those wards that Florence Nightingale used to wander through," Pat said.

"Which reminds me, nurse," I said, coming to her, "that we both require some attention." The day-long train trip from the boat dock, plus several previous days of rough weather on shipboard, had kept us from each other.

"We've got lots to do," she turned away, "before we think of anything like that." She opened a suitcase and began to unpack.

Without speaking, we moved from suitcase to the armoire, from trunk to armoire, occasionally meeting at this single storage closet, my haste to complete the task running into her sense of order. "Not there," she would say, or, "If you're going to do it, do it right."

The drawers and hanging space of the armoire finally filled, crammed is the word, she stuffed my arms with sheets, and I dutifully helped her with the bed. First one sheet, then its companion, and next, two pillows encased and plumped, followed by a blanket and spread. While trying to imitate her precision with the hospital corner, I wondered at her obsession with making a neatness of something that would hopefully, and imminently, be torn asunder.

"There now," she said, looking about for something else to put right, and I pulled her toward me before she could find another project. "Listen, I still have a lot to do," she protested. "I want to measure some of these windows for curtains."

"What is this with you," I said, "some sort of a nesting instinct?"

"Ugh." She gave me a slow stiff-arm in the chest, "Don't be disgusting. Anyway, it's still daylight and these mirrors put me down." She was still a bit self-conscious about the change in her body.

"Well, take your glasses off," I suggested helpfully. She let my lips find the soft, warm nook beneath her ear, and leaned against me with a placid indifference.

"Really not?"

"No, really not," she answered. "I do want to get settled in first. I want to see what the stores are like, I have to get some food in. There are just a zillion things that have to be done."

"Well, for Christ's sake," I said, as she pushed out of my grasp, "you couldn't wait to get between the sheets in Wellfleet."

"You're distressingly vulgar today," she answered, the full lips failing the attempt at primness. "Anyway, we weren't married then and it was different."

"Different, how was it different?"

"It was just different," she replied with a maddening certainty. She was at the small sink in the far corner, washing her hands. "Anyway, you should go check in at the University."

"Now don't start setting up a schedule for me. If you want to play house, it's all right with me, but save me the bit about planning well-balanced meals. I'm beginning to feel like I married a Kraft food commercial."

"Ah, poor Hamlet," she said, coming to me. Cool hands held my face for a hot-mouthed kiss, a whorish tongue at work. "I want to be your mistress, but I also want to be your wife. But you must help me, *cher professeur*. Now don't be greedy," she said, tapping my lips. "Go make your appearance at the academy and then come back and little mother will have some goodies for you. Maybe."

So, nibbling this crumb of a promise, I carried my hunger to the nearest bus stop. I took a bus that seemed to point toward the center of the city, where I knew the old University was located. The rain had stopped and the fronts of buildings were washed with chalky light that passed from pink to blue, now and then a west-running cross street of pure gold, and against this backdrop, masses of gray pedestrians moved like blundering supernumeraries from a more somber play.

Although the signs of the shops, the make of the automobiles moving slowly in traffic, the ancient appearance of the architecture—all these were different, were foreign—I had no sense of being a stranger in this European city; that is, I felt no more strange than if I had been in an unfamiliar American city.

As an American, I was naturally conscious of my surroundings, and my first view of this city outside the bus offered no "newness," no release from the sense of that old contact sport played in America—eyeball to eyeball. This was probably the reason Patricia and I used the local language and began to call the city Alclair though the name, of course, is spelled Atha Cliath. But Alclair is how it seemed to be pronounced, it was our ear-view of the sound, as all our perceptions probably changed what we actually experienced.

In fact, how it got this name was part of the same question, for it had only been called Atha Cliath, Alclair or whatever since the uprising, when the triumphant revolutionaries not only put down the English, but put down the English names as well. Perhaps one of the first steps, certainly symbolic if nothing more, a people take after achieving freedom is to rename the environment, as if to liberate it also; a step toward improving the surroundings by calling them something different. This might be worth a paper, I thought on the bus that first day, though historian caution pricked my enthusiasm: it may only apply to the twentieth century.

In any event, I got off the bus before the Georgian quadrangle of the old University, and here was a structure that was new to me because it so obviously predated my own history. Surrounded by an elaborate iron fence, it was an island unto itself within the commercial wash around it. Two great statues flanked its entrance arch, one of which had his head turtled in the high collar of a Regency cloak and presented some sort of a scroll that might have been the plans for the building or a code of law. The name meant nothing to me. In more medieval gown and cap, the other was of a poet, a figure of ambiguous stature who several centuries before had incurred his countrymen's wrath by telling them the truth about themselves. The tall iron fence did not protect him from contemporary feelings, for a rosette of red paint glazed the worn stone features.

Through the gate and into the hush of the inner yard, there were more statues and pedestaled urns, cracked and empty, and a few black-gowned fellows moving along a maze of paths. And all around, the many-windowed fort of knowledge dampened the outside city noise down to a sealike murmur. Directions from a passing don took me to the administration building, a completely oval building with a domed roof of verdigrised copper. There were statues inside also, dignified and handsome viceroys, offering the invariable hand of reason, while the other toyed with the hilt of a sword.

What the eighteenth-century architects had in mind for this place I do not know, perhaps a debating hall because of the sensitive acoustics of its sphered interior. Now twelve-foot-high partitions have cut it up into cubicles and typewriters clack and machines whir, grinding out the schema of academic policy. And surveying it all from above the partitions were marble busts, wigged and slightly contemptuous of eye, set in niches around the ceiling.

Though unwigged there was the same supercilious glint
in the eyes of the Dean, who received me in one of the
inner cubbies of this temporary maze. He had taken my
credentials, the letters of introduction, and with only
a cursory inspection returned them.

"I fear there's been a mistake," he said with a smile, his
voice calm and deliberate.

"A mistake?" I asked.

"Yes. You see," and he looked around the molded
plaster frieze of the ceiling dome, "you've come to the
wrong university. Your post is up the street, an entirely
different institution. Quite different," he added with a
smile.

"But on the forms it . . ."

"On the forms it says . . ." His finger pointed to the
appropriate line. "That's the other spot. There's a bit of
confusion now and then, but you'll like it there. It's really
an up-and-coming faculty. Hold on, I'll get you squared
away," he said, picking up the phone and speaking into
the receiver. "Get me Dean Morraugh over at the government college. There now. What's your subject, Mr. . . .
Phillips?"

"Medieval history specifically, though I was told I
would be teaching American history for the year."

"A whole year for American history," he said with
wonder. "But of course, we have enough medievalists here
already. I suppose it would be useful to have someone tell
us about your history, at that."

"I suppose so," I said, remembering Art Levy's tone of
voice when he asked me, "You're sure you this is the spot
you want?"

"What I mean is, we sometimes loan a professor now
and again to them up the street, and perhaps we can get

our own back now. You can come over and give us a bit of your time, if you would like. That's nasty bit of history going on in Vietnam right now, isn't it?"

"The responsibilities of power are not always pleasant."

"Yes, quite," he replied. "We've had so much of it over here, don't you know. You Americans have such a brief past, by comparison, and I expect you find it difficult to make the adjustment. It's comforting to have a long history, things are so easily named, put in their place, if one has a past. Nearly impossible to do that as they happen." Then he laughed soundlessly. "One can even mistake one thing or one place for another," and he picked up my forms and looked them over again. The phone rang.

"Yes. Hullo, Morraugh—Dudley here. Yes, fine. Look here, Gil, we seem to have one of your flock here. Yes, an American named Phillips. Thought he was coming here, but—worse luck—you seem to get him. Yes, that's right. Fine. I'll do that. And to you, too." The phone put down, he turns to me, handing back my papers and introductions. "Dean Morraugh will receive you tomorrow morning. Do you think you can find the place? Right across from Liberty Park? You won't get lost, now?" he said, rising and showing me out.

"You've got to be kidding," Patricia said when I told her. I had waited until she sipped her martini.

"Well, it may not be as bad as all that," I said. "Anyway, it's got us to Europe, expenses paid."

"Well, here's to sunny Spain," she said, raising her glass.

"It's going to be all right," I assured her. "What are you cooking?" There were marvelous herb smells in the kitchen.

"Some fish, if that oven works," she replied pessimistically.

There were candles on the dining-room table and flowers

on the sideboard. The shelves of the kitchen larder were filled with cans and packages and there were other indications that she had been busy during my absence. Her long hair swept up and over into a glistening bun behind one ear.

"What sort of place is this other university?"

"It's like a state university," I told her knowledgeably, stretching out my meager information as much as possible. "Actually a better place for me, in that there's more of a cross section of people in terms of the classes. And it's famous for . . ." and I stopped, sorry to have continued the buildup.

"Famous for what?" she said, peeking in the oven.

"Well, it has a world-renowned collection of stuffed birds . . ."

"Stuffed birds?"

"Yes, Arctic birds which are very . . ."

"Stuffed birds?" she hooted, her face becoming red with laughter. "Oh, Hamilton, you're the living end. When I think that I could have had my pick of the Columbia law class . . . stuffed birds," she repeated, shaking her head and then pecking at my lips as if to accompany the words. "Well, come on, cock robin, let's eat."

The wine I had purchased was pleasant and she looked beautiful in the candlelight. The meal was excellent, and I felt more guilty with each bite of *sole véronique*. My chagrin was enforced by the chocolate *mousse*.

In the darkened bedroom, I lay in bed watching her stand before one of the large windows facing the street. She was nude and the glow of the streetlights silhouetted the line of her back and sweep of hips, the undulation of the heavy breasts, as she undid her hair and shook it down.

"Come on," I said softly.

"Just a moment," she said. She walked around the dark room, tested the taps of the sink, rearranged the clothing on the one chair and, with a muttered curse, reset the matchcover wedge in the door of the armoire. Finally, everything in order, she settled in beside me. "Well, I suppose you're good for something," she whispered, her hands moving down my ribs.

"A small but perhaps meaningful accomplishment," I replied.

"Not so small," she answered.

"That suggests empirical comparison," I said. Her breasts enriched my hands.

"Don't be nasty," she replied.

"You've never told me about any . . ."

"And I'm not going to," she replied, adding in a tone that implied a smile, "it would only disgust you."

"Really?"

"Ah, my little naturalist," she said, kissing my ear, then suddenly her whole body quaking, the chuckling rising deep from her throat. "Stuffed birds." Laughter, especially tinged with ridicule, is not the best friend of passion.

"This is nothing to joke about," I replied.

"I can see that," she replied gravely. Then, "Do you like my belly?"

"Yes."

"It's getting big."

"A Botticelli belly," I answered, feeling her.

"But it will get bigger."

"Yes."

"What will we do then?" She turns over.

"You mean how?"

"Yes, how?" she replied, her voice distant.

"There are ways."

"*Mon cher professeur*, you will teach me these ways."

"Yes," I replied, aware it would be more of a refresher course. "But now, we will content ourselves with a few simple truths."

"Simple for you," she said, pulling me to her, "groovy for me."

Sometime in the night, it may have been only an hour later or it could have been toward morning, I was aware of her pulling away from me, an almost frantic untangling of legs and arms. Feet padded quickly over the carpet as she began to gag.

"What is it?" I jumped up, went to her at the sink.

"Just . . . just . . . just" she said between heaves.

I held her head as she vomited, our nude bodies spooned up tight but with no desire, her flesh rather chilled and clammy. "Wow," she said after rinsing out her mouth and straightening up. "I think I better go sit on the john." I escorted her out to the hall and we mounted single file up the narrow steps to the commode near the roof. "Go away," she said dully, sitting down on the seat. Then as if to soften the command, "Go get me my Amphojel. It's on the mantel in the dining room."

So I left her perched on the high seat, somewhat fearful she might roll off and into the black emptiness below, and went down to the dining room for the preparation. It was on the mantel and I noticed, for the first time, that Jack Kennedy still hung over the sideboard.

"Hamlet!" Her anguished voice came down from the commode, followed by more gagging. So I took the steps two at a time, naked and holding a spoon and bottle of medicine in one hand. In the dim light at the top, she knelt as a penitent before the toilet, the roundness of her buttocks resting on the elliptic soles of feet. In this way we spent our first night in Alclair.

It is in this small room, then, a room which under other circumstances would be comfortably cozy with its fire in the small grate, the worn but deep-cushioned chairs and heavy drapes, that the story comes to a pause. It resembles one of those tape recordings which uses an endless spool of magnetic ribbon that can play back and forth continuously and never really come to a conclusion.

Even the astringent antiseptic odor is gone, and there is a neutral ambivalence in the air, as if the smell of chloroform and the scents of the flowers on the bedside table had met and dissipated each other. The bed is an ordinary piece of furniture, and seemingly impossibly narrow, though wide enough to hold my wife, once again slim. Her breathing is quiet, peaceful, her face turned on the pillow away from me, and I wonder how long it would take to count the long, fine strands of black hair splayed on the white pillow.

I feel strangely emotionless, at zero, with neither regret, nor sorrow, nor even any relief beyond the easing of my initial anxiety. I start to laugh but nothing comes out and my eyes are wet. Not real tears, but just a gentle, moist residue of the clash between laughter and tears, the mind checkmating the heart. And so, I remain at null point, and for some reason think of Art Levy on his balcony, dancing to the strains of the bossa nova and looking down on the old seawall that was to keep out the Moorish pirates but was only effective against the waves of the Mediterranean.

It was the Moors who brought the cipher with them, maybe bouncing the big circle over the walls of Europe, and certainly this medieval concept of nothingness has been perfected today and is about to achieve a new dimension—if that is possible with naughts—when Arthur builds the high-rises, using the wall as a foundation. It will be an inland attack, you might say, joining the attack from the sea on the very point designed as the ultimate defense. Unit upon unit, cell upon cell forever expanding, and expanding, and expanding, and expanding.

Patricia stirs, her face turns toward the ceiling. The eyes are closed and resemble deep, soft wounds just barely healed. I cannot decide whether she looks younger or older than when I last saw her a few hours ago. Orderly progression, at once the pride and plaything of historians and mathematicians, begins with naught and would seem to reach endlessly, perhaps beyond the stars, in a series only measurable at last by machines and which, at last, comes back to naught and is measureless. It is possible, perhaps, to choke on zeros as one is consumed by zeros. As for the stars, they obviously have no need of us.

"He got tangled up in his little thing." Her voice is faint but firm, and how long she has been conscious, I do not know. "That's why he wanted to come out," she says. "He got all tangled up."

"Well, you're in fine shape," I tell her. "The doctor says you'll be able to have lots more babies."

"Sure," she answers. Her face cramps around a pain only I can feel. "This is very poor," she says softly. "Very poor." Then, "How's Jack? He was so upset."

"He's fine. Waiting at the corner saloon like always."

There's a tremor around her lips, perhaps an attempt to smile. "You know," she continues almost casually, "at the worst part of it—before we knew he was—well, I guess the doctor knew, but before I was sure—I kept try-

ing to think of your crazy prayer to the sun god—anything, you know?"

"Yes."

"And I got it all mixed up in my mind. I remembered
something about paying my vows in the presence of his
family, or your family—which is part of something I used
to read in Edna's prayer book, for new mothers, I think.
Then I got mixed up between paying vows and paying
dues—remember you saying something about paying dues
—so everything got mixed up with sun gods and paying
vows and paying dues. Anyway," and she takes a deep
breath, "none of it worked."

Her face turns away from me on the pillow and she
plucks at a tissue box, blows her nose. The other hand,
the one with my mother's wedding band, slips down to
mine. I recognize the ring more than the hand.

"Hamlet . . ."

"You must rest," I say, taking this hand.

"No, wait," she turns back to me. Her nose is pink
and her eyes luminous. "Hamlet, I don't feel bad. Not
really. I mean not guilty, not sorry for you or for me.
Maybe for . . . for the small descendant . . . maybe . . ."
She squeezes my hand. "But I haven't failed you, have I?"

"Where would I be without you?" Her eyes become
heavy with drugs or emotion or perhaps both.

"Back at Scott," she tells me, "teasing all them bitches.
But you would know where you are, maybe know what
you were going to do. Have some kind of a program."

"Or think I do."

"That's the same thing, isn't it?"

"Maybe."

"I'm not handling this very well," she tells herself as
much as me. And for a moment she seems to drift away,

eyes closed. Then back again. "Lana Turner was always great in these scenes. She always looked like she had been doing it too much."

"Cut it out. You're going to be all right."

"I know it," she says finally. "Well, that's the way it goes," she says softly. "Maybe I can sleep on my belly tonight. Won't that be a kick?"

"Do you want me to stay?" I ask.

"Do you want to go?"

"No."

"Well," she continues dreamily. "What now?"

"We'll go home," I tell her.

"Oh, you mustn't," she says, half rising and more upset by this idea than apparently by what has happened. "You mustn't say that . . . you mustn't do that just because . . ."

"That's not the reason," I tell her.

"Are you sure?"

"I'm sure," I answer, though I'm not.

"When?"

"As soon as you're able," I say, only then deciding.

"Let's fly back," she says. "Soundlessly, and effortlessly and . . ." She cannot think of another word.

"I'll make the reservations tomorrow."

"Well . . ." She stops. Her forehead wrinkles and her lips purse, childishly, with the taste of a new thought. "What's the weather like? Don't tell me it's clearing up."

"No, it's not," I tell her.

January 1968
Ancramdale, New York